Re-Views
by an
Evangelical Biblical Critic

Re-Views
by an
Evangelical Biblical Critic

Robert H. Gundry

CASCADE Books • Eugene, Oregon

RE-VIEWS BY AN EVANGELICAL BIBLICAL CRITIC

Copyright © 2022 Robert H. Gundry. All rights reserved. Except for brief quotations in critical publications or reviews, no part of this book may be reproduced in any manner without prior written permission from the publisher. Write: Permissions, Wipf and Stock Publishers, 199 W. 8th Ave., Suite 3, Eugene, OR 97401.

Cascade Books
An Imprint of Wipf and Stock Publishers
199 W. 8th Ave., Suite 3
Eugene, OR 97401

www.wipfandstock.com

PAPERBACK ISBN: 978-1-6667-4150-6
HARDCOVER ISBN: 978-1-6667-4151-3
EBOOK ISBN: 978-1-6667-4152-0

Cataloguing-in-Publication data:

Names: Gundry, Robert H. (Robert Horton), 1932-, author.

Title: Re-views by an evangelical biblical critic / by Robert H. Gundry.

Description: Eugene, OR: Cascade Books, 2022 | Series: if applicable | Includes bibliographical references.

Identifiers: ISBN 978-1-6667-4150-6 (paperback) | ISBN 978-1-6667-4151-3 (hardcover) | ISBN 978-1-6667-4152-0 (ebook)

Subjects: LCSH: Bible. New Testament—Criticism, interpretation, etc. | Books—Reviews.

Classification: BS2395 G86 2022 (print) | BS2395 (ebook)

11/15/22

Permissions

Lightly revised editions of the following titles are reprinted here with permission from *Books and Culture* / *Christianity Today*: "Postmortem: Death by Hardening of the Categories"; "You Can*not* Be Serious!"; "Jesus the *Halakic* Jew"; "To Plato or Not to Plato? Questions Theopsychological and Theopolitical"; "Smithereens"; "Tom's Targum"; "Frederick the Bruce"; "Josephus as a Pre-Raphaelite"; "*Zealot*, or Jesus as a Jewish *Jihadist*"; "Theological Seitz in Paul's Letter to the Colossians"; "Thinking Outside the Box—Pandora's, *i.e.*"; "Everything You Should Know about the Samaritans (Even If You Don't Want To)"; "Messed Up Memories of Jesus?"; from *Christianity Today*, "Reconstructing Jesus"; from *Bulletin for Biblical Research* / Penn State University, "Kingdom and Power, Love and Violence"; and from *Evangelical Studies Bulletin* / Wheaton College (Wheaton, IL), "In Response to Rich Mouw, Mark Noll, and Chris Smith." The essay "Trimming the Debate between Craig and Lüdemann" was adapted from and first published in *Jesus's Resurrection: Fact or Figment?*, by William Lane Craig and Gerd Lüdemann, ed. Paul Copan and Ronald K. Tacelli, copyright (c) 2000 by Paul H. Copan, Ronald K. Tacelli, Gerd Lüdemann, and William Lane Craig. It is here used by permission of InterVarsity Press, P.O. Box 1400, Downers Grove, IL 60515, USA. www.ivpress.com.

Contents

List of Abbreviations | ix
Introduction | xiii

Biblical Text and Translation
    Postmortem: Death by Hardening of the Categories | 3
    Re-Facing the Text | 10
    Tom's Targum | 17

Higher Critical Issues
    Thinking Outside the Box—Pandora's, *i.e.* | 27
    Messed-Up Memories of Jesus? | 34
    A Question of Interpretive Reliability in Defense of Historical Reliability | 45
    Tabor's Ossuary | 50
    Why Matthew, Mark, and Luke Are So Much Alike: The Synoptic Problem | 55
    Holes in the *Whole* Postcolonial *Story* | 61

Portrayals of Jesus
    Reconstructing Jesus | 81
    The Burden of Christ's Passion | 88
    Zealot, or Jesus as a Jewish *Jihadist* | 92
    Jesus the *Halakic* Jew | 99
    Kingdom and Power, Love and Violence | 107
    "You Can*not* Be Serious!" | 125

Bible and Tradition
    On *The Mind Behind the Gospels: A Commentary
        on Matthew 1–14* | 133
    Smithereens! | 137
    In Response to Rich Mouw, Mark Noll, and Chris Smith | 148
    Theological Seitz in Paul's Letter to the Colossians | 155
    To Plato or Not to Plato? Questions Theopsychological
        and Theopolitical | 161

People and Scripture
    Josephus as a Pre-Raphaelite | 171
    Everything You Should Know about the Samaritans
        (Even If You Don't Want To) | 183
    Trimming the Debate between Craig and Lüdemann | 189
    Ingmar Bergman and *The Seventh Seal* | 208
    Frederick the Bruce | 212

List of Abbreviations

1 Cor	First Corinthians
1 En.	First Enoch
1 Kgdms	First Kingdoms (LXX)
1 Pet	First Peter
1 Sam	First Samuel
1 Thess	First Thessalonians
1 Tim	First Timothy
2 Bar.	Second Baruch
2 Cor	Second Corinthians
2 Kgs	Second Kings
2 Macc	Second Maccabees
2 Tim	Second Timothy
4 Kgdms	Fourth Kingdoms (LXX)
4 Macc	Fourth Maccabees
aka	also known as
AD	in the year of our Lord
Ad. Gr.	*Oratio ad Graecos*
Ant.	*Jewish Antiquities*
Ascen. Isa.	Martyrdom and Ascension of Isaiah 6–11
AYBRL	Anchor Yale Bible Reference Library
BBR	*Bulletin for Biblical Research*

BC	before Christ
B.C.E.	before the Common Era
BETL	Bibliotheca Ephemeridum Theologicarum Lovaniensium
BGBE	Beiträge zur Geschichte der biblischen Exegese
Bib. Ant.	Biblical Antiquities
CE/C.E.	the Common Era
Cels.	*Contra Celsum*
cf.	compare
Civ.	*De civita*
Dan	Daniel
Deut	Deuteronomy
ed.	edition, or edited by
e.g.	for example
Eph	Ephesians
esp.	especially
et al.	and others
et passim	and here and there
ETL	*Ephmerides Theologicae Lovanienses*
EvQ	*Evangelical Quarterly*
Ezek	Ezekiel
Gal	Galatians
Gen	Genesis
Gen. Rab.	Genesis Rabbah
Hist. eccl.	*Church History*
Hist.	*Historiae* (*Histories*)
i.e.	that is
idem	the same
J.W.	*Jewish War*
Jas	James
JSNT	*Journal for the Study of the New Testament*
JSNTSup	Journal for the Study of the New Testament Supplement Series

JSOT	Journal for the Study of the Old Testament
KJV	King James Version
LXX	Septuagint
Matt	Matthew
N.B.	note well
NovTSup	Supplements to Novum Testamentum
NRSV	New Revised Standard Version
NT	New Testament
NTS	*New Testament Studies*
OT	Old Testament
Phil	Philippians
Ps(s)	Psalm(s)
Q	purported source of Jesus' sayings
rev.	revision, or revised by
Rom	Romans
Sib. Or.	Sibylline Oracles
SNTS	Society for New Testament Studies
Song	Song of Solomon
T. Ab.	Testament of Abraham
TDNT	*Theological Dictionary of the New Testament*
TJ	*Trinity Journal*
US/USA	United States of America
USSR	United Soviet Socialist Republic
v(v).	verse(s)
Vit. Const.	*Vita Constantini*
viz.	namely
Wis	Wisdom of Solomon

Introduction

REVIEW ESSAYS FEATURE ANALYSIS and elaboration—what scholars call "criticism"—largely missing from ordinary book and movie reviews. The present book contains review essays that were written almost entirely in the 2000s, appeared in a variety of publications, have recently undergone light revisions, and retain their relevance up to the present time. The hyphen in "Re-Views" links the newness of republication with the analytical character of the essays. They start with those dealing with the biblical text and its translation, proceed to some higher critical issues, graduate to literary portraits of Jesus, discuss the relation between the Bible and tradition, and conclude with some biographical portrayals of people associated with Scripture and its interpretation.[1]

"Postmortem: Death by Hardening of the Categories" appeared first in *Books and Culture* (hereafter *B&C*) 12 (2006) 8–9; "You Can*not* Be Serious!" in *B&C* 15 (2009) 12–14; "Jesus the *Halakic* Jew" in *B&C* 16 (2010) 11–13; "To Plato or Not to Plato? Questions Theopsychological and Theopolitical" in *B&C* 17 (2011) 25–26; "Smithereens" in *B&C* 17 (2011) 9–11; "Tom's Targum" in *B&C* 18 (2012) 22–24; "Frederick the Bruce" in *B&C* 19 (2013) 30–32; "Josephus as a Pre-Raphaelite" in *B&C* 19 (2013) 35–38; "*Zealot*, or Jesus as a Jewish *Jihadist*" in *B&C* 19 (2013) 14–16; "Theological Seitz in Paul's Letter to the Colossians" in *B&C* 20 (2014) 25–27; "Thinking Outside the Box—Pandora's, *i.e.*" in *B&C* 21 (2015) 24–25; "Everything You Should Know About the Samaritans (Even If You Don't Want To" in *B&C* 22 (2016) 22–23; "Messed Up Memories of Jesus?" in *B&C* (2016) 114–16; "Reconstructing Jesus" in *Christianity*

---

1. The transliteration of Greek words and phrases in essays dealing with the biblical text facilitates understanding for nonreaders of Greek.

Today 42 (1998) 76–79. Thanks to *Christianity Today* for permission to republish the preceding with minor adaptations.

"Kingdom and Power, Love and Violence" appeared first in *Bulletin for Biblical Research* 24 (2014) 37–73. Thanks to Penn State University Press for permission to republish the essay with minor adaptations. "Trimming the Debate Between Craig and Lüdemann" appeared first in *Jesus's Resurrection: Fact or Figment?* (Downers Grove, IL: InterVarsity, 2000), 104–23. Thanks to InterVarsity Press for permission to republish the critique with minor adaptations. "In Response to Rich Mouw, Mark Noll, and Chris Smith" appeared first in the *Evangelical Studies Bulletin* 19 (2002) 7–10. Thanks to Wheaton College (Wheaton, IL) for permission to republish the response.

Biblical Text and Translation

Postmortem: Death by Hardening of the Categories

THE FIRST THING TO say about Bart D. Ehrman's *Misquoting Jesus* is that the book has little to do with misquoting Jesus.[1] You'd think from the subtitle, *The Story Behind Who Changed the Bible and Why*, that the main title signals an exposé of postbiblical changes of what Jesus actually said as recorded in the Bible. But not only does Ehrman disbelieve that the Bible always records what Jesus actually said. He also devotes most of his book to parts of the Bible that don't pretend to be quoting Jesus at all. None of his three parade examples of textual changes—from Jesus' "becoming angry" to "feeling compassion" in Mark 1:41, from nothing at all about Jesus' blood-like sweat to its later insertion in Luke 22:43-44, and from Jesus' tasting death "apart from God" to doing so "by the grace of God" in Heb 2:8-9—deals with what Jesus purportedly said.

Of Ehrman's thirty-six lesser examples of textual changes, twenty-two have nothing to do with the reported words of Jesus. Not even John 7:53—8:11 does; for although Jesus is quoted there ("Neither do I condemn you. Go and sin no more," he says to the woman taken in adultery, for example), Ehrman rightly excludes the whole passage from the canonical text (see below) but doesn't argue that Jesus is misquoted in the passage. (Regardless of one's opinion concerning historical value, denying canonicity doesn't equate with denying historicity.) Four of the lesser examples represent omissions rather than misquotations of Jesus' words, and ten—only ten—represent textual changes in which Jesus is misquoted. Of these ten, moreover, only one (in Luke 22:17-19) poses

---

1. San Francisco: HarperSanFrancisco, 2005.

a serious question as to what the evangelist originally reported Jesus to have said, that is, whether he said his body was being given and his blood being shed for the disciples; and because of a partial parallel in 1 Cor 11:23–25, even this one hardly counts as a misquotation though *Luke* may not have recorded it. (Ehrman makes no argument that Paul misquoted Jesus.) Along with other textual critics, Ehrman seems certain of what the evangelists originally reported Jesus as saying in the nine remaining examples. So the misquoting of Jesus—which, I repeat, occupies only a small portion of *Misquoting Jesus*—has to do only with textual changes by later copyists.

This is exactly Ehrman's point, though: *later* copyists changed the text of the New Testament—usually accidentally, though sometimes deliberately and for theological reasons. In the latter case, for example, they changed texts to make them harmonize with other texts, to fortify texts against their use by those whom the copyists considered heretical, and to implement texts for use against the same. And so Ehrman has written *Misquoting Jesus* in part to introduce lay people to textual criticism of the New Testament, that is, to the ferreting out of copyists' changes. (To a considerable extent, this book popularizes his earlier, scholarly book *The Orthodox Corruption of Scripture*.[2])

As an introduction to New Testament textual criticism for lay people, *Misquoting Jesus* is very informative and often entertaining. But for more than one reason, such people are liable to get a misimpression from the book. The blurbs on its dust jacket talk about "the multitude of mistakes and intentional alterations . . . made by earlier translators [*sic*, 'copyists']," "mistakes and changes" that Ehrman shows had "great impact . . . upon the Bible we use today," thus "making the original words difficult to reconstruct," so that "many of our cherished biblical stories and widely held beliefs concerning the divinity of Jesus, the Trinity, and the divine origins of the Bible itself stem from both intentional and accidental alterations by scribes—alterations that dramatically affected all subsequent versions of the Bible."

Horsefeathers! So what if John 1:18 originally read in reference to Jesus "the unique Son" rather than "the unique God"? "The Word," who will be identified with "Jesus Christ" (1:17), has already been called "God" in 1:1; and doubting Thomas will call him "my Lord and my God" in John 20:28 (to make nothing of the fact that the King James Version, which

---

2. New York: Oxford University Press, 1993.

"was based on corrupted and inferior manuscripts" [so the dust jacket], translates what Ehrman considers the original reading in 1:18). So what if "the Johannine Comma" in 1 John 5:7–8 ("the Father, the Word, and the Spirit, and these three are one") represents a copyist's inference of the Trinity from authentic New Testament texts, not an authentic New Testament text itself? We have those authentic texts for our *own* inferring of the Trinity.

It's simply false that "for the first time Ehrman reveals where and why these changes were made" and that he "reveals" the inferiority of the manuscripts underlying the King James Version. We've known about this inferiority for a long, long time. It hasn't led to revolutions in church teaching, nor has it needed to. And though their text-critical judgments don't always match Ehrman's, the contemporary translations used nowadays by lay people don't depend on the inferior manuscripts. (Granted, however, that these translations deserve censure when they include—in any format whatever—Mark's long ending [16:9–20] and the story about the woman taken in adultery [John 7:53—8:11]; for those passages have poorer manuscript support than many readings completely overlooked in such translations.)

Not only the dust jacket but also Ehrman himself contributes to the misimpression lay readers will probably get to the effect that the text of the New Testament is largely uncertain. He begins and ends with a personal testimony according to which he turned away from evangelical Christian faith to agnosticism because "we have only error-ridden copies" of the New Testament. "We don't even have . . . copies of the copies of the copies of the originals." (Oh? How would we know that an early manuscript isn't a third- or fourth-generation copy?) And "the vast majority of these ['error-ridden copies'] are centuries removed from the originals and different from them, evidently, in thousands of ways." Indeed, "there are more differences among our manuscripts than there are words in the New Testament," perhaps upwards of four hundred thousand differences.

To be sure, Ehrman gets around to admitting that "most of these differences are completely immaterial and insignificant," that theologically significant ones appear only "occasionally," that "it is at least possible to get back to the *oldest* and *earliest* stages of the manuscript tradition," and that "this oldest form of the text is no doubt closely (*very* closely) related to what the author originally wrote" (emphasis original). But first impressions tend to be lasting, and Ehrman emphasizes what he self-contradictorily claims to be "lots of significant changes" by which the

New Testament text has been "radically . . . altered." Therefore lay people are preprogrammed to miss that Ehrman seems at odds with himself and to carry away the misimpression that they can hardly trust the New Testament to represent what its authors originally wrote. So the content as well as the title of *Misquoting Jesus* is almost bound to mislead the intended readers. I suspect that it's the deceptiveness of the title, especially the main title, that vaulted the book onto the *New York Times'* Best Sellers list. Are we dealing with a marketing ploy?

To his credit, Ehrman recognizes textual corruption in other ancient texts. But he makes nothing of the contrast between the poverty of those texts as to number and chronological proximity to the originals in comparison with New Testament texts. Nor does he take account of the possibility, even probability, that multiple copies of the originals were made and that in the second century the originals themselves were still available for checking (as mentioned in Christian literature of the period). Again to his credit, Ehrman relates the history of New Testament textual criticism to the history of early Christian literature in general, including books that didn't make it into the Bible. But he opines that earliest Christianity was a hodgepodge of competing views, so that orthodoxy, represented by the New Testament, came into being only later as the view that won the most adherents. This opinion neglects both the historical connections of New Testament books with Jesus' immediate disciples and their associates and the generally acknowledged earlier dates of New Testament books as compared with the noncanonical books of what Ehrman calls "lost Christianities."

Ehrman appeals to Luke's "many" lost sources and to Paul's "many" lost letters but gives us no reason to suppose that any of them represented lost Christianities or to suppose that such Christianities were already existing and producing their own literature. (How does Ehrman know that Paul wrote more lost letters than the two or three he refers to in his extant letters?) Yet again to his credit, Ehrman relates the history of New Testament textual criticism to the history of the New Testament canon. But Ehrman's repeated insistence on the nonprofessionalism and incompetence of Christian copyists during the second and third centuries may be overdrawn, for those Christian copyists' use of abbreviations for sacred names and of codices instead of scrolls inclines toward more professionalism and competence than he allows.

Furthermore, do the miscopyings that Ehrman counts significant carry so much significance as he claims? Take his first parade example,

Mark 1:41. Does a mistaken "feeling compassion"—even though it disagrees with Jesus' lack of explicitly stated compassion elsewhere in Mark—really demand overhauling our interpretation of the rest of Mark's Gospel ("the interpretation of an entire book of the New Testament," according to Ehrman)? I think not. Ehrman argues that a compassionate Jesus would clash with Mark's portrayal of him elsewhere as "a charismatic authority who doesn't like to be disturbed." But a compassionate Jesus in Mark 1:41 would clash with such a portrayal no more than does Mark 10:45, "For indeed the Son of Man has not come to be served, but to serve and to give his life as a ransom for many," a statement that not only exudes compassion and expresses servitude rather than disturbance, annoyance, irascibility, or what-have-you but also, unlike 1:41, suffers no text-critical doubt and does quote Jesus (in reference to himself, of course).

Would a mistaken reference to Jesus' being in such agony as to make his sweat like drops of blood (Luke 22:43–44) really demand overhauling our interpretation of the rest of Luke's Gospel? Or would it represent only a foreign body in a book that otherwise features a calm and collected Jesus? I think the latter. Besides, the Greek word that Ehrman treats as meaning "agony" can also (and perhaps better) be treated as meaning a contest or struggle in which, by virtue of an angel's strengthening him, Jesus was able to pray "more fervently" (hence the blood-like sweat) and thus overcome the temptation of avoiding the cross. Whether or not original, such a meaning would accord nicely with Luke's overall portrayal of him as a man of prayer and virtue.

And would Jesus' tasting death "by the grace of God" rather than "apart from God" (Heb 2:8–9) demand overhauling our interpretation of the rest of Hebrews? I think not. For although the author several times writes that Jesus offered up himself in a sacrificial death that we might be forgiven, he also writes that Jesus did so to do God's will (Heb 10:9). It looks pretty gracious of God to will his Son's self-sacrifice for our sakes. These parade examples of Ehrman's suffice to make my point: the textual corruptions he sees don't have nearly the interpretive significance that he attributes to them.

Earlier, I mentioned Ehrman's purpose "in part" to introduce lay readers to New Testament textual criticism. He makes quite clear his further and ultimate purpose to dysangelize them—in other words, to proclaim New Testament textual criticism as bad news to all who believe the Bible to be God's word. Thus Ehrman's leading question to such believers: "What if the book you take as giving you God's words instead contains human words?" There's the rub: Ehrman has so hardened the categories of humanity and divinity that since the Bible is "a very human book," for him it can't also be divinely inspired. The human authors' writing out of their "needs, beliefs, worldviews, opinions, loves, hates, longings, desires, situations, problems" somehow excludes the Holy Spirit's using those needs, beliefs, worldviews, and so on to convey divine revelation. As though God *could* have communicated in a vacuum, apart from such concomitants!

Ehrman also hardens the categories of literary genre, quotation, and copying to such a degree that he seems to think divine inspiration of the Bible would necessarily have produced historicity with no admixture of unhistorical elements, with quotations that always conform to originally intended meanings, and with errorless copying. There's no room for nuance, free play, or ambiguity. For scriptural inspiration to have worked, everything would have to have been cut and dried. As Ehrman says, "Given the circumstance that [God] didn't preserve the words [which have 'been changed and, in some cases, lost'], the conclusion seemed inescapable to me that he hadn't gone to the trouble of inspiring them."

If you take that line of reasoning further, divine inspiration would also have required errorless translations of the Bible or—since there's always some slippage of meaning in translation from one language into another—different Bibles, all equally inspired, in every human language; and also again—since one and the same language is in a continuous state of flux—a newly inspired Bible for all human languages every passing moment (compare Ehrman's statement that "if [God] wanted his people to have his words," he would "possibly even have given them the words in a language they could understand, rather than Greek and Hebrew"). And since Ehrman one-sidedly avers that "meaning is not inherent and texts don't speak for themselves" and that therefore readers "can make sense of the texts only by explaining them in light of their other knowledge," to understand God's word would require inerrantly inspired interpretation as well as inerrantly inspired writing, copying, translation, and updating. No wonder, then, that Ehrman's "journey" from evangelicalism came to what he calls "a dead end." His evangelical faith died by way of a hardening of the categories; and his self-reported postmortem stands as a warning to evangelicals, from whom he inherited some of that hardening of categories.

Postscript: Despite the foregoing criticisms, my sympathies often lie with Ehrman. The rigidity of the fundamentalism in which I grew up far exceeded anything he has described concerning his own such experience.

His inveighing against homogenizing the distinctive messages of biblical authors for the sake of historical harmony strikes in me a resonant chord. And at an early stage of my doctoral research on Matthew's use of the Old Testament, what increasingly seemed to count as misquotations—the usual suspects: reversing Micah's description of Bethlehem as small into a strong denial of that description (Matt 2:5–6), quoting Hosea's reference to Israel's exodus from Egypt as though it predicted the Messiah's stay in Egypt and exit from there (Matt 2:15), and so on—these seeming misquotations led me at one point to say aloud in the privacy of my study, "God, it's not looking good for you and your book." So why didn't I arrive at Ehrman's "dead end"? I have no explanation except to say that "by the grace of God" (the phrase Ehrman judges a textual corruption in Heb 2:8–9) I was spared a hardening of the categories through which Scripture is perceived. Or since they were already hard—*unreasonably hard*—I should rather say that the Spirit of God softened my categories so as to give them an elasticity that accommodates the human features of Scripture without excluding its ultimately divine origin. I pray that Ehrman and all others like him may enjoy such a softening. (Sadly, he has wandered into atheism since my writing of this review essay.)

Re-Facing the Text

My enjoyment of earlier publications by Sarah Ruden made me eager to read and review a new book of hers about translating the Bible into English. Since she has made her name as a translator of Greek and Latin classics, I wondered at first whether her title *The Face of Water*[1] might be alluding to the ancient myth of Narcissus, who fell in love with the reflection of his face in a pool of water. I was wrong. For such an allusion you'd expect *The Face on Water*. Ruden's subtitle, *A Translator on Beauty and Meaning in the Bible*, makes for a biblical allusion instead, "And the Spirit of God moved upon the face *of* the waters" (Gen 1:2c KJV), and signals an emphasis on beauty as much as on meaning.

The title of a preliminary poem, "After Reading *The Journals of George Fox*," furthered my anticipation, because Fox founded Quakerism, my mother grew up a Quaker and graduated from George Fox University (as it is now called), and I spent the most formative years of my boyhood in the little Quaker community of Greenleaf, Idaho, named after the Quaker poet John Greenleaf Whittier. Moreover, Ruden makes much of her own Quakerism.

To highlight the usually colloquial style of biblical Hebrew and Greek, Ruden adopts in her own language a similar style: chatty (like "Thing is," at the start of a sentence), zesty (like "for cryin' out loud" elsewhere), and sometimes edgy. So edgy, in fact, that after reading a number of pages, waking up in the middle of the night and thinking about the book, I predicted to myself that before long "shit" would appear in Ruden's text. Behold, there it appeared some pages later the very next day, though attributed to the "cogent" suggestion of an unnamed professor.

---

1. New York: Pantheon, 2017.

At that point it wasn't hard to predict a dropping of the F-bomb, as then happened right on schedule. Ruden offers "Shit!" as a replacement for the fossilized "Behold!" Occasionally used to express wonderment, however, "Shit!" usually carries an undertone of negation, as in "Damn it!" So how about "Wow!" for a slangy replacement, like Ruden's "For darn tootin'"? Reserve the scatology for Phil 3:8. (As Judy Davis says in the movie *One Against the Wind*, "Have your man look it up.")

Some surprising mistakes, not attributable to popular speech, turn up from time to time. Ruden puts *sic* after quoting a historically acceptable spelling of the Bible translator John Wycliffe's last name. "On behalf of" occurs where "in behalf of" is clearly required. More seriously, the Samaritans' temple is said to have stood "in the northern Palestinian city of Samaria," whereas it stood miles away on Mount Gerizim near the village of Sychar.

Ruden's breezy style suggests that she writes for nonscholarly readers, or at least for nonscholars when it comes to the Hebrew Bible and the Greek New Testament. Her self-description as a popularizer confirms this suggestion, as does also her noting "Hebrew's stark poverty of conjunctions," so that readers of the Hebrew Bible have to sort out for themselves the logical relations between statements connected usually by a mere "and." Biblical scholars would not need to be told that; nor would they need to be told that both Hebrew and Greek, being highly inflected languages (carrying *within* a verb its subject, to take but one of many available examples), generally require fewer words to express a thought than does English, in which separate words are usually required.

Grammatical explanations can help, but I suspect they often get into weeds so thick that the average nonscholar will wonder what's going on. Concerning the story of David's lament over the death of his first child by Bathsheba, for instance, Ruden says that an "overexplicit" pairing of the unusually independent Hebrew pronouns for "I" and "he" suggests emphasis: "*I* will go to him, but *he* will not return to me." A nonscholar is liable to puzzle over the description "overexplicit" in the relation between pronouns, a participle, and a finite verb, and then wonder why "this [emphasis] would be very hard, if not impossible, to show in English" when Ruden's use of italics seems to do a good enough job. Or what would a nonscholar make of her interlinear version of Ezek 37:2a, "*and-he-caused-to-pass-me beside-them round round*" in correspondence to the "dorky-looking" transliterated Hebrew, *veh-heh-eh-veera-nee ahlei-hem sahveev sahveev*, which she translates, "And caused me to pass by them round about"? (This sort of presentation fills the last thirty-nine pages.)[2]

Ruden draws a contrast between ancient literature as wedding form and content in equal measure and modern language as "serving mainly to convey information in explicit and interchangeable forms—but with a dimension called 'style' for artistic uses *on the side*" (emphasis added). Those who have showered accolades on the artistic style-cum-content of Ruden's English translations of *The Aeneid*, *Lysistrata*, and *The Satyricon* might well disagree. Moreover, there's plenty of relatively unartistic, mainly informational content in ancient Hebrew and Greek literature. As one of my children (about five years old at the time) asked me during family devotions upon our launching into the laws of sacrifice in Lev 1–7, "Of what interest is all this to me?"

Ruden's introduction contains a cursory survey of Old Testament, intertestamental, and New Testament history, a brief discussion of the way biblical books were put together for a canon, and some semi-theological opinions. She doesn't "ooh and aah" over the gnostic Gospels or, despite using feminine third person pronouns generically, deal in "'gendered perspectives' or other pseudo-political folderol." Nor does she credit canonization to "institutional authority," such as church councils—rather, to "popular favor." In line with such favor she goes on to claim that societies made sure their translations of the Bible "reflected their own current concerns more and the concerns of the texts' long-gone originators less." One could argue to the contrary that translations were designed to *affect* societal concerns more than to *reflect* them.

Ruden states that "Scripture has, over time and on balance, *not* been placed in the position of a tyrant [a prejudicial term for Scriptural authority, which she elsewhere affirms under the condition of communally evolving perceptions] but rather at the service of ideas [presumably arising out of human cogitation] about a just and protecting God" (emphasis original). It follows naturally that she chooses for treatment biblical passages not especially for their Jewish or Christian distinctiveness but because they "get from quarters both religious and nonreligious that almost erotic individual assent to great words, as well as a certain homey embrace in communal memory." These passages come in pairs, first from the Old Testament, then from the New Testament: David and Bathsheba and the Lord's Prayer under the rubric of "Grammar"; the Creation Account

---

2. Here and below in this review I follow Ruden's practice of transliteration.

and John's Prologue under "Vocabulary"; Ezekiel's Dry Bones and Revelation's Martyrs in Paradise under "Style"; the Twenty-Third Psalm and the Beatitudes under "Poetry"; Ecclesiastes on the Fragile Joys of Life and Paul on the Love of God Through Jesus under "Rhetoric"; the Ten Commandments and the Parable of the Good Samaritan under "Scripture as the Big Conversation"; and the book of Jonah and Paul on Circumcision under "Comedy."

Ruden treats these passages initially from the standpoint of their character. Then she goes through them again, making her own translations, and yet again with an explanation of her scholarly resources and methods. The question that readers will have to ask is whether she succeeds in recapturing the "tone and lyricism" of the selected passages. For she complains that most of what she sees in English Bibles is the "loss of sound, the loss of literary imagery, the loss of emotion," and "the loss of thought and experience."

It's "false," claims Ruden, that "Hebrew and Greek words had the kind of narrow meanings characteristic of English words." But it's false to say that English words have narrower, more "compartmentalized" meanings than do Hebrew and Greek words. In fact, the correspondences between words in different languages vary; and whatever the language, a word's range of possible meanings depends largely on context, which Ruden dismissively describes as "much touted." Not that context always clarifies meaning. But Ruden tends to underestimate contextual limitations on a word's meaning and therefore to commit the interpretive sin of "illegitimate totality transfer," or what she sanctifies as "large territories of meaning in a single [Hebrew or Greek] word." The Old Testament scholar James Barr famously warned against this sin. But Ruden remains unrepentantly stiff-necked: "No one is going to convince me that a reader should treat this Hebrew word as she would treat the English one ['beginning'], ignoring any possibility of an allusion to authority and superiority here [in Gen 1:1, where *reisheet*, she says, spans a temporal 'beginning,' a social and political 'chief,' ritual offerings of 'firstfruits,' and the quality of 'best']."

As she does with *reisheet* in Gen 1:1, Ruden attributes to *archei*, "beginning," in John 1:1a ("In the beginning was the Word [*logos*]" [KJV]) "shadings of sovereign power, and of excellence of several kinds." Illegitimate totality transfer again. Ruden similarly attributes to *logos* shadings of "financial reckoning," "argumentation," "storytelling," and "transcendent thought." Hence her translation: "In the beginning was the idea." But throughout John's Gospel *logos* occurs for verbal expression, for which "idea" does poor service. In this case, then, illegitimate totality transfer has pretty well erased the contextually intended meaning of *logos* (see John 1:18, "he hath declared him," and 5:24, "he that heareth my word" [KJV]). But Ruden does right to say that in John 1:13 "only 'husband' makes sense." So context rules after all!

Though characterized by some overinterpretation, especially of a psychological rather than linguistic sort, Ruden's treatment of the story of David and Bathsheba rates an A+. Included there and elsewhere is an important observation that the repeated expression, "And it came to pass" (KJV), far from carrying forward a narrative ploddingly, highlights the following in a variety of ways and therefore deserves lively translations.

To stress the compactness of Hebrew as compared with English, Ruden counts thirty-three words in the KJV of Ezek 37:1 "as opposed to the Hebrew's thirteen." But in a highly inflected language like Hebrew, as already noted, words tend to have more syllables, each one acting like a separate word in English. So the number of syllables in the Hebrew of Ezek 37:1 (35) comes within two whiskers of the KJV's number (37). Absent an appreciable difference, then, what happens to Ruden's point that "repetitive patterning [in Hebrew] is far less wearing [than in English]"? Nevertheless, she offers a scintillating commentary on Ezekiel's vision of dry bones.

In the Lord's Prayer, Ruden uses two ways of translating the jussive verbs, one with the helping verb "let," as in "let your kingdom come," the other with "must," as in "your kingdom must come." Trouble is, "let" connotes permission; and "must" connotes necessity. By avoiding these non-jussive connotations, "Thy kingdom come" (KJV) does better.

Because of Jesus' command to pray privately (Matt 6:6), Ruden deduces that despite the plural in "*Our* Father" and subsequent first person plurals, the pray-er is "supposed to be completely alone or even furtive." Perhaps she missed that Jesus has switched from a singular "you" in Matt 6:6 to a plural "you" in the lead-up to the Lord's Prayer (Matt 6:7–8).

In the book of Revelation, Jesus is portrayed as an *arnion*. This Greek word is diminutive, so that Ruden translates it with "little lamb" but says, "I don't want to ride this distinction [from a full-sized lamb], as diminutives seem naturally to replace ordinary words as languages evolve" (cf. *biblion*, a diminutive in Revelation for a book large enough to contain the names of the innumerable redeemed, I might add). But Ruden goes on to ride the distinction extremely hard: "only, and relentlessly, a 'little lamb'"; "the tiny animal" on "the majestic throne"; "this tiny creature";

"a single tiny divine lamb"; "the darling lamb" that is "tiny and pet-like"; "this tiny lamb in the center of the throne like a toddler on a CEO's office chair." Unfortunately, Ruden fails to note that according to Rev 5:6 "this weakest and most dependent of herd animals," as she calls him, sports no fewer than seven horns with which he will gore to death his and his people's enemies.

Ruden's explanation of Hebrew poetry will enlighten nonscholars. She correctly observes that in the KJV of Ps 23, "maketh me to lie down" sounds wrongly compulsive nowadays. But her interpretation of oil-anointing as designed for cleanliness raises questions: Why only the head? Why not the much dirtier feet? Why not oiling the head to make it shine joyously? And to me, "deepened 'wagon tracks'" for "paths [of righteousness]" sounds too specific. Yet Ruden brilliantly builds up to Ecclesiastes with a discussion of Hesiod versus Juvenal, though I wonder whether in Ecclesiasticus, Jesus the son of Sirach might give Juvenal a run for his money in respect to misogyny, for which she awards the palm to Juvenal.

As for the Beatitudes, to substitute "Happy" for "Blessed," as Ruden and many others do, puts the emphasis on a subjective feeling instead of an objective fact and thereby runs into trouble regarding those who mourn. For mourners aren't happy. So how about "Fortunate" in place of the outdated "Blessed"? Ruden does offer a nice explanation, however, of sound effects in the Greek of the Beatitudes and draws a marvelous contrast between the Parable of the Good Samaritan and a story in the Roman novel called *The Golden Ass*.

She denies that the Decalogue was dictated from on high and opines that it gives "a lasting impression of living voices working things out." Over against such commendable human collaboration on the part of ancient Israelites and their heirs, she cites with obvious disapproval dogmatically minded Christians: "whereas Christians—don't get me started." Perhaps we glimpse here the latitudinarianism of Ruden's Quakerism, which ranges from the evangelical to the Hicksite.

Her section on Comedy deserves high praise. She suggests that the ambiguity of *elōhim*, Hebrew for "gods" or "God," may have posed a puzzle for the pagan sailors and the Ninevites in the story of "cartoonish" Jonah, whom she calls (perhaps too cleverly) "Flitillary Joe," "Joe-Nothing," and "Busterfly." And then there's Paul's sarcastic humor in wishing that the person who's "arousing" Galatian Christians with insistence on circumcision "would get his own pair cut off," that is, get castrated (Gal 5:12). Maybe Ruden doesn't go far enough, though. Since circumcision (literally, "a cutting *around*" [<u>peri</u>tomē]) has to do with the penis, not the testicles, might Paul be wishing that the troublers would go to the extent of getting their circumcised penises "chopped *off* [<u>apo</u>kopsontai]"?

I'm sorry to have criticized *The Face of Water* more than I'd have thought needful. Despite its disappointing errors and misjudgments, however, it contains sizeable passages of brilliance. Dare I say that Ruden often proves herself a better commentator than translator? Last of all, a hurrah for her outlining the Christian gospel concerning Jesus Christ and confessing, "As unscientific as it makes us seem, I and two billion-plus other people say, 'Of course.'" Amen.

Tom's Targum

TIME WAS WHEN EVERYBODY understood a translation to be a more or less word-for-word transfer of meaning from one language to another—"or less" because words and grammatical constructions differ in languages foreign to each other and therefore sometimes require renderings looser than word-for-word. On the other hand, everybody understood a paraphrase to be recognizably freer: more thought-for-thought than word-for-word. But translation of the Bible increasingly into languages featuring grammatical structures far different from those of biblical Hebrew and Greek, and carrying cultural freight far different from that of the Bible, made word-for-word transfer a lot less feasible.

Along came the dynamic (aka functional) equivalence theory of translation. For the sake of languages and cultures exotic to those of the Bible, this theory incorporated paraphrase into translation, so that even in English versions of the Bible the boundary between translation and paraphrase became as porous as the border between the United States and Mexico. You can even hear Eugene Peterson's *The Message*, a paraphrase if there ever was one and self-identified as such, quoted as a "translation." The incorporation of paraphrase into translation may best be illustrated by the shift from the marketing of Kenneth Taylor's *The Living Bible* originally as "a paraphrase" to its being marketed now as *The New Living Translation*, though those who revised it (I was one of them) were told at the start to keep it recognizable as a paraphrase by Taylor.

In the wake of this development arrives *The Kingdom New Testament: A Contemporary Translation* (from here on *KNT*)[1] by N. T. Wright, identified effusively in its back ad as "the world's leading New Testament

1. New York: HarperOne, 2011.

scholar (*Newsweek*)" and accurately in its gatefold as "one of the world's leading Bible scholars." Duly distinguishing between translation and paraphrase, Wright asks, "Is this new version really a translation or a paraphrase?" and answers, "It's a translation, not a paraphrase" (xii). Why a new translation? Because language is constantly changing, so that "translating the New Testament is something that, in fact, each generation ought to be doing." (I leave aside the question whether for the present generation enough new translations have already been produced.)

KNT originally appeared in Wright's series of popular commentaries on the New Testament—*Matthew for Everyone* et al.—and therefore sports a colloquial style. I'll call *Everyone* "Joe the plumber" and "Jane the hairdresser." Or to suit today's woke culture, should I say "Jane the plumber" and "Joe the hairdresser"? Either way, "J&J." And since Wright calls me "Bob," I'll call him "Tom." Colloquialism all around, then, so that *KNT* is to be evaluated at the level of J&J's everyday speech.

Tom's preface helpfully alerts J&J (1) to translators' often having to take interpretive stances on controverted passages; (2) to the use of gender-neutral English in *KNT* when referring to human beings in general; (3) to the omission of some verses because they're missing from the best manuscripts, undiscovered as yet when verse-by-verse numbering was instituted; (4) to the desirability of reading in one sitting large chunks of the New Testament for their "flow and pull"; and (5) to the need in careful study for two or three English translations, not just *KNT*, even if you know the original Greek (as J&J do not).

KNT sparkles with many gems of spirited English. My favorites, in no particular order: "Were completely flabbergasted" (Matt 19:25). "Mr. Messiah" (Matt 26:68). "Hey, you!" (Luke 4:34). "Swapped" (Rom 1:26). "Get this straight" (Jas 1:19). "The real stuff, not watered down" (1 Pet 2:2). "Well then" and "There you are, then" (Matt 5:48; 7:11; Mark 10:8) instead of "Therefore." "Play-acting" and "play-actors" (Matt 6:2, 5) instead of "hypocrisy" and "hypocrites." "Fuss about" (Matt 6:32) instead of "seek after." "A tight squeeze" (Matt 7:14) instead of "narrow." "We're done for!" (Matt 8:25) instead of "We're perishing!" "Tell him off" (Matt 16:22) instead of "rebuke." "Salt is great stuff" (Mark 9:50) instead of "... good." "Eventually, Paul got fed up with it" (Acts 16:18). "God won't have people turning up their noses at him" (Gal 6:7). "Put Jesus on the spot" (Luke 10:25). "Face it" (Luke 11:13) instead of "If therefore." "You have no idea" (Jas 4:14) instead of "You don't know." "Wine ... fine" (Matt 16:2). "Refused ... used" (Luke 20:17). "Guzzling and boozing" (Matt 11:19, though "guzzling" is rare for eating, as required here). "Silly . . . sensible" (Matt 25:2). "Legion . . . there are lots of us" (Mark 5:9). "He hadn't the guts to refuse her" (Mark 6:26).

Balancing the foregoing hits, though, are some misses: "Yes, I know that's weird, but there's more" (Phil 3:8), instead of a simple "More than that," is too clever by half. "What d'you . . . ?" "Where d'you . . . ?" and "How d'you . . . ?" (Luke 22:9 and often) are *too* colloquial. "Woe betide . . ." (Matt 23:13 and often) is pedantic. "Without him knowing how he did it?" (Mark 4:27) is awkward. "Stone-cold sober" (Mark 5:15) makes an ex-demoniac seem to have been formerly drunk. To an American's ear, "Chloe's people have put me in the picture about you" (1 Cor 1:11) sounds as though they've included Paul in a photo of the Corinthians rather than that they've informed Paul about the Corinthians. Though traditional, Jesus' being "a high priest according to the order of Melchizedek" (Heb 5:6 and following) will sound to J&J as though Jesus became a high priest at Melchizedek's command. (How about "in alignment with Melchizedek," which corresponds to the Greek word's use for a line or rank of soldiers?)

"That indeed is what we are [viz., 'God's children']" (1 John 3:1) doesn't have the oomph of a literal translation: "And we are!" The characteristically British use of "lot"—as in "A fine lot [= amount] of faith you've got!" (Matt 14:31); "This lot [= group] who came in last" (Matt 20:12); "cut the whole lot [= male sexual organs] off" (Gal 5:12); "you double-minded lot" (Jas 4:8); "Why do you lot eat and drink . . . with tax-collectors and sinners?" (Luke 5:30)—will befuddle American readers. Tom dislikes "whom" where good grammar requires it, as in "I will show you who [instead of 'whom'] to fear" (Luke 12:5, also elsewhere), and regularly positions "only" too early, as in "only lasts a short time" (Matt 13:21) instead of "lasts only a short time" (plus further examples). But whether deliberately or not, in these cases he's following popular usage.

KNT is peppered with words, phrases, and whole clauses that have nothing corresponding to them in the original Greek and that aren't needed for understandable English. Here are just a few of many such insertions: "And let everybody know it" (Matt 20:25). "What had happened was this" (Mark 6:17). "Something new" (Mark 8:31). "Now look" (Luke 11:19). "After all" (Luke 19:11). "Really?" (John 1:46). "Oh, really?" (John 5:12). "Wait a minute" (John 1:50). "Come on" (John 4:31). "Well I never" (1 Cor 5:1). "It's Passover-time, you see" (1 Cor 5:7). "Well, well!" (John 3:10).

Repetitions of legitimately translated words make up a special class of insertions: "For me, for me" (Luke 1:49). "Men, men" (Acts 14:15).

"Kill him! Kill him!" (Acts 21:36). "Please, please" (Acts 21:39). "Welcome, welcome, welcome with a blessing, they sang" (Luke 19:38, plus an omission of "the coming one"). Admittedly, these insertions often add zest. They're the sprightly way Tom expresses himself. But they don't represent even loosely what the New Testament authors actually wrote.

Inconsistencies of translation also abound in *KNT*. But variety is the spice of life, and according to Ralph Waldo Emerson "a foolish consistency is the hobgoblin of little minds, adored by little . . . divines." And Tom is no little divine. Nonetheless, inconsistency can cause confusion and obscure connections, as happens in the following: A tunic is an undergarment, a cloak an overgarment; and Tom uses "tunics" for the undergarment (Acts 9:39), but also both "shirt" and "cloak" for the undergarment (Matt 5:40; 10:10; Luke 9:3). Confusing! "Colleague," "servant(s)," and "slave(s)" alternate with each other for the same Greek word and even in the same parable (Matt 18:23–35; Luke 19:12–25). "The Righteous One," "Lord," and "God" get capitalized regularly (see Jas 5:1–11, for example), as does "our Lord and Master" for the Roman emperor (Acts 25:26). But "the father" (in reference to God), "the son" (in reference to Jesus), and "the holy spirit" (in reference to the third person of the Trinity) don't get capitalized. Are J&J to infer nondivinity versus divinity?

Tom makes a point of his translating the Greek conjunction *gar* variously (xii–xiii) and notes that English versions often translate it with "for" in the sense of "because." (It needs adding that a conjunctive "for" often introduces an explanation other than causal.) Judging this sort of "for" to be formal, stilted, and nonconversational, Tom translates *gar* variously with a semicolon, "So," "yes," "of course," "after all," "No way!" "Why not? Because . . . ," "Look at it like this," "You see" (tiresomely often), and even with elliptical dots (. . .) or not at all. For example, Mark 8:35–38 sets out four parallel reasons for the cross-taking demanded in 8:34. Jesus introduces each reason with *gar*. Tom translates the first *gar* with "Yes," the second with "After all," and the third and fourth not at all. So J&J may miss the parallelism of reasons given for cross-taking.

Tom's saying, "I have tried to stick closely to the original" (xii), almost forces a reviewer to judge the closeness of *KNT* to its underlying Greek text. First, then, some outstandingly close and accurate translations: "Leaven" (a bit of fermenting dough) rather than "yeast" (Matt 13:33 and later). "Born from above" (John 3:3, 7) rather than "born again." "Crossbeam" (Luke 23:26) rather than the whole cross as carried. "Life of the age to come" (usually) rather than "eternal life" (though the aspect of eternality is not to be denied), and "assembly" rather than "church" (the latter of which tends to mean a building). "The Messiah, the son of God, is . . . Jesus" (John 20:31) rather than "Jesus is the Messiah, God's Son." "The spirit-animated body . . . the nature-animated one" (1 Cor 15:46) rather than "the spiritual [= ethereal] body . . . the natural [= physical] body."

Second, some questionable or disappointing translations: "After the Babylonian exile" in Matt 1:12, leaving the misimpression that "Jeconiah became the father of Salathiel" after the seventy years of Babylonian exile rather than becoming so right after the deportation to Babylon at the start of the seventy years. "Some wise and learned men" (Matt 2:1) for the Magi, who were astrologers (and in other contexts dream-interpreters, magicians, or even quacks). "God's kingdom," connoting territory, without a complementary translation, "God's reign," connoting activity. "Corn" (Matt 12:1 and later), which will make J&J think of corn on the cob rather than wheat or barley. "Anything remarkable," being weak tea for "miracle" at Mark 6:5. "Mattress" (Luke 5:18–19, 24; John 5:8–9, 11), which will suggest to J&J something too cumbersome to carry. "Time" instead of "hour" (Matt 24:36; Luke 12:39–40), so that the specificity of an hour as the shortest unit of time named by ancients is lost. "I'm your friend" instead of Peter's "I love you [Jesus]" (John 21:15–17) and despite Tom's translating the Greek verb with "love" seven out of eight times earlier in John's Gospel (the sole exception appearing in 15:19: "The world would be fond of its own"). "Plenty of room" and "home" instead of "abodes" and "abode" in John 14:2, 23, so that the connection with "abiding" in Christ (John 15) is severed, a further severance occurring in the translation "remain" instead of "abide." "With . . . no god" (Eph 2:12) for gentiles prior to their conversion, in seeming contradiction of their former polytheism. There are also frequent failures to bring out prolonged and repeated actions in the past and present, as in "Ask [rather, 'Keep asking'] and it will be given to you" (Matt 7:7) for beggars' wisdom.

Third, some tendentious and outright erroneous translations: "My friend" (Matt 15:28) for Jesus' addressing a Canaanite with "Woman." "Oh, Mother!" (John 2:4) for Jesus' addressing his mother Mary with "Woman," which introduces exactly the same question used by demons in an attempt to fend him off, as in Mark 5:7: "What do you and I have to do with each other?" Also John 19:26, where Jesus addresses Mary with "Woman" rather than "Mother" (as falsely again in *KNT*) when putting distance between himself and Mary by calling the beloved disciple her son, and her the beloved disciple's mother.

"You and your silver belong in hell!" (Acts 8:20) turns a wish (so the original) into an exclamatory statement of fact. "Do it quickly, won't you?" (John 13:27) turns the original's firm command, "What you're doing, do very quickly," into a whimpering question (compare *KNT*'s "Why don't you give them something [to eat]?" instead of the original's "You give them [something] to eat" [Mark 6:37]). "Heal yourself, doctor!" (Luke 4:23) isn't a "riddle." It's a "proverb." Against the original of Mark 7:2–4 Tom treats immersing as though it were the same as washing. "Giving wedding parties" (Luke 17:27) disagrees with "being given in marriage [as daughters are]" (so the original).

Tom speaks of "God's word" as a sword that "can pierce right in between soul and spirit, or joints and marrow" (Heb 4:12). But the original has no "right in between," and a sword doesn't pierce in between joints and marrow. So, according to the original, "piercing to the point of a division *of* the soul and *of* the spirit, and *of* joints and *of* marrow," depending on whether the sword strikes between two jointed bones or elsewhere deeply into the marrow of one bone. Therefore penetration into the soul and into the spirit, not between them.

"Several" occurs erroneously and often for the Greek word *polloi*, which means "many," and this despite the nonuse of a Greek word that does mean "several" (*tines*). The use of "fox" (Luke 13:32) where the original may mean "vixen" (a female fox) misses a possible slur on Herod Antipas. The use of "Adulterers!" where the original has "Adulteresses!" misses a similar slur on the addressees in Jas 4:4. And "shake you into bits like wheat" (Luke 22:31) is puzzling for "sift you like wheat."

Following are some examples of the effect of Tom's interpretation on his translations: "Took a deep breath" (Acts 8:35; 10:34) interprets "opening his mouth." "Will you please tell me how I can get out of this mess?" (Acts 16:30) interprets "What must I do to be saved?" in terms of avoiding execution (despite Paul's having assured the jailer that all the prisoners were present) rather than in terms of escaping God's wrath. "Practicing homosexuals" (1 Cor 6:9; 1 Tim 1:10) interprets homosexuality in terms of behavior as distinct from inclination. "Or any intermediate state of" interprets "'angel' or 'spirit'" (Acts 23:8) as referring to dead and therefore disembodied human beings rather than to nonhuman angels or spirits. (I agree.)

Since in Tom's opinion "righteousness" tends now to mean "self-righteousness" and sound like "a proud, 'churchy' sort of word" (xiii), he repeatedly uses "God's covenant justice" (Rom 1:17 and following) to interpret "God's righteousness" (compare "your covenant behavior" [Matt 5:20] for "your righteousness"). But will J&J, who haven't read Tom's scholarly publications, understand this new translation any better than the traditional one? Never mind the disputability of Tom's interpretive translation and its sounding at least as "churchy" as "God's righteousness." Similarly in regard to "the faithfulness of Jesus" (Rom 3:22–26; Gal 2:16; Phil 3:9) rather than "faith in Jesus" as an interpretation of "faith of Jesus" (so the Greek), though Tom translates Mark 11:22, which exhibits the very same grammatical construction, "Have faith in God."

Almost always (and extremely often even in short passages), Tom prefers "King Jesus" over "Christ Jesus," and "Messiah" over "Christ." "Christ/Messiah" means "Anointed One," of course; and the Christ/Messiah was to be a king. But for "king" Greek uses a different word (*basileus*). So "King" for "Christ/Messiah" comes by way of inference more than by way of translation and despite the fact that others than kings were also anointed (priests most prominently).

"She will, however, be kept safe through the process of childbirth" adopts one of several possible interpretations of 1 Tim 2:15 by translating "She will be saved" as "She will . . . be kept safe" and by injecting "the process of" into "through childbirth." Perhaps the most obvious example of a translation slanted by interpretation appears earlier in 1 Tim 2:11–12, which Tom renders as follows: "They [godly women] must study undisturbed, in full submission to God. I'm not saying that women should teach men, or try to dictate to them; rather, that they should be left undisturbed." Tom first replaces learning (from men) in quietness with studying undisturbed (by men). Then he imports "to God," with no support in the Greek text, to make God rather than men the object of women's submission—against the making of men, especially husbands, the objects of women's submission according to Tom's own translations of 1 Cor 14:34–35; Eph 5:22–24; Col 3:18; Titus 2:5; 1 Pet 3:1, 5. Finally, he changes Paul's "I don't permit [a woman to teach men or dictate to them]" into a wishy-washy "I'm not saying that . . ."

One more textual matter requires mention. Tom rightly rejects what he calls "two extra 'endings' for Mark's gospel," because "they are not found in the best manuscripts" (xvi). Yet he includes these extraneous materials in translation, the shorter in single square brackets, the longer in double square brackets (the reverse of what he says in his preface). On the other hand, he includes the story of the woman taken in adultery (John 7:53—8:11) without noting its absence from the best manuscripts, without enclosing it in any brackets, and without mentioning that in the inferior manuscripts it occurs willy-nilly after Luke 21:38; 24:53; John 7:36, 44; 8:12; 21:25 as well as after John 7:52. This inconcinnity may appeal to the nonjudgmentalism that's prevalent nowadays even on moral matters ("'Well, then,' said Jesus, 'I don't condemn you either!'" [John 8:11, often quoted without the follow-up: "'From now on don't sin again!'"]). If only the inauthentic longer ending of Mark hadn't encouraged snake-handling in the Appalachians, maybe that ending would have shed its square brackets.

Does *KNT* work, then, as a translation in the sense taken for granted by J&J when reading both *KNT*'s subtitle, *A Contemporary Translation*, the back ad's description of *KNT* as "modern prose that stays true to the character of the ancient Greek text ... conveying the most accurate rendering possible," and Tom's own statement of having "tried to stick closely to the original"? No, not even by the standards of dynamic/functional equivalence, of which J&J are ignorant anyway. Too much unnecessary paraphrase. Too many insertions uncalled for. Too many inconsistencies of translation. Too many changes of meaning. Too many (and overly) slanted interpretations. Too many errant renderings of the base language.

But there is a body of religious literature characterized by all those traits, namely, the ancient Jewish targums, which rendered the Hebrew Old Testament into the Aramaic language. So *KNT*'s similar combination of translation, paraphrase, insertions, semantic changes, slanted interpretations, and errant renderings—all well-intentioned—works beautifully as a targum. Which apart from the question of truth in advertising isn't to disparage *KNT*. For the New Testament itself exhibits targumizing, as when, for example, Mark 4:12 has "lest ... it be forgiven them" in agreement with the targum of Isa 6:10 rather than "lest ... one heals them" (so the Hebrew) and as when 2 Tim 3:8 has "Jannes and Jambres" in agreement with a targum of Exod 7:11—8:19, which in the Hebrew original leaves Pharaoh's magicians unnamed. Hence, *Tom's Targum*. Trouble is, J&J won't know they're reading a targum.

Higher Critical Issues

Thinking Outside the Box—Pandora's, *i.e.*

THE HACKNEYED EXPRESSION "THINKING outside the box" derives from the nine-dot puzzle in which you are supposed to connect all the dots by drawing a continuous set of no more than four straight lines. Underlying the puzzle is a natural tendency to imagine that the corner dots represent the corners of a square, so that connecting the dots requires a continuous set of at least five lines. The solution lies in thinking outside those corner dots so as to imagine only four lines of a bisected triangle.

But a box is three dimensional. A square is only two-dimensional. So why do we speak of thinking outside the *box* instead of thinking outside the *square*? Maybe, just maybe, the Greek myth of Pandora's box comes into play.

Whether or not it does, that myth likewise starts with a puzzle. For a wedding present Pandora, the first human female, is given a box with contents unknown to her.[1] She is not supposed to open it, but she puzzles over its contents. Then curiosity gets the better of her. She opens the box, and out fly all the evils that afflict human beings: hard toil, noisome diseases, the miseries of old age, early death, and countless other plagues.

In his book *Pandora's Box Opened*,[2] New Testament scholar Roy A. Harrisville likens to Pandora's still *un*opened box the traditional treatment of biblical books as a breed apart from other literature, as closed off from historical-critical questions of authorship, dates of writing, textual fidelity, factual accuracy, theological consistency, moral probity, and so

---

1. Actually the box was a jar, but the mistranslation has become traditional.
2. Grand Rapids: Eerdmans, 2014.

forth. In modern times, though, historical critics have opened the box by asking those questions about biblical books. (Compare the statement of Benjamin Jowett in his famous essay, "On the Interpretation of Scripture" [1860], that an interpreter "is to read Scripture like any other book.")

The relatively recent asking of historical-critical questions has engendered a host of answers pestilential in their effect on many people's faith in the Bible as God's word, or even as containing or becoming the word of God. If Moses did not write the Pentateuch, as many historical critics of the Old Testament aver, for example, what is to be made of Jesus' saying that Moses wrote about him (John 5:46), even if it be accepted that Jesus made such a statement? If Old Testament saints did not rise bodily from the dead and appear to many in Jerusalem at the time of Jesus' death and resurrection in accord with Matt 27:51b–53, as many historical critics of the New Testament aver, how can we be sure that Jesus himself rose bodily from the dead in accord with Matt 28:1–20? Since late copyists inserted the story of the woman taken in adultery at several different locations in the New Testament (most often in John 7:53—8:11), what is to keep us from doubting the textual integrity of other passages too? You get the idea.

Since the Enlightenment, and along with more recent developments in literary criticism, the pestilential effect of these and similar questions has caused a backlash against historical criticism of the Bible. The backlash threatens to displace historical-critical interpretation of biblical texts not only with contemporary nonhistorical-critical interpretations but also with the allegorical, anagogical, and tropological interpretations offered by the early church fathers and medieval scholastics. Sometimes these premodern interpretations are touted as superior to modern interpretations arising out of historical criticism.

Publishers are riding the premodern wave with series such as the Ancient Christian Commentary on Scripture (InterVarsity), emphasizing the early church fathers, and the Church's Bible (Eerdmans), emphasizing medieval commentators. Even in traditionally historical-critical series, attention to premodern interpretations has become both common and celebrated, as for example in Ulrich Luz's three-volume commentary on the Gospel according to Matthew (Fortress; Hermeneia Series). Moreover, theological interpretation of the Bible in the form of commentaries written by contemporary theologians rather than by biblical scholars is invading the market, as in the Brazos Theological Commentary on the

Bible (Baker) and Belief: A Theological Commentary on the Bible (Westminster John Knox).

Harrisville describes these developments as "the ['ten thousand times ten thousand'] voices that challenge or dismiss the historical-critical method" and complains, "The synchronic is thrown against the diachronic, orality against textuality, the text against authorial intent, the intratextual against the referential, reader-response against text autonomy, feminist against patriarchal interpretation, and so on and on." To this list can be added postcolonial criticism, LGBTQIA+ criticism, other advocacy criticisms, and even *lectio divina*.

Against those developments, Harrisville defends the historical-critical method on the ground that biblical religion arises out of God's dealing historically with humankind. As others have put it, the biblical God is not a god of mythmakers or the God of philosophers—rather, the God of Abraham, Isaac, and Jacob, of Moses and Joshua, of Jesus and the apostles. So if we are to make sense of the Bible, whether or not we believe in its divine inspiration, it behooves us to ask of it historical questions, and to answer those questions. Thus the subtitle, in part, of Harrisville's book: *An Examination and Defense of Historical-Critical Method*.

Why the need for a defense right now? Answer: because of what Harrisville identifies as a current malaise in that there is no longer any agreement on method among biblical interpreters. No longer do they speak the same hermeneutical language with each other, as they used to do when aiming to determine the historically, authorially intended meaning of biblical texts. Harrisville's complaint leads him to discuss an extraordinarily broad range of interpretive issues, most of them related to the Bible in particular, but some of them having wider relevance.

With apologies for its length, here is a catalog of those issues that gives some notion of the breadth of discussion:

- a closed biblical canon versus openness to further revelation;
- the Old Testament as contributory to the New Testament versus the Old Testament as opposed, or at least inferior, to the New Testament;
- accommodation versus nonaccommodation to cultural limitations in human understanding;
- naturalism (as in demythologization) versus supernaturalism (as in accepting the possibility of miracles);
- biblical errancy versus biblical inerrancy;

- verbal versus conceptual infallibility;
- harmonizing of biblical texts versus acceptance of disharmony;
- biblical perspicuity versus opacity;
- the letter versus the (so-called) spirit of biblical texts;
- literal versus figurative interpretation;
- preunderstanding versus neutrality in the process of interpretation;
- the hermeneutics of suspicion versus the hermeneutics of charity;
- reason versus faith and revelation;
- truth as correspondence to reality versus truth as subjective;
- the advantage versus disadvantage of faith and obedience for biblical interpretation;
- biblical texts as interpreted by human beings versus human beings as interpreted by biblical texts;
- interest in what lies behind a biblical text (its author's psychology, for example) versus interest in a biblical text for its own sake;
- interest in an author's intention versus interest in interpreters' often different intentions;
- the Spirit's interior witness to Scripture versus external authority;
- individual interpretation (as in Pietism, for example) versus ecclesiastical interpretation (as in Roman Catholicism, for example);
- exegesis according to historical analysis versus exegesis according to a theological system;
- historicism versus allegory and typology.

Lying between these opposing poles, of course, are mediating positions, which Harrisville also discusses.

The subtitle's remainder, *and Its Master Practitioners*, telltales the main structure of *Pandora's Box Opened*. After comparatively brief treatments of interpretive methods in ancient history, the Reformation era, and the period of Protestant orthodoxy and Pietism, Harrisville pays most attention to the Enlightenment, the modern period (up through the nineteenth century), and the twentieth century.

Slotted into the chronological periods are accounts of the interpretive positions taken by well-known influential figures such as

Luther, Calvin, Bengel, Reimarus (often overrated), Spinoza, Locke, Semler, Schleiermacher, Strauss, Baur, Edwards, Hodge, Barth, Bultmann, Cadbury, and Gadamer. Other figures, some of them perhaps lesser known (especially in English-speaking circles), also come into view: Müntzer, Flacius, Wolff, Haman, Baumgarten, Edelmann, Ewald, and Schlatter (finally getting his due), plus Stuart, Harper, Burton, Mathews, Case, and Lake in the United States. There are many others as well. Thus Harrisville's treatment of historical-critical method is itself historical-critical in regard to biblical interpretation.

Harrisville has provided such a feast of information and argument, much more than can be detailed here, that it would be churlish to fault him for omissions. So I shall compliment him with complements. Fitting splendidly into the discussion would be some attention to Martin Kähler's *The So-Called Historical Jesus and the Historic Biblical Christ* (1892). The historical-critical contributions of J. B. Lightfoot, Theodor Zahn, H. J. Holtzmann, and B. H. Streeter may also deserve attention. Since form criticism, represented most outstandingly by Rudolf Bultmann, did gain attention, perhaps C. H. Dodd's kerygmatic alternative needs some too. Likewise in regard to Oscar Cullmann's emphasis on salvation history and Raymond E. Brown's advocating a biblical *sensus plenoir* in addition to hypothesizing, historically-critically, five stages (later, three stages) in the production of John's Gospel.

Since text criticism is admittedly a subset of historical criticism, one might welcome at least a mention of B. F. Westcott and F. J. A. Hort (for the NT) and workers on the Dead Sea Scrolls (for the OT). Notably, the early historical-critical publications of Richard Simon caused stirs in the Roman Catholic Church, as did the later controversy over Alfred Loisy at the turn of the nineteenth and twentieth centuries. Also worthy of mention may be the work of M.-J. Lagrange and others at the École Biblique in Jerusalem, plus the historical-critical effects of Cardinal Bea's work on the papal encyclical *Divino afflante Spiritu* and at the Second Vatican Council. The effect on historical-critical method of biblical archaeology, with standout names such as that of William Foxwell Albright, would further enrich an already rich discussion.

But does Karl Barth really count as one of the historical-critical method's *Master Practioners*? Whether true or not, the word at Basel University during my time there was that Oscar Cullmann, who also taught there, considered him a great theologian but a lousy exegete, whereas Barth considered Cullmann a great exegete but a lousy theologian.

As generally agreed, the main blame (if you will) for opening Pandora's box of historical-critical questions rests at the feet of Baruch Spinoza. According to the ancient Greek myth, however, hope remained in the box. It did not escape. At the outset of his book Harrisville notes this remainder but does not return to it explicitly at the end. Nonetheless, he does find hope for the future of historical-critical method, especially in the views of his former teacher Otto Piper. He admits with Piper that readers' presuppositions and purposes inevitably cloud authorially intended meanings and generate other meanings, as often in New Testament usage of the Old Testament. Yet despite the consequent cutting down to size of historical-critical method, argues Harrisville, we need the method for a focus on the historical reality, however much or little it may be blurred around the edges, out of which emerged the gospel as God's word.

Here a qualification is in order: for Harrisville, Piper, and many others the Bible is not to be equated with God's word. It only, but importantly, "attests" to that word, which consists in the gospel (so the very last statement in *Pandora's Box Opened*). Welcome, then, to a canon within the canon, the interior canon of the gospel being the truly decisive one.

How to distinguish the gospel as God's word in the Bible from the rest of the Bible? This question throws us back onto questions of private versus communitarian versus creedal versus ecclesiastical judgments. And back onto the question whether to interpret the gospel expansively in terms of the whole Bible, or whether to separate out a gospel for use as a tool to critique the rest of the Bible (as in Martin Luther's treatment of the epistle of James, for instance). If to separate out a gospel, will this gospel be pedobaptistic and covenantal? Or fidebaptistic and conversionist? Or pneumatic and charismatic? Will it be individualistic or socialistic?[3]

Whose version of the gospel gets to be the scalpel that cuts away whatever is deemed extraneous or inimical to that version? Will it be a Roman Catholic version? An Orthodox version? A Lutheran version? A Calvinistic version? An Arminian version? A Pentecostal version? A Marxist version? Some other version? Presumably a Christian gospel arises out of the life, death, and resurrection of Jesus. But out of him as a teacher? As a reformer? As a prophet? As an example? As a substitutionary

---

3. At lunch in the refectory of Manchester University an English clergyman once told me that to be a Christian I had to be a Socialist, a statement that reminds me of another of Benjamin Jowett's famous sayings: "My dear child, you must believe in God despite what the clergy tells you." Not that Jowett's brand of theology is to be adopted, however. He himself was a clergyman!

sacrifice? As a victor? As some of the above but not all, or as all the above and perhaps more?

In other words, to distinguish the gospel within the Bible from the rest of the Bible is to pose the question of plenary inspiration versus partial inspiration—and, if partial, the further question of how to identify the inspired parts (or inspiring parts, if you think the Bible *becomes* God's word for you in a crisis). As for me, I'm pinning my Pandoran hope on the Bible as a whole. Despite my disagreement with the Lutheran Harrisville at this point, I have to say that his dense and learned discussion deserves a close reading by every biblical scholar, church historian, theologian, and seriously minded lay Christian.

Messed-Up Memories of Jesus?

IN HIS BOOK *JESUS Before the Gospels: How the Earliest Christians Remembered, Changed, and Invented Their Stories of the Savior*,[1] Bart Ehrman writes for readers uninitiated into modern scholarly study of the New Testament and other early Christian literature. Such readers, he assumes, view the canonical Gospels of Matthew, Mark, Luke, and John as presenting fairly or wholly harmonious and reliable portrayals of the historical Jesus, that is, Jesus as he would have been videotaped had the necessary technology been available in the first century. Ehrman is at pains to disabuse his readers of that view, so that his own portrayal of the historical Jesus makes only a minimal appearance in the book. Emphasis falls instead on what Ehrman takes to be the *un*historicity of stories that evolved in oral traditions prior to the writing of the canonical Gospels and that then made their way into them.

To flesh out that emphasis, Ehrman posits "a mysterious period of oral transmission, when stories [about Jesus] were circulating, both among eyewitnesses and even more, among those who knew someone whose cousin had a neighbor who had once talked with a business associate whose mother had, just fifteen years earlier, spoken with an eyewitness who told her some things about Jesus." (By itself, Ehrman's introduction contains nine such rhetorical flourishes; and I've counted at least ten more in the rest of the book.) Then Ehrman asks how "those people at the tail end of the period of transmission" were "telling their stories about Jesus." "Did they remember very well what they had heard from others (who had heard from others who had heard from others)?" Think the game "Telephone," in which a message whispered from one person to another, then

---

1. New York: HarperOne, 2017.

to another and another, and so on till the message ends up much distorted. That is to say, many distortions characterized the oral stories about Jesus that the evangelists eventually wrote down. Not that the stories contained no reliable information whatever. The "gist" of his life comes through "pretty well," says Ehrman, but "the details get messed up."

Enmeshed in Ehrman's argument are a number of distinctions: First, a personal distinction between the evangelists traditionally identified as Matthew, Mark, Luke, and John, and those whom Ehrman regards as the actual, unknown authors of the canonical Gospels. Second, a geographical distinction between Palestine, the location where Jesus' first disciples lived, and the rest of the Roman Empire, where the Gospels' true authors lived. Third, an educational distinction between Jesus and his first disciples as all uneducated, illiterate peasants and the true authors of the Gospels as highly educated literates. Fourth, a linguistic distinction between Jesus' first disciples as Aramaic-speakers who knew little or no Greek and the evangelists as Greek-speakers who knew little or no Aramaic. Fifth, a chronological distinction between Jesus' first disciples as having lived for the most part before the fall of Jerusalem in AD 70 and the actual evangelists as having written not until about AD 70 and the decades following. Sixth, an informational distinction between true details known about Jesus at first and untrue details that came about through messy storytelling. Seventh, a historiographical distinction between writing what probably took place and writing what probably did not take place. Often these distinctions consist in unargued assertions; so I will take occasion below to point out Ehrman's repeated failures to mention for uninitiated readers even the existence of arguments countering the assertions.

For now I proceed to what Ehrman considers his special contribution: the application to Jesuanic oral traditions of modern secular studies of human memory from the standpoints of psychology (concerning individual memory), sociology (concerning collective memory), and anthropology (concerning memory in wholly or largely illiterate and therefore oral cultures). These studies have exposed the unreliability of memories. Not total unreliability, but astonishing unreliability. So we cannot trust the Gospels entirely, says Ehrman, and probably very little, because their written reports about Jesus rest on memories of memories of memories. Why, even the testimony of eyewitnesses has sometimes turned out to be unreliable, as shown for example by the well-known use of DNA evidence to overturn criminal convictions based on eyewitness testimony. So the

Gospels would not be reliable even if they were written by eyewitnesses to Jesus' life. The same conclusion is to be drawn if as non-eyewitnesses the evangelists had drawn on the testimony of eyewitnesses. And to illustrate the way shifting cultural conditions affect collective memories, Ehrman cites the remembering of Columbus during the past colonial era as the celebrated discoverer of America, and the remembering of him during the present postcolonial era as a ruthless and therefore despicable latecomer. Shifting memories of Abraham, Lincoln, and Masada come in for similar treatment.

Returning to ancient times for further examples of shifting memories, Ehrman cites outlandish, postcanonical stories about Peter, Judas Iscariot, Pontius Pilate, the Virgin Mary, and Jesus as a baby, a boy, and an adult—stories that everybody, including evangelical Christians and hidebound fundamentalists, considers unhistorical. Why? Because they're . . . well, just plain silly. An excess of the miraculous for its own sake, for example. But Ehrman adds that modern people reject the historicity of those apocryphal stories because they don't want or expect to see historical reliability in them. Conversely, they accept the historicity of canonical stories about Jesus, including those about his miracles, exorcisms, and resurrection, because they do want and expect to see such reliability in them. Thus Ehrman sows a seed of doubt concerning readers' motives and expectations and then proceeds to cite a bevy of historical implausibilities, discrepancies, and outright contradictions in the canonical Gospels as evidence both that the details concerning Jesus' life got "messed up" through faulty and inventive memories and that theories of formally and informally controlled traditioning fail to satisfy. Here's a sampling:

- In the Synoptic Gospels of Matthew, Mark, and Luke, Jesus doesn't attract his first disciples till after the imprisonment of John the Baptist. In John's Gospel he attracts his first disciples before the Baptist's imprisonment.
- In the Synoptics, Jesus proclaims God's kingdom over and over again but keeps his messiahship under wraps until the night before Good Friday. John's Jesus says very little about the kingdom but proclaims in public his messiahship and much else about himself over and over again from the very start of his ministry.
- In Matt 12:38–42, Jesus refuses to give a "sign," except for that of Jonah, whereas Jesus gives multiple "signs" throughout John's Gospel.

- The who, when, and where of a woman's anointing Jesus differ from one Gospel to another.
- In the Synoptics, Pilate delivers Jesus to his (Pilate's) soldiers for crucifixion. In John, he delivers Jesus to the Jews for crucifixion.
- In Luke, the curtain of the temple is rent before Jesus dies, but after he dies in Mark and Matthew.

Along with other examples, the foregoing are cited by Ehrman in much more detail than present space allows for analysis. But nothing new is to be seen in them, for they and similar differences between the Gospels have long been noted. How then should evangelical and other conservatively minded Christians respond? Not, I think, by straining for pure historicity where historical implausibility, discrepancy, and contradiction seem reasonably obvious. Instead, note should be taken that differences between the Gospels, troublesome as they are to pure historicity, commonly fall into patterns distinctive to, or at least characteristic of, the evangelists' various emphases.

To take but one of many available examples, consider Ehrman's highlighting as "strikingly different" the Synoptics' placement of Jesus' cleansing the temple in the last week of his life, whereas the Gospel of John places it at the very beginning. Ehrman concludes that two cleansings seem implausible. Well and good, and let us agree with him that the Synoptics present a historically accurate chronology (though he reduces the event to "some kind of disruptive activity in the Temple"). But is John's unhistorical chronology necessarily the result of messy storytelling that took place over much time and in many different locations? Hardly, for a theological purpose underlies the chronological shift.

In John's Gospel alone, John the Baptist has proclaimed Jesus to be God's Lamb who takes away the sin of the world (John 1:29, 36). Jesus has then gone up to Jerusalem for a Passover festival, when lambs were to be sacrificed (John 2:13). There he cleanses the temple, but only in John's account is Jesus said to drive out the animals being sold for Passover sacrifice. Why does he drive them out? Obviously, to make theological room for himself as God's recently proclaimed sacrificial Lamb, who makes animal sacrifices obsolete. To continue the theme of Passover, John mentions this festival several more times and, not as in the Synoptics, has Jesus going to it at least once again before the end of his life (John 6:4; 11:55; 12:1; 13:1; 18:39; 19:14). Then in another chronological shift, John has Jesus dying as God's Passover Lamb on the very afternoon when

Passover lambs are to be slain—as against the Synoptics' historically accurate placement of Jesus' death during the following afternoon. Finally according to John but not the Synoptics, a soldier pierces Jesus' rib cage with a spear "in order that the Scripture might be fulfilled: 'Not a bone of him [the Passover lamb in the OT context] shall be broken'" (19:19–37).

Do those differences from the Synoptics look like the result of messy storytelling? No. They look instead like deliberate editing on the part of an author. At the loss of some historicity? Yes, but to a great theological gain. *What we have in the Gospels, then, isn't historically messed-up memories—rather, theologically dressed-up portraits.* When it comes to further historical implausibilities, discrepancies, and contradictions among the Gospels, evangelicals and other conservatives would do well to engage in the foregoing theological hermeneutic rather than in text-contorting harmonizations for the sake of pure historicity. The same is to be said against pleas that we would see harmony if only we had more information than is presently at hand.

To his credit, Ehrman recognizes editorial patterns in the Gospels; but he's mesmerized by the notion of messy storytelling prior to the evangelists' writing. As a result, he fails to see that such storytelling is likely to have produced helter-skelter differences among the Gospels rather than differences that fall neatly into recognizably distinctive patterns. And if the evangelists imposed distinctive patterns on a hodgepodge of disparate oral traditions, how is it that the first three Gospels are so much alike that we call them "Synoptic"? (John's Gospel is a special case about whose relation to the Synoptics all sides dispute.) Nevertheless, Ehrman insists, "We need to know what was happening to the memories of Jesus precisely during that time gap ['forty to sixty-five years separating Jesus's death and our earliest accounts of his life']."

Therein lies a problem, though: we don't have any oral traditions concerning Jesus. We have only written records. So at this point the argument has to mutate into literary questions of date, authorship, early church tradition, and exegesis, as Ehrman also recognizes. But except in regard to the early church fathers Papias and Irenaeus, he defers without argument to the shared opinion of fellow higher critics outside evangelical and other conservative camps. Unfortunately, this deferral leaves the general readers for whom Ehrman writes ignorant of contrary higher-critical opinions and the arguments supporting those opinions.

The early church father Papias, whom Ehrman does discuss, recorded a tradition that in anecdotal form Mark wrote up the apostle Peter's reminiscences of Jesus' life and ministry. Because this tradition tends to support a high level of historicity in Mark's portrayal of Jesus, Ehrman tries to undermine the tradition. He dates Papias's writing not till AD 120 or 130. But recent scholarship has mounted impressive arguments for a date in the very first decade of the second century. Ehrman pays no attention to these arguments. Furthermore, Papias was recording a tradition passed on to him from an earlier, even apostolic time period; and the earlier the tradition, the greater a likelihood of its trustworthiness. Though disputed also among conservatives, there is even the possibility (a likelihood in my opinion) that the "elder/disciple John" to whom Papias ascribed the tradition of Mark's writing up Peter's reminiscences was none other than the apostle John.[2]

Against reliability in the tradition passed on by Papias, however, Ehrman cites the later church father Eusebius of Caesarea's scorn of Papias. But Papias wasn't recording only his own view of Mark's writing. He was recording an earlier and therefore *pre*-Papian tradition. And Ehrman doesn't mention Eusebius's opposition to chiliasm (the belief in a coming millennial rule of Christ on earth) as a reason for the scorning of Papias, a chiliast who also stated his preference for oral reports over books. Ehrman then uses this preference to argue against Mark's Gospel as stemming from the apostle Peter's reminiscences. But the fact that Papias preferred oral reports supports the reliability of the tradition he passed on concerning a book. For apart from the tradition's reliability, a preference for orality would likely have led him *not* to cite a tradition favoring the apostolicity of a *book*'s contents.

Inveighing further against the pre-Papian tradition that Mark "gives an exhaustive account of everything Peter preached," Ehrman declares "there is no way" that "anyone could think that the Gospel of Mark in our Bibles today gives a full account of Peter's knowledge of Jesus." But according to the tradition, Mark wrote only "*some* things" (Greek: *enia*) that Peter remembered. Since "the vast majority" of stories in Mark "have nothing to do with Peter," declares Ehrman further, Mark's Gospel must not derive from Peter's reminiscences. But the Gospel is predominantly about Jesus! Even so, it quickly introduces Peter and his brother Andrew as Jesus' very first disciples and almost as quickly relates Jesus' entering their house and healing Peter's mother-in-law.

2. See the essay "The Apostolically Johannine Pre-Papian Tradition concerning the Gospels of Mark and Matthew" in my book *The Old Is Better* (Eugene, OR: Wipf & Stock, 2010), 49–73.

According to the theory of a messianic secret in Mark, the evangelist or someone before him invented Jesus' attempts to keep his messiahship secret and did so to explain why Jesus was not widely acknowledged as the messiah during his lifetime. Ehrman uses this theory to undermine yet further the historicity of Mark's Gospel as a record of Peter's reminiscences of Jesus' ministry: "One of the overarching organizing principles in the Gospel was not at all historical." Sadly, general readers are left uninformed that recent scholarship of the critical kind with which Ehrman aligns himself has left the theory in tatters.

Ehrman also tries to dissociate what Papias passed on concerning Matthew, another disciple of Jesus besides Peter, from our canonical Gospel according to Matthew. He does so by translating the Greek *ta logia* with "the words," as though the pre-Papian tradition were referring to a collection of Jesus' sayings rather than to our narratival Gospel according to Matthew, and also by arguing that "in a Hebrew dialect" excludes a reference to our Greek Gospel according to Matthew. But the pre-Papian tradition uses *ta logia* also for Mark's Gospel; and nobody thinks that tradition was describing it, or another writing by Mark, as a collection of Jesus' sayings rather than a narratival Gospel. Besides, *logia* is better translated with "oracles" (relating in this case to an authoritative book as a whole) than with "words" (relating to a book's contents as consisting in individual sayings). As to Matthew's "Hebrew dialect," a strong argument has been mounted for "Hebrew *style*," which would fit our Matthew perfectly, rather than "Hebrew *language* [or '*tongue*,' in Ehrman's translation]," which would not fit our Matthew even as a Greek translation of a Hebrew original. Again Ehrman omits to mention such considerations.

"If Papias did have our first two Gospels [Matthew and Mark] in mind," says Ehrman, his imaginatively grotesque account of Judas Iscariot's death—though it "overlaps with an account found in Matthew"—shows clearly that Papias "does not consider Matthew's version to represent the Gospel truth." But again, it was the earlier elder/disciple John who had in mind our first two Gospels. If Papias followed suit, as apparently he did, it may have been his preference for oral tradition that led him to accept the grotesque account over Matthew's. Be that as it may, Ehrman doesn't consider that imaginative expansions of early tradition imply a *high* view of that tradition, just as the many noncanonical, unhistorical expansions of the Old Testament in Second Temple Jewish literature evince reverence for the Old Testament, not a discrediting of it.

Another early church father, Irenaeus, titled the canonical Gospels as according to Matthew, Mark, Luke, and John and described himself as a personal disciple of the earlier church father Polycarp, who in turn was a disciple of the apostle John. This pedigree makes for a strong argument, seconded by the Muratorian Fragment (an early list of NT books), supporting reliability in the titles. Matthew and John were among Jesus' first disciples. Mark and Luke were associates of Jesus' first disciples. Naturally, then, Ehrman needs to undermine such a historicity-favoring tradition. So regarding Matthew, Mark, Luke, and John, Ehrman says, "Those are the apostolic names that came to be associated with these books all over the Christian map," the implication being that such names were mistakenly attached to the Gospels to give them authority. But neither Mark nor Luke was an apostle, as Ehrman quickly admits. And given geographical spread on the Christian map, why the absence of diversity in authorial ascriptions if Irenaeus's are false?

Given the truth in those ascriptions, the weight of what Papias passed on concerning Mark and Matthew, and arguments undiscussed here but favoring a pre-AD 70 date of writing for the Synoptics (and certainly of the traditions they incorporated), the amount of historically worthwhile material that the evangelists worked with looks to have been very much larger than the minimal amount suggested by Ehrman's thesis of messed-up memories. And this is not even to enter current scholarly discussions of historicity in the Johannine tradition.

Back to Jesus and his disciples: Ehrman doesn't *know* that none of them were literate. There's plenty of evidence for a higher rate of literacy than he acknowledges. Besides, ancient authors often dictated to a scribe, as even an illiterate could do. As noted already in the pre-Papian tradition, Mark's Greek doesn't bespeak a high education such as Ehrman ascribes to all the evangelists; and John's Greek is so simple that beginning students of Greek regularly start there. Moreover, contemporary research is turning up more use of Greek among first-century Palestinian Jews than used to be thought.

Trying to undermine historicity yet again, Ehrman asks about the Sermon on the Mount, "How could a massive crowd possibly hear anything he [Jesus] had to say if he was in an outdoor setting on a mountain [or standing 'on a level place' (Luke 6:17)]?" Has Ehrman never read a skeptical Ben Franklin's on-the-spot calculation that George Whitefield could be heard by more than thirty thousand people? I myself heard Tommy Titcombe, a diminutive early missionary to Nigeria, speak to several thousand in a voice so booming that the loudspeaker system had to be turned off.

Ehrman correctly notes that Luke 1:1–4 doesn't say the evangelist interviewed eyewitnesses or based his account "on what he directly learned from eyewitnesses." But Ehrman doesn't notice that Luke's wording leaves open these possibilities, which would fit Luke's purpose to convince readers of "the certainty" of the Gospel's following contents. Also, Ehrman gratuitously says that in the prologue of John's Gospel the "we" who saw the incarnate Word dwelling among them were "the community of Jesus's *later* followers" (emphasis added). But how does Ehrman know that they were only "later," that they didn't at least include Jesus' first followers, or even that they didn't consist solely of the first followers (cf. 1 John 1:1–4)?

Ehrman casts doubt on the historicity of Jesus' triumphal procession by arguing that the Roman soldiers stationed in Jerusalem would have put an immediate stop to the procession. But the procession is said to have taken place on the road outside Jerusalem, not on the streets inside Jerusalem, where the soldiers would have been stationed.

"The Jews did not kill Jesus," asserts Ehrman. "The Romans killed Jesus." Consequently, Ehrman omits Jesus' hearing before the Sanhedrin from his list of historically accurate "Gist Memories of Jesus's Death." In line with Ehrman's own emphasis on ways the recent past corrupts memories of the distant past, you wonder whether a widespread feeling of guilt over the twentieth-century Holocaust has led him to disremember Jesus' hearing before the Sanhedrin, their accusing him before Pilate, and the Jews' clamoring for his crucifixion.

Inferring that Jesus never performed miracles, Ehrman writes that "with the passing of time Jesus's miracle-working abilities became increasingly pronounced in the tradition, to an exorbitant extent." In the apocryphal Gospels, to be sure. But increasingly in the canonical Gospels? The reverse, I think. The earliest of them, Mark, emphasizes Jesus' miracles as acts of brute power, as when the evangelist says that to staunch a woman's chronic flow of blood, "power had gone out of him [apparently without his having willed it to do so]" (Mark 5:30). Matthew scales down his accounts of Jesus' miracles to foreground the accompanying words of Jesus. At the expense of brute power Luke emphasizes the humanitarian element in Jesus' working of miracles. And John, writing last, avoids "miracles" (literally, "powerful acts") altogether and refers instead to Jesus' "signs" and "works" as symbols of the salvific changes that happen to believers in Jesus: from emptiness to fullness, darkness to light, and death to life (to mention several examples).

Ehrman declines to discuss in this book any evidence for the historicity of Jesus' miracles and resurrection. Why? Because historians discuss only "what probably happened in the past," and "by definition" miracles and resurrections are "utterly improbable." But historians also discuss what probably did *not* happen in the past; and to distinguish between the probable and the improbable they have to judge the quality of all testimonial evidence. Philosophical presuppositions affect that sort of judgment, of course. So by refusing to examine testimonial evidence in favor of Jesus' miracles and resurrection, Ehrman has followed philosophically in the train of David Hume even while denying an antisupernaturalistic presupposition. Unfortunately, Ehrman neglects to note for his readers both a considerable philosophical critique of Hume's reasoning and Craig Keener's investigations into reports of ongoing miracles.[3]

Moving away from the Gospels, Ehrman emphasizes a dearth of information about Jesus' life and teaching in the apostle Paul's letters, as though to say that at the early date of those letters not very much truly historical information was available to Paul even though he spent time visiting with Peter and James the brother of Jesus (Gal 1:19). But scholars disagree widely over how much those letters reflect Jesus' life and teaching. Aside from that disagreement and Ehrman's failure to mention it, by common consent Paul was a literate, highly educated Greek-speaker—in contrast with Jesus' first disciples according to Ehrman. And a self-confessed and zealous persecutor of the church was Paul: "I was persecuting God's church outrageously and wreaking havoc on it" (Gal 1:13; see too Phil 3:6). Yet very shortly he converted into an equally zealous Christian missionary at stupendously great personal cost to himself (see esp. 2 Cor 11:16–29). And he refers to similar activity by "the rest of the apostles and the Lord's brothers and [particularly] Cephas [Peter]" (1 Cor 9:5). According to Mark, Matthew, and John, not even Jesus' brothers believed in him during his lifetime. So how plausible is it that they, the apostles, and Paul turned into empire-wide preachers of a shamefully crucified Jesus as the Messiah and world's Savior if in fact the historical Jesus was no more than a Jewish teacher who happened to get in trouble with the Romans? And how is it that Paul and the others converted so radically,

---

3. See Craig S. Keener, "Miracle Reports and the Argument from Analogy," *BBR* 25 (2015) 475–95, with considerable bibliography.

quickly, and even immediately, not after decades of memory-corrupting storytelling? Yeah, let's talk about implausibility!

Finally for the present review, Ehrman illustrates different *recent* memories of Jesus with Reza Aslan's book *Zealot* (Jesus as a revolutionary against Rome) and Bill O'Reilly's book *Killing Jesus* (Jesus as a sort of politician who "wanted smaller government and lower taxes"). Here the meaning of "memories" strays into the meaning of "interpretations." You could say, of course, that all memory is interpretive. But surely the degree of interpretation varies from one memory to another. In my opinion, Ehrman does not take sufficient account of this variation and thereby betrays that he is judging the Gospels almost exclusively according to a modern criterion of strictly factual accuracy. His concluding "paean" even to historically *in*accurate memories for their aesthetic beauty and moral uplift slights, tragically, the glory of the gospel.

A Question of Interpretive Reliability in Defense of Historical Reliability

IN A SECOND, HEAVILY updated edition of his book *The Historical Reliability of the Gospels*,[1] the author, Craig L. Blomberg, mounts a conservative defense of the canonical Gospels' historical reliability and notes by way of contrast the nonconservatism of his religious and educational upbringing. The defense of reliability ranges widely through harmonization of the Gospels (starting in the early church), various criticisms (source, form, redaction, midrashic, literary), philosophy (regarding miracles and resurrection), the question of contradictions (among the Synoptics and between them and John), Jesus-tradition outside the Gospels (as to apparent historical errors, non-Christian testimonies, Christian traditions in Acts through Revelation and outside the NT), and historiography (in respect to genre, burden of proof, and criteria of authenticity). Rounding out the volume are appendices on archaeology and text-criticism in relation to the Gospels' reliability; a massive bibliography, with whose contents Blomberg displays an admirable firsthand acquaintance; and indices of authors, Scripture, and ancient sources.

Detailed, fair expositions of the strengths and weaknesses of various positions characterize Blomberg's discussions of the aforementioned topics. Budding theological students will learn much from the expositions, and scholars of all stripes are also likely to learn. Blomberg makes much of a rising tide of historiographical conservatism in the last few decades, but

---

1. Downers Grove: InterVarsity, 2007.

exceptions such as the Jesus Seminar and especially Bart Ehrman come in for occasional jabs. On the basis of secular historiographical methods, Blomberg argues that the burden of proof rests properly on skeptics of historical reliability, though he seems to accept a burden of proof when it comes to miracles and Jesus' resurrection while citing big bang and intelligent design theories as possible scientific supports for a theism that makes reasonable an acceptance of supernaturalism in human history.

On the one hand, modesty conditions many claims made by Blomberg. Though believing in the complete inerrancy, infallibility, and inspiration of Scripture, he does not presuppose them in his defense of the Gospels' historical reliability. Instead, he argues on purely historical grounds for a strong likelihood of historicity. Sometimes the argument self-confessedly supports only the core details of a passage, though other details may in fact be likewise historical. So Blomberg argues for "*overall* historicity" and "*general* trustworthiness" and allows for "*minor* modifications" and (of course) the paraphrasing of Jesus' words. For example, Matthew may have "recognized that Jesus' self-understanding included the idea of unity with the Father . . . and the Spirit . . . *whether or not* Jesus ever encapsulated that concept in an explicit trinitarian formula" such as is found in Matt 28:19 (159; emphasis added).

On the other hand, immodesty attaches to other of Blomberg's claims. Early on he writes, "It is fair to say that all the alleged inconsistencies among the Gospels have received at least plausible resolutions" (56). Hence "one can answer with confidence that they [the Gospels] have emerged unscathed" (87). "Most of the charges have been answered adequately many times over" (152); and "in every case, it has been concluded that an even-handed treatment of the data does not lead to a distrust of the accuracy of the Gospels in what they choose to report" (297).

Underlying these immodest claims is a persistent attempt to harmonize differing details in the Gospels' parallel accounts. As to the disciples' having no faith in Mark 4:40 and little faith in Matt 8:26, for instance, Blomberg grants that "Matthew has *softened* the force of Mark's wording *somewhat*, and he does on the whole paint the disciples in a *slightly* more positive light than Mark. But this hardly produces an irreconcilable contradiction, as if Matthew had made Jesus praise the disciples' great faith" (155; emphasis added to point up the attempt to minimize difference). What commentator has interpreted little faith as great faith, though? And who but an excessively determined harmonizer would interpret the difference between no faith and little faith as merely "perspectiv[al]"?

To harmonize Jesus' cursing of a fig tree and its withering, seemingly on the spot according to Matt 21:18–20, with the account in Mark 11:12–14, 19–21, where the withering isn't noticed till the next day, Blomberg sees "no reason to exclude an interval of time between verses 19 and 20 [in Matthew]" and agrees with H. Ridderbos that "Matthew's use of 'immediately' 'does not mean that [the tree] became barren at once, but merely that it began to wilt from that moment on'" (178). No mention is made of Matthew's usual practice of eliminating immediacy as compared with Mark, of his inserting "immediately" here not just once but twice, of his using a word for immediacy (*parachrēma*) quite possibly more emphatic than Mark's usual word for it (*euthus*), of Matthew's dropping the next day's notice of the withering (so Mark) because of the immediacy in Matthew, or of Matthew's having just advanced the cleansing of the temple to Palm Sunday from the next day, where Mark placed it.

To get rid of the discrepancy between Jesus' prohibiting the Twelve from taking sandals or a staff in Matt 10:10 (so too Luke 9:3 in regard to a staff) and allowing both in Mark 6:8–9, Blomberg hypothesizes—on the supposed likelihood of an inclusion of the Twelve among the seventy-two in Luke 10:1–24—that "Matthew has combined some of Jesus' instructions to the Twelve with some of those to the seventy-two," so that "on the one occasion [of the Twelve alone] staff and shoes were permitted; on the other [of the seventy-two], they were forbidden" (187–88). What to do with Luke, then? For he distinguishes the mission of the seventy-two from that of the Twelve yet agrees with Matthew against Mark in prohibiting a staff for the Twelve.

Blomberg favors two cleansings of the temple, the first one early in accordance with John 2:13–22, the second one late in accordance with the Synoptics. No consideration is given to the possibility of John's having advanced the cleansing for a close connection with the Baptist's pronouncing Jesus in 1:29, 36 to be the Lamb of God that takes away the world's sin. For John's is the only account of the cleansing in which Jesus drives out the sacrificial animals, now rendered obsolete by his arrival as God's Lamb. Nor is any consideration given to John's other chronological advancements for theological reasons—of Jesus' open self-revelations, judgment, and eternal life, for example.

To harmonize the accounts of Judas Iscariot's death in Matt 27:3–10; Acts 1:15–20, Blomberg resorts to the traditional explanation that the rope broke and that the chief priests acted as Judas's agents in the purchase of a field. It remains unexplained how or why Matthew calls it the

Field of Blood because of Judas's having betrayed the innocent blood of Jesus whereas Luke calls it the same because of Judas's blood. Many other problems of harmonization exist, as in the accounts of Jesus' resurrection and subsequent appearances; but limits of space both here and in the book prevent very detailed discussions.

Blomberg allows for Jesus' recorded discourses to be somewhat composite, but he generally favors that they are "substantially abbreviated accounts of much longer messages of Jesus" (181)—this because Jesus' "having ended *these* sayings" (Matt 7:28–29; 13:53; 19:1; 26:1; cf. 11:1) "easily misleads his [Matthew's] readers into assuming that he has narrated unified sermons of material already spoken by Jesus" (emphasis original). How misleading, then, are the two instances of "immediately" in Matthew's account of the fig tree's withering, and the statement in Matt 1:17 that "*all* the generations . . . from David to the deportation to Babylon [are] fourteen generations" (emphasis added) when 1 Chr 3:1–16 knows of four more generations? Apparently the limitation to "fourteen" applies to Matthew's text, not to history. The possibility of "longer messages" remains, however.

For all his devotion to scriptural inerrancy (24n1) and desire to understand inerrancy as much as possible in historical as well as theological terms, Blomberg occasionally allows theology to overcome, or at least to cloud, historicity, as when he has Luke changing a parabolic landlord's certainty that tenants would respect his son (so Mark 12:6) into the mere possibility that they would (Luke 20:13) "to make sure that no one misinterpreted the parable by thinking God did not realize what would happen when he sent *his* son" (99; emphasis original). In Luke, therefore, the theology of divine omniscience trumps what Jesus historically said according to Mark. Similarly, "the Evangelists' redaction" clouded with faith the fig tree's symbolizing Israel in Jesus' intention, "since their [the Evangelists'] emphases lie elsewhere: faith in the context of prayer and forgiveness more generally (Mark 11:24–25)" (131). Would that Blomberg had let the evangelists' theological concerns encroach on their historical concerns a bit more often. As it is, his resistance to loosening up the category of historical writing in the Gospels may lead many who take the evangelists' wording with arguably greater seriousness than he does to regard his harmonizations as special pleading and then be psychologically disposed to dismiss his sterling defense of the Gospels' historical reliability in other respects and on the whole. 'Twill be a pity should it happen so.

To balance the eight beatitudes recorded in Matt 5:3-10, Blomberg imagines four unrecorded woes in addition to the four recorded in Luke 6:24-26. He also omits defending the historicity of the Old Testament saints' resurrection in Matt 27:51b-53; ambiguates the public self-identifications of Jesus in John so as to avoid a contradiction of his public reserve in the Synoptics; treats the disciples' baptism in the Holy Spirit at Pentecost (Acts 1:5; 2:1-4) as "not just . . . an initiatory experience" (214) despite the initiatory connotation of baptism and for the sake of avoiding a conflict with the disciples' reception of the Holy Spirit fifty days earlier (John 20:22); and fails to deduce from Jesus' infusing the disciples with the Holy Spirit on the first Easter Sunday evening that he ascended to the Father earlier that day in accordance with John 7:37-39; 20:17.

The following would not matter very much but for their making of gaps in Blomberg's arguments for historicity: he equates Matthew with Levi without reference to a contrary opinion among many scholars; regards 16:8 as the original end of Mark without noting recent defenses of a lost original ending; understands Papias's Matthean *logia* as sayings of Jesus despite considerable, unmentioned opinion to the contrary; assumes without discussion that Luke traveled with Paul in the "we"-passages of Acts; and neglects the Leuven school of thought according to which John used one or more of the Synoptics.[2]

---

2. Errata: on line 9 of p. 6 a cross-reference should be supplied; in note 39 on p. 255 "Jesus" should be changed to "Josephus"; and on p. 43 "Robert Gundry" should not be cited "for Matthew's supposed use of Luke" (the other way around, in fact; see "Luke's being influenced by Matthew" in my *Matthew: A Commentary on His Handbook for a Mixed Church under Persecution*, 2nd ed. [Grand Rapids: Eerdmans, 1994], 683; Gundry, "Matthean Foreign Bodies in Agreements of Luke with Matthew Against Mark: Evidence That Luke Used Matthew," in *The Four Gospels 1992: Festschrift Frans Neirynck*, ed. F. Van Segbroeck et al., BETL 100 [Leuven: Leuven University Press / Peeters, 1992], 1467-95; idem, "A Rejoinder on Matthean Foreign Bodies in Luke 10,25-28," *ETL* 71 [1995] 139-50; idem, "The Refusal of Matthean Foreign Bodies to Be Exorcised from Luke 9,22; 10,25-28," *ETL* 75 [1999] 104-22).

Tabor's Ossuary

THERE'S AN ELEMENT IN the discussion of Jesus' family tomb, so-called, that needs some detailed scrutiny. I have in mind the agreement or disagreement between the earliest oral and literary traditions of what happened to Jesus' corpse, on the one hand, and the interpretation of an ossuary found at Talpiot, Israel, as having contained the secondarily buried bones of Jesus of Nazareth, on the other hand.[1] If I understand Professor James Tabor correctly, he believes that

- the said ossuary probably contained Jesus' bones;
- Jesus' brother James revived and carried forward a messianic movement started by John the Baptist and taken over by Jesus;
- because of the removal of Jesus' corpse from the tomb into which Joseph of Arimathea had put it and because of a secondary burial of Jesus' bones about a year later, James and others in the revived messianic movement knew that Jesus hadn't risen from the dead physically, nor did they proclaim that he had;
- because of visions which Paul claimed for himself, he proclaimed that Jesus had risen from the dead;
- Paul presented Jesus' resurrection (and ours to come) as spiritual rather than physical; and
- in the Pauline offshoot from the messianic movement then headed by James, the notion of a spiritual resurrection morphed into legendary stories of a physical resurrection, such as we have in the canonical Gospels.

1. See James Tabor, *The Jesus Dynasty* (New York: Simon & Schuster, 2006); idem, jesusdynasty.com/blog/ (no longer available).

With such an understanding, there's no disagreement between the earliest literary version of Jesus' resurrection—that is, Paul's presentation of it as spiritual rather than physical—and an ossuary's having contained the bones of Jesus. It would be problematic, though, if the earliest oral and literary versions of Jesus' resurrection presented it as physical. For the earlier the notion of a physical resurrection of Jesus, the greater the tension between that notion and the knowledge of Jesus' original followers that his bones lay in an ossuary of nearby, known location—especially if those who held the notion of a physical resurrection and those who had contrary knowledge of Jesus' ossuary-interred bones were in conversation with each other. On so fundamental a point we should expect some literary evidence of disagreement among them. And the tension becomes even more severe if the original followers of Jesus knew about his bones and some of these followers had themselves interred those bones yet proclaimed him as physically resurrected.

Tabor affirms correctly that Paul and Jesus' original followers were in conversation with each other: "There is little doubt that the apostle Paul was accepted into the inner circles of Jesus' original followers," and they "publicly endorsed his missionary preaching to the Gentile Roman world (Gal 2:9). It was *what* he preached and taught that began to create problems."[2] But Tabor immediately goes on to discuss Paul's view of "a heavenly Christ," including a nonphysically resurrected one, as though that view of him created problems for Jesus' original followers. Not so! As Paul clearly points out in Gal 2, the problems had to do with issues of circumcision, law-keeping in general, and table fellowship. There's nothing about a problem of disagreement over whether Jesus was physically resurrected.

To support a Pauline presentation of a nonphysically resurrected Jesus, though, Tabor states that Paul "claimed to hear a disembodied 'voice' that he identified as 'words' of Jesus."[3] But the texts cited by Tabor—that is, 2 Cor 12:9; 1 Thess 4:15; 1 Cor 11:23—say nothing about a *disembodied* voice. Nor, for that matter, does the word *voice* appear in those texts despite Tabor's putting quotation marks around it.

Tabor's view that Paul presented a nonphysically resurrected Jesus rests above all, however, on Paul's statements in 1 Cor 15:44, 46, 50, about which Tabor states, "Paul, our earliest witness to the resurrection, speaks

2. Tabor, *Jesus Dynasty*, 262.
3. Tabor, *Jesus Dynasty*, 262.

of a 'physical body' and a 'spiritual body,' and though it is a body, he clearly presents both the resurrection of Jesus and the future resurrection of the dead at the end of the age, as putting off the flesh like a garment and being transformed into a higher spirit life."[4] Likewise, Tabor writes that according to Paul, at the second coming the Christian dead will be resurrected "in gloriously transformed spiritual bodies," that Christians still living at the time "will likewise be instantaneously changed from flesh to spirit," and that "Paul seems to be willing to use the term 'resurrection' to refer to something akin to an apparition or vision. And when he does mention Jesus' body he says it was a 'spiritual' body. But a 'spiritual body' and an 'embodied spirit' could be seen as very much the same phenomenon."[5] (Actually, Paul talks about a spiritual body only in connection with Christians' resurrection, but the parallel with Jesus' resurrection, which Tabor draws, is to be accepted.)

Has Tabor understood Paul's discussion of resurrection correctly? I think not. In the first place, Paul contrasts "a spiritual body" with "a soulish body," not with a "physical body" (1 Cor 15:44, 46). But what do these expressions mean? Take first the adjective "spiritual." When Paul describes some Christians in Corinth as "spiritual" rather than "fleshly" or "carnal," he doesn't mean that some Christians in Corinth are floating around its streets in a ghostly form as opposed to others who are pounding the pavement with their feet. No, he's describing some Christians as taught, filled, and led by the Holy Spirit, whose temple is their present physical bodies, as opposed to others dominated by their sinful proclivities despite the indwelling Spirit (1 Cor 2:10–16; 3:1; 6:19; 14:37; Gal 6:1). When Paul speaks of "spiritual gifts," he means gifts given by the Holy Spirit (Rom 1:11; 1 Cor 12:1; 14:1). The manna, the water-supplying rock, and the Mosaic law—all in the Old Testament—are "spiritual" in that the Holy Spirit gave them to the Israelites (Rom 7:14; 1 Cor 10:3–4). And the gospel is "spiritual" as given by the Holy Spirit (Rom 15:27; 1 Cor 9:11).

So we should capitalize the adjective *Spiritual* and dismiss the notion that it indicates nonphysicality. In Paul's view, that is to say, the resurrected body is Spiritual not in the sense of nonphysicality (he even switches back and forth between "body" and "flesh" in 1 Cor 15:35–41) but in the sense of its having been raised by God's Spirit, which is none other than Christ's Spirit, rather than procreated, as in the case of our

---

4. jesusdynasty.com/blog/.

5. Tabor, *Jesus Dynasty*, 232, 264.

present bodies, animated as they are by the soul—hence the contrast with "soulish bodies." But let Paul speak for himself to the effect that in resurrection a Spiritual body is a body raised by the Holy Spirit: "The last Adam [Christ] became a life-making Spirit" (1 Cor 15:45); "But if the Spirit of the one who raised Jesus from the dead dwells in you, the one who raised Christ from the dead will make alive also your mortal bodies through his Spirit that dwells in you" (Rom 8:11).

Ah, but what about 1 Cor 15:50, "Flesh and blood cannot inherit the kingdom of God"? Tabor appeals also to this text for a nonphysical understanding of resurrection on Paul's part.[6] Well, the immediately following statement reads, "Nor does perishability inherit imperishability." These two statements parallel each other, so that the phrase "flesh and blood" corresponds to "perishability." Together, the terms refer to the present body in respect to the perishability of its flesh and blood, not in respect to the physicality of its flesh and blood. For Paul proceeds to say that it is "*this* perishable body" that will put on imperishability and "*this* mortal body" that will put on immortality (1 Cor 15:51–55, esp. v. 53). And since for Paul the resurrection of Christians will follow the pattern of Christ's resurrection, as Tabor recognizes, Paul must have thought that when Christ was raised, it was the perishable, mortal body of his earthly lifetime that put on imperishability and immortality, not that he was raised and exalted to heaven in some nonphysical form.

According to 1 Cor 15:1–7 Paul "received" information about Jesus' death, burial, resurrection, and appearances as resurrected to Cephas (Peter) and others, including James. On the basis of Gal 1:10–23 Tabor interprets this reception as a direct revelation from heaven rather than as the passing on of tradition by one or more earlier followers of Jesus.[7] But in Galatians Paul is talking about the gospel he preached before going to Jerusalem and conversing with Cephas three years after that direct revelation, whereas in 1 Corinthians he's talking about the sort of information he'd get from one or more earlier believers. So contrary to Tabor's earlier cited identification of Paul as "our earliest witness to the resurrection," our earliest witnesses to it are the ones or one (probably Cephas) who passed this information on to Paul. Or, rather, our earliest witnesses are those who claimed to have seen Jesus as resurrected before Paul did, as admitted by Paul himself in his phrases, "And last of all . . . also to me" (1 Cor 15:8).

6. Tabor, *Jesus Dynasty*, 264.
7. jesusdynasty.com/blog/.

Therefore we have to investigate not only Paul's understanding of Jesus' resurrection, whether it was physical or nonphysical, but also what was the understanding of it by the earlier witnesses and traditioner(s).

"Cephas," the Aramaic form of "Peter," and the two instances of "according to the Scriptures" in 1 Cor 15:3–7 favor that the tradition stemmed from Jesus' original followers, Jews still closely tied to their ancestral faith, Judaism. Now Tabor correctly writes,

> In Judaism to claim that someone has been "raised from the dead" is not the same as to claim that one has died and exists as a spirit or soul in the heavenly world. What the gospels [here we might substitute the witnesses and traditioners behind 1 Cor 15:3–7] claim about Jesus is that the tomb [in which he "was buried," according to the pre-Pauline tradition] was empty, and that his dead body was revived to life ["raised," according to that same tradition]—wounds and all. He was not a phantom or a ghost.[8]

So it looks as though those witnesses and traditioners, given their Judaistic upbringing, would have understood Jesus' resurrection as physical just as Paul did, and just as we should expect, in that by definition "resurrection" means the "standing up" of a formerly supine corpse.

We're left with this question: If Jesus' bones were known to be lying in an ossuary near Jerusalem, how is it that the earliest literary tradition in 1 Cor 15:1–7, the even earlier oral tradition stemming from Jesus' original disciples, and Paul's properly exegeted understanding—how is it that all of them presented Jesus' resurrection as physical? This question seems to me hard to answer.

---

8. Tabor, *Jesus Dynasty*, 232.

Why Matthew, Mark, and Luke Are So Much Alike: The Synoptic Problem[1]

FULL DISCLOSURE: THOUGH STARTING my doctoral research on Matthew's use of the Old Testament with the intention of supporting Matthean priority over Mark and Luke as a solution to the synoptic problem, I quickly converted to the Mark-Q solution and have more recently come to view Luke as subsidiarily reflective of Matthew as well as mainly reflective of Mark and Q (the latter a putative sayings-source reflected in Matthew and Luke). To honor the memory of Michael Goulder, who once told me that Austin Farrer's solution is just as much a Two Gospel solution as the Griesbach solution is, I'll use the designations Griesbach, Farrer, and Mark-Q. It's been said of one synoptic scholar that he would die for his solution to the problem, and of another such scholar that he would kill for his solution. But suitably to the gentle spirit of Christopher Tuckett, the honoree of *New Studies in the Synoptic Problem*,[2] the essays in his Festschrift display no synoptic jihadism of a violent sort. Following are my takes on some of the essays in the volume.

Tuckett's survey, "The Current State of the Synoptic Problem," includes a perceptive discussion of simplicity as an argument in favor of this or that solution to the problem. For example, solutions that get rid of Q, which is only a hypothesized source, are often said to gain the advantage of simplicity over the Mark-Q solution. But Tuckett points out

1. This review assumes on readers' part some technical knowledge concerning the synoptic problem and suggested solutions to it.
2. Leuven: Peeters, 2011.

that the Griesbach and Farrer solutions have to hypothesize oral, written, and redactional sources, so that the simplicity of extant sources breeds a complexity of hypothetical sources similar to Q in this respect.

John Kloppenborg's discussion of "Synopses and the Synoptic Problem" addresses the history of synopses but centers on the currently most popular, those of Kurt Aland and Huck-Greeven. Kloppenborg concludes that all solutions work from synopses that are prejudicial (though not necessarily deliberately so) as regards pericope divisions, alignments, and the sequencing of parallel columns.

In the light of modern research on human memory, Andrew Gregory's "What Is Literary Dependence?" underscores the ancient preference for paraphrase over verbatim copying; oral tradition as deriving from oral performances variously suited to different occasions; and the question of stability versus instability in authors' memory of both oral traditions and written texts.

In "Textual Criticism and the Synoptic Problem," Peter Head complains that scholars dealing with the synoptic problem falsely assume, against textual critics, that the Greek text in Aland's synopsis "is, to all intents and purposes, what Mark and Luke originally wrote."

In "The Synoptic Problem Without Q," Eric Eve argues that because of Mark-Q overlaps, Q might as well be Matthew; that reliance on memory may well have led a Luke using Matthew to jumble Matthew's order; and that to explain Matthew's jumbling of Q's order as due to the use of a codex, whose pages could easily be flipped back and forth, allows the same sort of explanation for Luke's jumbling of Matthew's order under the Farrer and Griesbach solutions. Maybe Luke used a codex of Matthew.

In "Looking at Q through the Eyes of Matthew," Ulrich Luz describes Q as "soft" or "open," that is, "not . . . as a 'literary' document, nor as the book of an author with a defined profile, with a distinct theology representative of a specific community"—rather, as "a collection of Jesus' sayings . . . relatively close to the oral tradition" and existing "in several different versions" but not as the result of successive redactions.

In "The M-Source: Its History and Demise in Biblical Scholarship," Paul Foster reads a historically informative obituary over the corpse of M as a special Matthean source and replaces the corpse with a ghostly combination of Matthean redaction and multiple short traditions.

In "Proto-Luke and What Can Possibly Be Made of It," Joseph Verheyden takes a jaunty romp through the woods of what he considers to be the fantasyland of proto-Luke and drops some well-chosen Latin phrases along the way to mark his trail for a return to reality, all the while wondering why any current scholars take proto-Luke seriously. Well, maybe they've been reading too much of J. K. Rowling. Notably, the tortuous number and length of Verheyden's footnotes diminish markedly as his romp proceeds. Proto-Luke is obviously fatiguing as well as fantastical.

Now I focus on features of the three most prominent solutions to the synoptic problem:

The Griesbach solution has Mark microconflating Matthew and Luke. The Farrer solution has Luke microconflating Mark and Matthew. The Mark-Q solution has Matthew microconflating Mark and Q.

The Griesbach solution has Luke reordering Matthew a lot. So too does the Farrer solution have Luke reordering Matthew a lot, but Mark a bit as well. The Mark-Q solution has Matthew reordering Q a lot, plus Mark a bit.

The Griesbach solution has Luke often quoting Matthew verbatim, and Mark often quoting Matthew or Luke verbatim. The Farrer solution has Matthew often quoting Mark verbatim, and Luke often quoting Mark or Matthew verbatim. The Mark-Q solution has both Matthew and Luke often quoting Mark or Q verbatim.

But the physical difficulties entailed in ancient authors' nonuse of desks on which could be laid both the scroll being written on, which lay on the lap or hip and required two hands to control, and any other scroll or scrolls being used as sources—those difficulties make it hard to explain how microconflation, reordering, and verbatim quotation came about. Since all three main solutions to the synoptic problem share the suppositions of microconflation, reordering, and verbatim quotation of earlier documents, all three have to explain how these supposed phenomena came about despite the physical difficulties. The rarity in ancient literature of microconflation, reordering, and verbatim quotation makes the explaining all the harder.

The use of codices instead of scrolls could lessen the physical difficulties equally well for all three solutions. The same goes for the possibilities of an author's using notes, revising an early draft, echoing feedback from auditors of an early draft, relying on oral traditions, remembering earlier texts, having assistants, and employing an amanuensis (so that the author could roam around consulting various written sources). Hence, none of these possibilities favors one solution of the synoptic problem over another.

Our knowledge has been expanded, then, our mistaken notions corrected, our conversation enriched. But the expansion, correction, and enrichment haven't brought us closer to agreement. So far as I can tell, they lack the *capability* of bringing us closer to agreement.

Finally, some odds and ends: Tuckett writes that "it is ludicrous to think of each of the later evangelists having access to exactly the same physical copy of the proposed source." Head writes similarly about "the fact that Matthew and Luke could not have had access to identical copies of Mark." Maybe so; but given the extensive travels of Paul, his companions, the rest of the apostles, and Jesus' brothers (Acts 1–28; 1 Cor 9:5) and the requested transport of "the books, namely the parchments" (2 Tim 4:13), whatever the identity of those books, I'm not sure we can rule out the possibility of an evangelist's having perused the autograph of an earlier Gospel or two. Nor are all textual critics so skeptical as Eldon Epp and David Parker, at least not to the degree of dealing a fatal blow to synoptic solutions.

Apart from Mark-Q overlaps and contrary to the description of minor agreements between Matthew and Luke against Mark as "tiny" and "trivial," I'd like to see more attention paid to substantive, as distinct from stylistic, Mattheanisms in Luke—and Lukanisms in Matthew, if there are any.[3]

The characterization of Q as basically a collection of wisdom-sayings dominates the discussion at points. I'd like to see more attention paid to the possibility of a Q modeled after an Old Testament prophetic book: the call of a prophet, plus his words, but no account of his death. Such a Q might look more Jewish-apocalyptic than Cynic-like.

Some arguments assume that Mark's Gospel ends with 16:8. In my commentary on Mark I provided a dozen arguments, almost entirely literary critical rather than text critical, for a lost ending;[4] and Clayton Croy has more recently advocated a lost ending.[5] I'd like to see what effect on synoptic arguments the theory of a lost ending might have—for example, on whether a lost ending, if it could be hypothetically reconstructed, might help explain the similarities and differences between Matthew and

---

3. See, for example, Robert H. Gundry, "A Rejoinder on Matthean Foreign Bodies in Luke 10:25-28" and "The Refusal of Matthean Foreign Bodies to Be Exorcised from Luke 9:22; 10:25-28," *ETL* 71 (1995) 139–50 and 75 (1999) 104–22.

4. Robert H. Gundry, *Mark: A Commentary on His Apology for the Cross* (Grand Rapids: Eerdmans, 1993), 1009–21.

5. N. Clayton Croy, *The Mutilation of Mark's Gospel* (Nashville: Abingdon, 2003).

Luke subsequent to discovery of the empty tomb. Verheyden mocks the possibility of using Matthew and Luke that way but avidly supports using them similarly to reconstruct a Q!

Some of the essayists in *New Studies* seem to identify Matthew's *ta logia*, in the tradition passed on by Papias, with the Gospel of Matthew. Other essayists do not. But if the identification is to be made and if the tradition's "therefore" makes Matthew "arrange" *ta logia* because Mark didn't write Jesus' words and deeds "in order" (two very big "if's," admittedly), then we'd have astonishingly early church tradition favoring Markan priority. Perhaps some attention should be paid to this possibility.

Because Mark and Luke lack a parallel to Matt 16:17–19, this lack often plays a part in arguments concerning the relationship of Mark and Luke to Matthew. Why don't Mark and Luke contain the passage if they used Matthew, for example? On all sides, the arguments assume a broadly positive portrayal of Peter in Matthew, not just in 16:17–19. But Matthew's Peter uniquely has "little faith" in 14:31 and therefore may be among those who doubted Jesus' resurrection in 28:17.

More to the point, in contrast with the other Gospels, Matthew has Peter deny Jesus the first time "before all" (Matt 26:70), whereas Jesus said that whoever denies him "before people" will be denied by Jesus before his Father in heaven (10:33). Then Matthew alone has Peter deny Jesus the second time "with an oath" (27:72) in flagrant violation of Jesus' prohibition of oaths (5:33–37, unique to Matthew) and in contrast with Jesus' refusal to answer Caiaphas under oath (26:63–64: "*You* have spoken," again unique to Matthew). As though that weren't enough, Matthew then uniquely juxtaposes Peter's bitter weeping, after denying Jesus a third time, and Judas Iscariot's remorse and suicide (26:75—27:5). So Matthew's Peter looks to be a representative apostate. No wonder Matthew has "Go tell his disciples" (as in Mark 16:7) but lacks Mark's additional "and Peter" (28:7), as well as lacking a special appearance to Peter of the risen Jesus (Luke 24:34; 1 Cor 15:5).

Never mind Matt 16:17–19; for at the level of Matthew's Greek text *Petros* likely means a loose stone in contrast with the *petra*, or bedrock, on which Jesus will build his church, "*this* rock" corresponding to "*these* words" of Jesus that form "the bedrock" on which the wise man builds his house in Matt 7:24–25. Besides, for Peter as the church's bedrock we'd expect Jesus to say, "You are Peter/Rock, and on *you* I will build my church." So synoptic arguments may need to adjust to Matthew's ultimately negative portrayal of Peter as a tare not to be weeded out from among the wheat until the end (so Matthew alone in 13:24–30, 35–43).[6] If negative, it would be hard to pit Matthew as a pro-Peter Gospel against Mark as a pro-Paul Gospel, or vice versa, depending on which of these Gospels reacted to the other.

In *New Studies* several corrections of fact need to be noted:

- It's the western side of the Sea of Galilee, not the "eastern," that is Jewish (against 198).
- It's the Griesbach solution (2GH), not the Mark-Q solution (2DH), that needs two separate synoptic displays, one placing Luke beside Matthew and another placing Mark between Matthew and Luke (against 58).
- It's Farrer, not Streeter, who "paid some attention to Streeter's arguments" (against 135).
- It's Jesus, not his disciples, who distributed bread to the five thousand according to John 6:11 and in accordance with laying down his life *on his own* (John 10:17–18), since the bread represents his self-sacrificed flesh (John 6:33, 52–58; against 676).

---

6. See Robert H. Gundry, *Peter: False Disciple and Apostate according to Saint Matthew, Second Edition with Responses to Reviews* (Eugene, OR: Wipf & Stock, 2018).

Holes in the *Whole* Postcolonial *Story*

IN A SERIES OF early books Richard A. Horsley treated the political economy of first-century Palestine. Those books greatly influenced an important segment of the so-called third quest of the historical Jesus. In his more recently published book *Hearing the Whole Story: The Politics of Plot in Mark's Gospel*,[1] Horsley shifted his attention from the political economy that he thinks explains the historical Jesus to the political economy that he thinks explains the Gospel of Mark, which represents "one branch of the Jesus movement" (23). So much emphasis falls on the economic that at a session of the Society of Biblical Literature in Toronto on November 23, 2002, I suggested he change the subtitle of his book to the electoral slogan, "It's the economy, stupid!" He laughed graciously at my suggestion—I dare say, appreciatively. My description of the book's slant as "postcolonial" echoes both his own use of the term (30) and a recommendation in the back ad by Adela Yarbro Collins. The need for a review essay arises especially out of Stephen D. Moore's accompanying recommendation of the book as "an astonishing achievement" which is so "electrifyingly original and eminently accessible" that it "has opened up a genuinely new chapter in Markan criticism."

According to Horsley, Mark's story of Jesus, taken as a whole, presents him as a Moses- and Elijah-like prophet who launched a movement of renewal among peasants living in the villages of Galilee and nearby regions. Negatively, the movement entailed resistance to economic

[1]. Louisville: Westminster John Knox, 2001. I recommend that readers of the present review essay read also, perhaps even first, Richard A. Horsley, "A Response to Robert Gundry's Review of Hearing the Whole Story," *JSNT* 26 (2003) 151–69.

exploitation by Roman rulers and the Judean elites sponsored by them. Positively, the movement entailed an egalitarian invigoration of village and family life over against the disintegrating effects of the economic exploitation, and in accordance with popular Mosaic and prophetic oral traditions as opposed to the elites' written tradition. Divine intervention through the coming of a heavenly Son of Man different from the earthly Jesus was expected to bring release from foreign domination.

To support this thesis, Horsley plays down Christology in Mark and plays up economics; plays down the male disciples of Jesus and plays up his female followers; plays down individual discipleship and plays up village culture and family stability; plays down scribal tradition and plays up oral traditions. Regretfully, I can agree with almost none of these downs and ups, for they seem to me distortive of Mark's story.

DOWN WITH CHRISTOLOGY?

I agree with Horsley's rejection of Mark as correcting a Christology of glory with a Christology of suffering (74–75), but unlike him I see Mark as redolent with a Christology of power.[2] Horsley, on the contrary, thinks that recognition of Mark as story does away with all theology, including Christology: "Whatever theological doctrine is supposedly found in Mark . . . is the creation of theologians. The Gospel of Mark itself can now be recognized as story" (x).[3] But stories can carry theology, as the current popularity of narrative theology shows; and, on the flip side, economics is sometimes just as storyless as the kind of theology Horsley disdains.

Because of its christological reference, then, Horsley regards Mark 1:1 as probably a copyist's addition (250). But there is no external support for omission; and omission would leave the *kathōs*-clause of 1:2 ("As it's written") standing first, whereas seven times elsewhere in

---

2. Cf. Robert H. Gundry, *Mark: A Commentary on His Apology for the Cross* (Grand Rapids: Eerdmans, 1993), 1–15, 1022–26 et passim.

3. Horsley argues that New Testament scholars discovered theology in Mark only because of their social location in theological schools (see, for example, 5–6). But it could equally well be said that he discovers political economy in Mark because of his social location in a secular university (the University of Massachusetts). Such arguments do not advance the discussion, however; they only example the elementary logical error of "poisoning the well." Horsley cites Wilhelm Wrede's *The Messianic Secret* in support of an overall "design" in Mark (5), but Horsley's denial of Markan Christology strikingly contradicts the christological design that Wrede saw in Mark.

Mark—including two other instances of *kathōs gegraptai*, as in 1:2—a *kathōs*-clause depends on the preceding.[4]

"Jesus rebukes Peter for believing he is the 'messiah,'" says Horsley (92). But in Mark 8:31–33 Jesus rebukes Peter for objecting to the coming passion and resurrection of the Son of Man, not for confessing Jesus as the Christ.

At the transfiguration, according to Horsley, Mark "pointedly" puts Jesus on the same level as Moses and Elijah; and Peter's impulse to build three booths suggests that Jesus is being "compared and ranked" with Moses and Elijah (107). But Mark says Peter was wrong: "he didn't know what he should answer, for he was terrified" (Mark 9:6). The heavenly declaration of Jesus' divine sonship and the command to hear him (9:7) promote him ahead of Moses and Elijah. He has appeared in glory, but they have not (9:2–4). The identification of Jesus as Elijah in Mark 6:14–16 and 8:28 appears among people's other mistaken identifications. And 9:11–13 puts John the Baptist, not Jesus, in parallel with Elijah.

Horsley doubts the messianic overtones in Jesus' being called the Son of God (250). But Mark 14:61–62 puts "the Son of the Highest" in apposition to "the Christ" and has Jesus answer, "I am," to the question whether he's "the Christ, the Son of the Highest." So after suggesting that 14:62 just might contain "a questioning answer," that is, "I am?" (but then why the high priest's charge of blasphemy?), Horsley uses the synoptic parallels to say that an earlier version of Mark "almost certainly had Jesus reply, 'You say so.'" Consequently, Mark's Jesus "never claims be 'the messiah' and never even admits to the designation as appropriate" (252). But the manuscript tradition favors "I am" overwhelmingly. Matthew 26:64 changes "I am" to "You say so" to keep Jesus from violating his own prohibition of oaths (Matt 5:33–37, unique to Matthew among the Synoptics), for only in Matthew is Jesus put under oath (26:63). And "You say that I am" in Luke 22:70 looks like a conflation of Mark and Matthew.

Horsley thinks that the centurion at the cross calls Jesus "'a son of a god' . . . in mockery and sarcasm, or at least ironically, and in a phrase that may not be an allusion to the messiah at all" (252 in reference to Mark 15:39). But we're dealing with *Mark's* story, not with what a historical centurion may have meant. So in view of Jesus' earlier "I am," the centurion's declaration is to be taken straightforwardly, in a Christian sense of "Son of God." Besides, mockery, sarcasm, and irony wouldn't fit the centurion's

---

4. Mark 4:33; 9:13; 11:6; 14:16, 21; 15:8; 16:7. Horsley accepts 1:2–3 as original to Mark's Gospel (44, 231).

making his declaration because he saw "the way" (*houtōs*) Jesus died, that is, with a loud shout at the rending of the temple veil and return of daylight after three hours of supernatural darkness (Mark 15:33–38). And the whole story of Jesus as God's Son includes, in addition to what has already been mentioned, the baptismal voice, the panicky declarations of demons, Jesus' often relating himself as Son to God as his Father, and the possibly original "Son of God" in Mark's superscription.[5]

For Mark, the chief priests' and scribes' mocking Jesus as "the Christ" (Mark 15:31–32) unintendedly expressed the truth. To avoid this understanding, Horsley ignores both the probable implication of Jesus' true christhood in the warning Jesus issued against false christs (13:21–22) and his explicitly christological statement, "You are Christ's" (9:41). The latter is preceded by the receiving of children in Jesus' name (9:37), by the casting out of demons in Jesus' name (9:38), and by the doing of a miracle in Jesus' name (9:39). Then Mark 9:41 follows up with people's giving the disciples ("you") a cup of water "in name, because you are Christ's" (literal translation). The phrase "in name" is interruptive. The text could have read more smoothly without it: "whoever gives you a cup of water because you are Christ's." But the phrase "in name" intrudes to make the point that Jesus' name, which he has just mentioned three times, isn't the name which *is* Jesus but the name which he *has*, that is, "Christ." You can't get more christological than this self-designation by him.

Mark "clearly rejects" the Messiah's Davidic sonship, writes Horsley, citing Mark 12:35–37 (20). It's true that Mark's Jesus doesn't affirm Davidic sonship; but the question isn't *whether* the Messiah is David's son, but "*how come*" (*pōs*) the scribes say he is. From what scriptural source (*pothen*) do they derive this designation? The Scripture doesn't contain it.[6] Notably, on the other hand, Jesus doesn't correct Bartimaeus's repeatedly calling him "Son of David" but responds favorably (Mark 10:46–52).

Horsley tells us that "in Mark 'son of man' appears only as a self-reference by Jesus or as a future figure 'coming with the clouds of heaven' and never as a 'christological title' of or for Jesus" (20). But this denial stands only if we accept that Mark distinguishes between the earthly Jesus as a son of man and a heavenly Son of Man yet to come. For the latter usage is titular, having lost "like" in the Danielic phrase, "one like a son of

---

5. Mark 1:1, 11; 3:11; 5:7; 13:32; 14:36, 39.
6. See the discussion in Gundry, *Mark*, 717–24.

man," and also having gained the definite article.[7] By referring to God as the Father of the coming Son of Man, Mark 8:38 favors a Markan equation of the earthly Jesus with the heavenly Son of Man; for throughout Mark, as noted above, God and the earthly Jesus appear as Father and Son.[8] Similarly, the ignorance of the Father's Son concerning the day and hour of the Son of Man's coming seems to equate Jesus as God's Son with the coming Son of Man (Mark 13:24–32). Jesus' resurrection three days after his death, so that he can come (again), makes this equation possible and attractive.[9]

Horsley suggests that the Son of Man's coming in Mark 14:62 intimates a speedy restoration of Israel's sovereignty (44). But why then did the Sanhedrin judge Jesus' statement blasphemous? Did they misunderstand him? More confidently, Horsley says that in 2:10, 27–28 "son of man" "appears to signify . . . people generally" (127–28; cf. 149). But in 2:10 the Son of Man's authority to forgive sins on earth is tied to Jesus' ability to heal a paralytic, not an ability shared by people in general. Healing by Jesus doesn't prove other human beings' authority to forgive sins on earth. In Mark no other human being is said to share Jesus' authority. And in 2:27–28 the Son of Man's *lordship* over the Sabbath seems stronger than humanity's *benefiting* from the Sabbath.

UP WITH ECONOMICS?

As to Jesus' and the Twelve's making Galilean village life socially, politically, and economically egalitarian now and God's intervening to make it free of foreign domination in the near future, it's hard to see that prior to the divine intervention egalitarianism would decrease the burden of taxes, tribute, tithes, and offerings imposed on the peasants by Rome and the Judean elites, or that Jesus' healings, exorcisms, and teaching would do so. In what way, then, or to what degree is "deliverance . . . already happening" through these activities of Jesus? Horsley does say that Jesus provides the people with healing of leprosy or forgiveness of sins that makes it unnecessary for them to obtain those from ruling institutions, which would cost them some of their precious economic resources, and then

---

7. Mark 8:38; 13:26; 14:62; Dan 7:13; cf. Rev 1:13.

8. On p. 128 Horsley does allow that at 14:62 Mark may have fused the earthly Jesus and the heavenly Son of Man.

9. Mark 8:31; 9:31; 10:33–34; 16:6.

cites Mark 1:41–44 but fails to include 1:45, where Jesus tells a healed leper to make an offering for his cleansing—at a cost to his precious economic resources (to use Horsley's own phraseology on page 109).[10]

Since the mustard seed grows into a mere shrub, not into the imperial image of a tree (cf. Ezek 31:4–6), Horsley sees anti-imperialism in the shrub (104; Mark 4:30–32). But in Mark there's no contrast with a tree; rather, with "all the shrubs." Inappropriately for an anti-imperial image, it's a contrast that emphasizes the largeness of a mature mustard plant, which Mark doesn't explicitly call a shrub anyway.

According to Horsley, "stories of sea crossings . . . would evoke the memory of the exodus" and of Elijah's and Elisha's water-crossings, all in the service of establishing and reestablishing the Mosaic covenant free of foreign domination (64). But Moses, the Israelites, Elijah, and Elisha crossed on dry ground, not as Jesus and the Twelve in a boat (still less by walking on water). Not much of a parallel!

The exorcism of Legion "tells of the people's liberation from the Roman legions and the destruction of those legions," writes Horsley (140–41; Mark 5:1–20). But Jesus' not knowing at first the name "Legion" sits uneasily on what Horsley calls an "obvious allusion to the Roman army" (50). Did Jesus have to ask the Romans who they were? Mark's text makes "Legion" represent numerousness ("we are many"), not the Roman army. And why do the "subject peoples," as Horsley calls them, ask Jesus to leave if, symbolically, he has freed them from Roman oppression? Horsley answers that "the demon's [*sic*, demons'] possession of the man functioned as the diversion of the whole community from blaming and striking out against the Roman order," so that "far from feeling liberated by the exorcism . . . they found Jesus' exorcisms a threat to their delicately balanced adjustment to the Roman order" (144–45). But to maintain his view Horsley would have to suppose that the locals didn't attribute the demoniac's violent behavior to demon-possession till after their attempt to tame him—a doubtful supposition. Otherwise, their attempt was—in Horsley's terms—a striking out against the Roman order *rather than* a psychological adjustment to it. And if a psychological adjustment, why didn't Jesus' other exorcisms draw similarly negative reactions instead of accolades (Mark 1:21–28; 3:7–12; 6:14–16)? And why the requests for exorcisms (7:24–30; 9:14–29)?

---

10. Despite Horsley's making much of cities' drain on the economic resources of villagers, it isn't necessary to discuss here the alternative possibility of an economically symbiotic relation between cities and surrounding villages.

Holes in the Whole *Postcolonial* Story 67

According to Horsley, "Jesus flat-out excludes the possibility that a rich man, who would have to be someone in collaboration with the Roman-imposed political-economic 'new order' in Palestine, can 'enter the kingdom of God' (10.17–25)" (43). But over against a human impossibility Jesus sets a divine possibility: "With human beings it's impossible, but not with God; for all things are possible with God."

In Mark 10:29–31, says Horsley, "the restoration of houses and fields is to occur in 'this age', not in the next" (123). True, but *leaving* your house, brothers, sisters, mother, father, children, and fields for the sake of Jesus and the gospel sounds like a relinquishment of inherited property and like a breakup, not a renewal, of biological families in favor of new, fictive kinship.

To stress present economic concerns at the expense of concern about the hereafter, Horsley treats the reference to "eternal life" in Mark 10:30 as a "'throwaway' line" that indifferently echoes the rich man's "unreal" question, as though only the rich would be interested in eternal life. Peasants would be interested only in "how they could support their families" from day to day (190–92). But apart from the common observations that rich people tend to enjoy present life so much that they take little thought of eternal life, and that poor people have it so bad now that they tend to long for *pie in the sky bye and bye*, in 9:43, 45 Jesus on his own initiative lays down conditions for entering eternal life. There contrast with entering Gehenna shows that eternal life is in view. So much for Horsley's claim that "Mark gives no indication anywhere else in the Gospel [outside 10:30] of interest in 'eternal life'" (192). Apparently Mark's Jesus *is* interested in people's fate hereafter. No throwaway line in 10:30, then. (Compare Jesus' reference in Mark 12:25 to people's resurrection.)

"'Taking up your cross' is . . . suffering for a political cause, the goal of which is the ending of submission and suffering," writes Horsley (228; see Mark 8:34–38). But losing your life—that is, dying—"for the sake of Jesus and the gospel" so as to save your life makes nonsense unless the life you save is eternal life rather than the present life you lose. The ultimate goal, then, is eternal life, not the end of submission and suffering in this life.

Horsley calls Jesus' cleansing of the temple "a blatantly revolutionary act . . . the reason Mark gives for the condemnation of Jesus at his trial before the high-priestly rulers in Jerusalem" (41; Mark 11:15–18; 14:53–65). Wrong! The temple-*cleansing* makes no appearance whatever in that trial. Mark brands as false the testimony according to which Jesus said he would *destroy* the temple. And the high-priestly rulers dropped this false charge and condemned Jesus only on the religious charge of *blasphemy*, not also on a political charge of revolution.

With many others, Horsley regards Jesus' cursing a fig tree and its withering as a sign of the temple's coming destruction (18; Mark 11:12-14, 20-25). But Mark makes out of the event only a lesson of faith in prayer, so that W. R. Telford, who shares Horsley's view, correctly feels forced to rid Mark's text of 11:24-25 and reinterpret 11:22-23 as a reference to the temple's being thrown into the sea, so to speak.[11] Not likely.

Horsley says that "'giving to Caesar what belongs to Caesar' means they [people] should not pay tribute, since according to Israelite tradition everything belongs to God and nothing to Caesar" (43; also 113, 150–51; Mark 12:13-17). Finally something really revolutionary! But what then is the point of Jesus' asking for a coin and calling attention to Caesar's image on it? If Jesus had meant what Horsley says he meant, we'd expect Jesus' answer to have become a charge against him before the Roman governor. As it is, the Pharisees and Herodians can only "marvel at him." And whereas Jesus was asked whether to *give* tribute to Caesar (*dōmen*), he answers in terms of giving *back* to Caesar (*apodote*), so that the tribute really does belong to Caesar. Contrary to Horsley's claim, moreover, Mark's Jesus doesn't engage in a "sustained confrontation" with the "Roman sponsors" of "the Jerusalem rulers" (130; cf. 109–10).[12] There's only a brief trial before the Roman governor on the morning of crucifixion.

A poor widow's giving all she had to the temple treasury examples the scribes' devouring of widows' houses, says Horsley (151; Mark 12:41-45). But it is priests, not scribes, who get money given to support the temple cult. So it is the widow's poverty, not her giving all she had to the temple treasury, that examples the scribes' devouring of widows' houses.

Concerning Mark 13, Horsley claims that Mark's Jesus knows nothing of "the end" or of an "end time," warns his followers to expect persecution for "faithfully developing their movement," and makes "no apparent allusion to [God's] judgment against Rome" (123, 129–30). But the tribulation's being unprecedented later as well as earlier and the Son of Man's coming after it make "the end" in Mark 13:7, 13 sound strictly eschatological. Persecution for the sake of Jesus and on account of his name (13:9, 13) sounds more christological than "movement"-oriented. And an allusion—no, an outright prediction—of God's judgment against

---

11. W. R. Telford, *The Barren Temple and the Withered Tree*, JSNTSup 1 (Sheffield: JSOT, 1980), 676–78.

12. Mark 10:42 speaks of rulers' lording it over gentiles, not over Israelites.

Rome is what we'd *expect* to hear if Mark's story were attacking the economic imperialism of Rome (cf. Rev 18).

According to Horsley, the Sanhedrin "condemned him [Jesus] . . . for threatening to destroy the temple" (100; Mark 14:55-59). But in connection with the temple-cleansing we've already noted that Mark brands this charge as false and has the Sanhedrin drop it. So Jesus doesn't oppose the temple as such, for his cleansing was reformative. As a result, the prediction of destruction in Mark 13:2 takes on a tone of regret rather than opposition.

To heighten the political element in his economic thesis, Horsley makes the Roman rulers join the Jerusalem rulers' "plot to destroy him [Jesus]" and denies that Pilate condemned Jesus to death "either on trumped-up charges or in order to please the crowd of 'Jews' that had been stirred up by the chief priests" (100, 112). But whether or not we believe it to be historically true, Mark's story affirms explicitly what Horsley denies (see Mark 15:1-15). And where does any Roman join in the Jerusalem rulers' plot? Where does Mark make a point of Roman sponsorship of those rulers? And if he writes against Roman domination, why does he have Pilate recognize Jesus' innocence and the chief priests' envy in the delivery of Jesus to Pilate? Why does he portray Pilate as wanting to release Jesus? Horsley thinks that "Mark presents Jesus as a provincial rebel ['king of the Judeans'] executed by the military governor of the Roman occupying forces in Judea" (42). More accurately, however, Mark presents Jesus as crucified, not because the governor thought him a provincial rebel, but because he didn't want to displease a crowd stirred up by chief priests envious of Jesus.[13]

---

13. Though the Markan Jesus spends most of his time preaching nonviolent revolution among villagers in Galilee, according to Horsley, Mark's writing in Greek shows that the Gospel isn't addressed to those villagers; rather, "to ordinary Greek-speaking people" living in areas surrounding Galilee, "such as Tyre and the Decapolis"—in other words, "most likely" to non-Galilean but nearby "villagers" who "identified with Israelite tradition" (44-51, 137). But the preaching of the gospel "to all the nations" (Mark 13:10) and "in the whole world" (14:9) resists a regional limitation, and the nations living farther away from the immediate environs of Galilee would hardly identify with Israelite tradition (cf. the Latinisms in Mark). Horsley dismisses Mark's worldwide purview by saying it is mentioned "twice *in passing*" (180, emphasis added).

DOWN WITH THE MALE DISCIPLES OF JESUS?

To make the twelve male disciples look worse than they already do in Mark, and thus to advance his thesis of egalitarianism, Horsley reverses the order of those disciples' sending the children away and Jesus' saying to welcome them, as though the disciples deliberately disobeyed the command of Jesus: "He insists that they welcome children; they send them away" (91; contrast the order in Mark 10:13–16). Furthermore, says Horsley, in Mark the Twelve and Peter "never find out about Jesus' rising," for "they are no longer part of the unfolding Gospel story of the kingdom of God" (94, also 81). But according to Mark 13:9–13, they will preach the gospel far and wide. We have there not just a command that might be broken; rather, a prediction by Jesus that will in fact be fulfilled. And the command, "Go tell his disciples and Peter" (16:7), shows that even at the end of Mark's story the male disciples haven't been written off.

The twelve males do display nonegalitarian ambitions, but in relation to each other, not in relation to women (Mark 9:33–37; 10:35–45). On the other hand, Horsley writes that "women are the only figures who faithfully follow and serve" (xv). By contrast, Jesus omits fathers from the list of his family members (i.e., those who do God's will [3:33–35]). So Horsley treats this omission as an egalitarian "challenge to the norm of the patriarchal family under a male head—except insofar as Jesus or God in effect replaces fathers as the male authority figure" (224–25). But the exception provides all the explanation that's needed: inclusion of fathers would have implied among Jesus' disciples figures having authority over *him*. So less patriarchalism among Christian families (in the biological sense of "families") isn't to be found here.

UP WITH THE FEMALE FOLLOWERS OF JESUS?

Because the number *twelve* calls to mind the twelve tribes of Israel, Horsley plays up the healing of the woman with a twelve-years-long flow of blood and the raising of a twelve-year-old girl as symbolizing the renewal of Israel, with women in egalitarian roles (18–19, 204, 206; Mark 5:21–43). Possibly symbolic of Israel's renewal—yes; but not to the effect of egalitarian roles for women any more than the use of "daughter of Zion" in biblical texts implies such roles for them. Mark puts the blood-flow in a multifaceted description of the woman's wretchedness and gives the girl's age as an explanation for her ability to stand up

Holes in the Whole *Postcolonial* Story

and walk around once Jesus has raised her. And since the woman approached him "from behind" and furtively touched "his garment(s)," not Jesus himself (against 204), doesn't Horsley exaggerate to say that she approached Jesus "boldly"?[14]

To play up a contrast between the Syrophoenician woman's dialogical victory over Jesus and her marginalized status, representing peasantry, Horsley somehow knows that because she appears without a husband or a son, she is poor and either widowed or divorced (213–14; Mark 7:24–30). But she might have been *called* a widow if she really was one; and the larger question is whether the nonappearance of husbands and sons with the woman who anointed Jesus, with Mary Magdalene, and with Salome implies that they too were poor and widowed or divorced (14:3–9; 15:40, 47; 16:1). Isn't Horsley reading into the text rather than out of it?

According to Horsley, a woman's pouring perfume on Jesus' head at Mark 14:3–9 is the action "of a prophet in anointing (literally 'messiah-ing' or 'christ-ing') Jesus" (207–8, also 217–18). But a king, such as the Messiah would be, was anointed with olive oil, not with perfume.[15] Mark doesn't use *chriō*, the verbal cognate of *christos*, as might be expected for the connotation of "christ-ing" or "messiah-ing."[16] The anointing is for burial, for which perfume is suitable, not for messianic kingship, for which (as noted) perfume is unsuitable. And it is Jesus, not the woman, who makes the anointing prophetic of his burial. Even Horsley says that Mark's Jesus "twists" the significance of the woman's anointing him, so that it represents messiahship "only in a highly qualified and ironic sense," one that includes "martyrdom" (253). Well, then, if he had to twist the anointing to correct her misconceived messianic hope, she does no better than Peter, whose confession of Jesus' messiahship likewise shows no recognition of messianic martyrdom.

Horsley says nevertheless that at the end of Mark's story "women . . . appear as paradigms of faithful understanding" (2). Of *faithless ignorance* might be a truer description. For just as a woman's ignorance

---

14. Horsley, *Hearing the Whole Story*, 204; cf. 210. By saying that divine healing power was "mediated [to the woman] through Jesus" (211) rather than saying that the power had its immediate source in Jesus, Horsley continues his downplaying of Christology in Mark.

15. 1 Sam 9:27—10:1; 16:1–13; 2 Kgs 9:1–13.

16. Cf. 1 Kgdms 9:27–10.1; 16:1–13. The coming of God's Spirit on Saul and David when they were anointed for kingship suggests that in Mark the coming of the Spirit on Jesus at his baptism constituted an anointing to messianic kingship (1 Sam 10:6; 16:13; Mark 1:9–11; cf. Horsley, *Hearing the Whole Story*, 218).

necessitated Jesus' twisting the significance of her anointing him, so also the women who come to the tomb to anoint his corpse are ignorant not only of his resurrection, which he has predicted, but also of the fact that by his own statement he has already undergone an anointing for burial (Mark 16:1–8). Horsley might be tempted to excuse the women's ignorance by saying they hadn't heard Jesus predict his resurrection or heard his interpretation of the anointing. But excusable or not, ignorance is ignorance; and Horsley has claimed paradigmatic understanding for the women. According to Mark 15:40–41, moreover, they had followed Jesus in Galilee and come with him up to Jerusalem. So it is narratively probable, indeed almost certain, that they had heard at least his interpretation of the anointing; for nothing in the account of that episode indicates a limitation to the Twelve. On the contrary, it was a woman who anointed him, he was dining in the house of Simon the leper, and the nonmention of the Twelve joins the indefinite "some" who indignantly criticized the anointing to disfavor such a limitation (14:3–9). In this case, the women's ignorance—like that of the twelve males—consists in a failure to understand, not in a failure to hear.

The women's response to the message and commission given them at the empty tomb is one of faithless fear and disobedience.[17] Contrariwise, Horsley thinks "the women plan to anoint Jesus because, in the 'dishonorable burial' of a Roman-executed rebel given him by Joseph of Arimathea, he remains unanointed" (282n49). Even so, they plan in ignorance of the earlier anointing for burial; and the notion of a "dishonorable burial" makes exceedingly strange the complimentary description of Joseph of Arimathea in Mark 15:43 ("a respected member of the council, who was also himself waiting expectantly for the kingdom of God") and also his "daring" (*tolmēsas*) to ask Pilate for Jesus' corpse.

"At the climax of the story," Horsley notes, "women are . . . the only witnesses to the crucifixion and empty tomb—and the only links to the implied continuation of the movement in Galilee and outwards." They are "the only ones who have the message that Jesus will meet them back in Galilee." In Mark's "open ending" they are directed back to Galilean

---

17. Here my argument presupposes Horsley's position that Mark's Gospel originally ended at 16:8. I myself set out a number of reasons, internal as well as external, for thinking that the original ending has been lost except for redacted parallel versions in Matthew and somewhat in Luke (Gundry, *Mark*, 1009–21). Such an ending would improve Mark's portrait of the women in Mark 16, but it would spoil Horsley's notion of their upcoming role in Galilee.

villages, "where the risen Jesus has supposedly gone ahead of them—apparently [for the women] to pick up where Jesus and the twelve had left off in advancing the movement." "Mark has transformed Jesus' 'resurrection' into an instruction to continue the movement back up in Galilee without them [the male disciples]" (xv, 208, 42, 96, respectively). Horsley's putting scare quotes around "resurrection" reduces Jesus' bodily resurrection to a continuation of the movement he had started.[18] But the women weren't told that *they* should go to Galilee; rather, that the *male* disciples should go there. They weren't told that *they* would see Jesus there; rather, that the *male* disciples would see him there. Nor were they told to *continue the movement* there; rather, that the male disciples would *see Jesus* there. So Mark gives no indication whatever that the women actually went to Galilee, saw Jesus there, or continued the movement there. (Since Horsley uses Luke-Acts to argue for the male disciples' staying in Jerusalem rather than going to Galilee, he should accept Luke-Acts as evidence that the women did the same.)[19] "Just as he told you" in Mark 16:7 refers back to Jesus' statement to the Twelve in 14:28 (cf. 14:17) and thereby shows that "There you will see him" is *not* addressed to the women.

If Mark's Gospel ends with 16:8, "the movement" stops dead in its tracks because of the women's fleeing in fear and saying nothing to anyone. Horsley responds, "The hearers [of Mark] . . . know that they [the women] eventually did tell the story—or it could not be retold—including 'to the disciples and Peter'" (208). Does Horsley then mean us to suppose that the women stopped their report at the point where they fled in silent fear? Or that they continued it but Mark or his source chopped off the continuation? But with an "omniscient narrator" like Mark, as Horsley takes him to be (16), who needs a report by the women anyway? If they did eventually tell the story to the disciples and Peter, Horsley has to say either that the women told them too late for seeing Jesus in Galilee (in which case the women delayed till too late their own supposed trip to Galilee, or they went in time to see Jesus there and then returned to Jerusalem to tell the disciples and Peter) or that having been told in time, the disciples and Peter refused to go. Sticking to Mark's text so far as

---

18. Cf. Horsley, *Hearing the Whole Story*, 95: "Mark deemphasizes the resurrection at the end of the Gospel [and] presents merely an empty tomb, with no resurrection appearances to anyone." What then of the announcement, "He is risen," and the promise, "There [in Galilee] you will see him" (Mark 16:6–7)?

19. See esp. Acts 1:14.

we have it makes us regard the women as mere message-bearers, though failed ones, for the benefit of Jesus' male disciples. Some egalitarianism!

DOWN WITH INDIVIDUAL DISCIPLESHIP?

I agree with Horsley that Mark isn't primarily about discipleship[20] but disagree with his exalting village and family life to the exclusion of individual discipleship, as in his statement, "Mark's Jesus addresses his program of teaching and healing to village communities, not individuals" (40). Horsley supports this statement by noting that the disciples "are to 'shake the dust off their feet' as a testimony against a whole 'place' or village that refuses to welcome them (6.7–13)," by limiting to the Twelve Jesus' call to leave house, family, and fields (Mark 10:28–30), and by taking *hoi par' autou* in Mark 3:21 as referring not to Jesus' biological family but to those who were with him, perhaps his disciples, and were coming to restrain him because they had heard that on account of crowd-pressure he couldn't eat and had consequently gone berserk (40, 178–83, 224).

Horsley doesn't cite Mark 10:31 in this connection, but it broadens Jesus' purview beyond the Twelve: "Yet many first ones will be last, and last ones first." Jesus also tells a rich man to sell all his possessions and come follow him (Mark 10:21), and 15:41 names women who were following him in Galilee. The parable of different soils indicates differences of individual response (4:3–9, 13–20, also 25). And with multiple instances of "anyone" and "whoever," individuals in a "crowd" are summoned to follow Jesus (8:34–38; cf. 9:33–50). So much for the supposed lack of individuation in Mark.

UP WITH VILLAGE CULTURE AND FAMILY STABILITY?

Taking a nonlimiting and therefore different tack on Mark 10:28–31 (N.B. the inclusion of v. 31 this time), Horsley declares that the passage deals with "*restored* households, not new communities" (emphasis original), and that the restoration is to occur through "observance of egalitarian economic principles, where no one seeks to become wealthy by taking advantage of others' vulnerability." The result will be an "abundance for all in the community, albeit with no illusions about political realities in

---

20. Horsley, *Hearing the Whole Story*, 28, 77–78; cf. Gundry, *Mark*, 1025-26 and, earlier, 440–42, 453.

the larger world."²¹ As argued earlier, however, if most of the poverty is due to tribute, taxes, tithes, and offerings, the patching up of relations between fellow villagers can hardly produce "abundance." And the notion of *restored* households clashes with the *leaving* of households, unless we are to imagine without textual support a return after the leaving.

If in Mark 3:21 *hoi par' autou* means not the biological family of Jesus but his disciples and other adherents, as Horsley opines (see above), we need to ask how they could think him berserk and remain disciples and adherents. (The berserk *auton* hardly refers to the crowd.) And what would it mean that they "came *out*" to restrain him? They were *with* him. And they shared his inability to eat. Since this inability implies an immediate presence of the crowd (Mark 3:20), how is it that they "hear" of that inability? They don't have to hear about their own inability to eat, do they? Better that *hoi par' autou* refers to Jesus' biological family who came out of Nazareth to restrain him on hearing of the crowd-pressure and consequent inability to eat. Then their inferring that he has gone berserk puts them, standing outside, in a contrast with his fictive discipular family, sitting around him in a circle (3:31, 34; cf. 4:10), so that Horsley's merging of biological and discipular families in village communities lacks conviction. Also, where is evidence in Mark that "following his [Jesus'] execution his followers . . . continued organizing the people and revitalizing village communities" (1)?

DOWN WITH SCRIBAL TRADITION?

To play up the orality of Jesus' peasant culture at the expense of writing in the culture of elites, Horsley says that "over against the Pharisees' written law of Moses from the Jerusalem great tradition [as found, for example, in Deuteronomy, which Jesus and his movement supposedly didn't regard as authoritative], Jesus looks to and defends the popular and, in this case [of marriage and divorce], common Israelite tradition of God's creation of humanity" (175). But part of what Jesus looks to and defends in Mark 10:6 ("male and female he made them") comes from Gen 1:27, usually assigned to a priestly and therefore elitist rather than popular source.

---

21. Horsley, *Hearing the Whole Story*, 192; cf. peasants' resolving of "petty disputes [such as those over 'borrowing and lending'] rooted in their deteriorating economic circumstances" (186).

Horsley posits that the scribal and priestly elites took over popular traditions of the exodus, conquest of Canaan, and Elijah's and Josiah's reforms "but framed them in a larger story that led to the establishment of a monarchy and temple in Jerusalem," and that "Mosaic covenantal law that had been cultivated among Israelite villagers for centuries was adapted into monarchic or temple-state law" (158–59; cf. 37). Apart from the highly speculative character of these statements, Samuel-Kings remains so highly and frequently critical of the monarchy and temple-state as to call in question an incorporation of peasants' oral traditions by the criticized elites into their writings. And if the great tradition incorporated popular traditions that included those critical of the ruling classes, how can we tell the difference between oral and written traditions (cf. Horsley's statement that "even elite circles had adopted Elijah" [238])?

UP WITH ORAL TRADITIONS?

Horsley regards differences from biblical texts where it is usually thought that Mark is quoting or reflecting those texts as evidence of his drawing on *un*written popular traditions (156–76). Does the same phenomenon in the Gospel of Matthew, whose author is usually considered scribal and therefore by Horsley's criterion elite, provide evidence that Matthew too is drawing on unwritten popular traditions? If not, why should Mark's differences imply a drawing on popular oral traditions rather than on the written great tradition? And don't the writings of Jewish scribal elites—*The Genesis Apocryphon*, Pseudo-Philo's *Biblical Antiquities*, and Josephus's *Antiquities of the Jews*, to name just three—exhibit differences from parallel texts in biblical material just as Mark's Gospel does? Horsley tries to have his cake and eat it too when he pits unwritten popular Israelite traditions, represented by Mark and his Jesus, against the written great tradition of Judean elites and then says that when Mark and his Jesus do cite the written great tradition they are only turning the elites' weapon against them. That the Pharisees were developing an oral tradition related positively to Scripture makes even more questionable Horsley's strong disjunction between popular unwritten traditions of peasants and the written tradition of elites.

How far Horsley takes this disjunction shows up in his comments on Mark 2:23–28, where according to him the dependence of Jesus on popular oral traditions is shown by his assuming and implying "fairly clearly" that young David, fleeing from King Saul, entered "the house of God"—that is, "the Temple in Jerusalem"—to eat the bread of presentation, as "confirmed by the identification of Abiathar as 'high priest'" (164-65). But it is hard to believe that an Israelite popular oral tradition had the temple standing in Jerusalem already during Saul's reign; and the reference to Abiathar is probably locative rather than temporal, for nowhere else does Mark use *epi* in a temporal sense.[22]

We might think that Horsley would consider Jesus' "declaring all foods clean" in Mark 7:19c an example of peasants' popular oral tradition, set against the elites' written laws of diet. But no, Horsley thinks that this reading in 7:19c is "somewhat flimsy" (172-73). Again, however, external evidence overwhelmingly favors the reading he doubts; and its well-known grammatical difficulty, evident in copyists' ill-attested efforts at improvement, add internal evidence favoring it. So leaving *Mark's* story of Jesus for once, Horsley resorts to familiar historical-critical arguments: (1) the notion that Jesus declared all foods clean must derive from later gentile Christians' resistance to Jewish food laws, and (2) Christians wouldn't have debated over food laws if Jesus had declared all foods clean. But later Christian debate over table fellowship, as in Gal 2:11-14, doesn't deter critical scholars from believing that Jesus ate with tax collectors and sinners!

"The Gospel of Mark . . . must have *begun* and continued in oral performance." That is to say, "Mark's story was composed in an oral communication environment and would *originally* have been repeatedly performed orally to communities of listeners." So writes Horsley by way of situating Mark in a culture of illiterate peasants (61 and xi, respectively, with emphasis added). But how does he know that Mark's story of Jesus wasn't written down *first*, and only then performed orally and repeatedly by a reader? "Let the reader understand" (Mark 13:14), which Horsley doesn't mention, favors this possibility over his and provides our only hard evidence of the way Mark was performed.[23]

---

22. See Gundry, *Mark*, 146.

23. This command probably means that a public reader of Mark should resist the temptation to which Matthew fell prey, namely, to change the gender of "standing" from masculine to neuter for agreement with the modified noun "abomination" (cf. Matt 24:15). The tradition cited by Papias from the Elder John has Mark drawing on the oral but *un*arranged anecdotes of Peter concerning Jesus, not on a plotted oral narrative (Eusebius, *Hist. eccl.* 3.39.15). The most recent assessments of the rate of literacy both inside and outside first-century Palestine put that rate higher than what Horsley accepts (see, for example, Michael Owen Wise, *Language and Literacy in Roman Judaea: A Study of the Bar Kokhba Documents*, AYBRL [New Haven, CT: Yale University Press, 2015]).

In sum, it would have been one thing for Horsley to write a postcolonial critique of Mark's story. But for him to treat that story as itself a premodern but postcolonial or, better, anticolonial critique of Roman imperialism is quite another thing. Especially so far as Christology is concerned, Horsley's version of Mark's story leaves a big hole. And if *Hearing the Whole Story* presents a fair example of postcolonial biblical criticism, little is to be gained from such criticism. For the whole story is a lot bigger than the *Whole Story*.

Portrayals of Jesus

Reconstructing Jesus

ASSIGNING THE CANONICAL GOSPELS to the genre of Greco-Roman popular biography and reviving the quest of the historical Jesus enjoy a symbiotic relationship. Following is an analysis of the side of this relationship devoted to reconstructing the historical Jesus, with special attention going to one such reconstruction—an extremely popular one among conservative Christians: that of N. T. Wright in *Jesus and the Victory of God*.[1]

Wright's book makes up volume 2 in a series titled *Christian Origins and the Question of God*, ambitiously projected to run to five volumes. Volume 1, *The New Testament and the People of God*, occupied itself mainly with background and method. Volume 3, *The Resurrection of the Son of God*, has now appeared and offers a stout, convincing defense of Jesus' bodily resurrection. Later volumes will take up the Gospel of John through the book of Revelation—above all, the epistles of Paul. But it is the aforementioned volume 2 that offers Wright's detailed reconstruction of the historical Jesus.

With a sweeping and imaginative proposal, *Jesus and the Victory of God* treats the figure of Jesus as portrayed in the Synoptic Gospels of Matthew, Mark, and Luke. Arguably, nevertheless, and despite some self-description to the contrary, the treatment does not represent biblical theology in a strict sense. For Wright is not interested in the synoptic portrayals of Jesus for their own sake so much as for what they can tell us about the Jesus of history who stands behind them. As already implied, Wright sees little difference between those portrayals and the historical Jesus, so that for the most part biblical theology and history merge into each other. But this merger prompts, in turn, another merger, that of the

---

1. Minneapolis: Fortress, 1996.

plural Jesuses of Matthew, Mark, and Luke into one synoptic Jesus. Thus the distinctive lineaments of the various portrayals are blurred almost to the vanishing point. Wright's main interest remains historical rather than biblical, and historicity is insulated against the doubts that differences between the Synoptics often raise (to say nothing about greater differences between these Gospels and the Gospel of John).

To some, the insulation will seem facile insofar as the neglected differences fall into patterns, thereby suggesting that other-than-historical concerns led the evangelists to write unhistorically more often than Wright concedes. Repeatedly, for instance, he explains differences between parallel sayings of Jesus as due to Jesus' own variations, spoken on more than one occasion, and neglects the significant fact that, throughout, the sayings in Matthew tend toward rigorism, those in Luke toward humaneness, and so on.

Given his main interest, though, Wright starts appropriately with the nineteenth-century quest of the historical Jesus and moves next to the new quest inaugurated in 1953 by E. Käsemann and revived more recently in North America by the Jesus Seminar. Wright's skewering of that seminar and its construction of a nonapocalyptic, almost non-Jewish Jesus occupies considerable space and shows Wright at his jousting best. Lastly, he associates himself with the third quest, represented also by E. P. Sanders and others who, on the whole, value synoptic historicity higher than does the Jesus Seminar and see the historical Jesus as solidly Jewish in outlook. The rest of Wright's book is devoted to spelling out the details of that outlook. What are they?

They are, Wright proposes, that whereas the Jews regarded themselves as still living in exile because of Roman domination, Jesus announced that the divinely promised and long-awaited restoration was underway. So he appeared less a teacher of wisdom than a prophet. According to him, moreover, the restoration was taking place in and through his ministry. How so, given that he was not throwing off the Roman yoke?

Well, Jesus had redefined the problem of Jewish exile and its solution. The problem lay not in Roman domination but in the Jews' satanically inspired zeal to free themselves from it by armed revolution instead of carrying out their divinely appointed task of leading gentiles to worship the one true God. The solution lay in repentance from that nationalistic sin and in belief in Jesus as the focal point of a renewed people of God that included Jewish outcasts and gentiles. As such a focal point, Jesus spoke and acted messianically as well as prophetically, though neither for him nor for the Jews did messiahship entail deity.

To renew God's people more inclusively, Jesus also redefined the Torah along lines of mercy and forgiveness as opposed to Israelite ancestry, food laws, and such like. The temple he redefined in terms of himself and his followers. And so it became unnecessary to obtain forgiveness through offering a sacrifice at the temple in Jerusalem, to observe Mosaic restrictions on diet, or to observe other practices demarcating Jews from gentiles.

No wonder that the leaders—Torah-centered Pharisees and temple-centered chief priests alike—opposed Jesus. He was dismantling the main symbols of Jewish national identity! It did not take omniscience for him to see the opposition mounting; so he made his last journey to Jerusalem under the conviction that there he would be put to death and thus suffer the Great Tribulation, which was expected to befall Israel just before God ushered in his kingdom.

Then Jesus did something that galvanized his opponents, especially the chief priests. He physically assaulted the sacrificial system of worship that took place in the temple. The assault was no mere attempt at reformation. No, it was an acted-out prophecy of judgment, of coming destruction. And reports came that Jesus had predicted such destruction verbally too.

In fact, he had. Earlier warnings of coming wrath had dealt not with the eternal judgment of individual sinners hereafter but with God's using the Romans to judge the Jewish nation here and now for their insurrectionism. More recently and specifically, Jesus had cleared the ground for a redefined temple by predicting that the old, corrupt one would be destroyed within a generation. Furthermore, this destruction would make obvious that he and the renewed people of God now constituted the true temple, that God had returned to it, and that for his renewed people, the exile, the real one, had ended.

What to do with Jesus? Get rid of him, naturally, and use the Romans to do so. His constant talk of God's kingdom and his own kinglike deeds and words could be misrepresented as insurrectionary. The Romans crucified Jesus as "King of the Jews," then. Only it was not so easy to get rid of him. He rose from the dead. That event, too, Wright treats as historical, not as fictional or eschatologically excluded from critical investigation.

Finally, Jesus came again at the destruction of Jerusalem and the temple in AD 70. Not in the way a traditional view of the second coming has it, of course. All that language about the sun's darkening, the moon's turning to blood, the stars' falling, and the Son of Man's coming in clouds derives from the Old Testament, where it is used metaphorically not to describe an end to the space-time universe but to invest human events with theological significance.

So talk of celestial disasters painted the destruction of Jerusalem and the temple in colors of divine judgment, and seeing the Son of Man coming in clouds meant a recognition that the destruction both demonstrated Jesus' having already ascended to God's right hand, as distinct from descending to earth in the future, and vindicated God's renewed people still living on earth. So Jesus did not make a chronological mistake when he said that everything would happen before the contemporary generation passed away (Mark 13:30). Everything *did* happen, right on schedule. For the events of AD 70—the destructions of Jerusalem and the temple—were all that Jesus was predicting, and they took place within a generation of his prediction. Furthermore, these events marked the victory of God over those who had engineered the death of his Son Jesus (hence the title of Wright's book).

There is much to learn from this reconstruction of the historical Jesus, and we may laud Wright for some sterling contributions: his maintaining Jesus' Jewishness; his defending Jesus' messianic self-consciousness (though self-consciousness of a uniquely divine sonship gets shortchanged); his resisting the separation of faith from history; his enlarging the historical base of our knowledge concerning Jesus; and his sharpening our tools of historiography, especially his developing a criterion of double similarity-cum-double dissimilarity: what is credible in first-century Judaism and as a starting point for Christianity, but sufficiently unlike both to be a mere reflection, is likely historical.

But there is also much to question. Most of it has to do with the possibility that Wright presses his thesis too far, makes it all-encompassing. In other words, does he give the theme of exile and return a prominence unjustified by the records we have of Jesus' teaching and of Jewish consciousness at the time? Can all the synoptic and related texts tolerate the controlling story of reinterpreted exile and restoration that Wright places on them? For example, can the prodigal son, who wanted distance from his home and wasted his substance in riotous living, represent Israel, who did not want to go into exile and had no substance to waste there (Luke 15:11–32, esp. 13)? Or can the sower's sowing of good seed stand for God's causing true Israel to return from exile, even though Jesus describes as good, not any seed, but *soil* (Mark 4:8, 20)?

Why are Jesus' sheep scattered when he is struck (Mark 14:27)? In Wright's view is not the striking of the shepherd supposed to effect the opposite, namely, the sheep's being *gathered* from exile? How is it that the elect are not gathered till after the great tribulation—that is, till after the Jewish War of AD 66–73, again in Wright's view—if Jesus was already gathering them from their exile forty years earlier (Mark 13:24–27)? How is it that Paul put "our gathering together to him" not till a future "coming of our Lord Jesus Christ" (2 Thess 2:1)? How is it that James and Peter addressed the recipients of their letters as exiles in the Diaspora rather than as returnees from it (Jas 1:1; 1 Pet 1:1)?

According to Wright, Jesus thought that in his passion he would suffer the great tribulation vicariously and thereby enable his followers living in Judea to escape the coming Roman slaughter, as they later did by fleeing Jerusalem before its destruction (cf. Mark 13:14). Is not this restriction of the benefits of his suffering to Judean disciples too severe? Does not his expanding to "all" the addressees of his command, "Watch," imply a larger group (Mark 13:37)? The destruction benefited disciples outside Judea by putting a stop to persecution emanating from there, yet this benefit did not derive from *Jesus'* suffering but from that of *unbelieving Jews*; and the benefit was erased by a shift to Roman persecution.

If Jesus thought he would suffer the great tribulation for his disciples, why did he put it after the abomination of desolation and link it with their later experience rather than with his own immediate experience (Mark 13:14–20)? And how is it that he called on them to take up their crosses and follow him (Mark 8:34–38)? Of what did their restoration from exile consist if they were not only going to continue living under Roman domination but also endure persecution for Jesus' sake? Does not answering that their restoration consisted in deliverance from the sin of insurrectionism spiritualize the restoration in a way analogous to the doctrine of "abstract atonement" on which Wright repeatedly pours scorn? Does not most of Jesus' pacifistic teaching have to do with nonretaliation against Jewish persecutors rather than with nonrebellion against Roman overlords?

Does it not turn scriptural emphasis upside down to interpret the plural "sins" that people repentantly confessed as primarily the singular sin of nationalistic insurrectionism, only secondarily of individuals' sinning in various ways that Jesus discusses at length in his moral teaching (Mark 1:5)? And has not Wright's fixation on redefined exile and restoration likewise led him to ignore and even deny Pharisaic legalism as an object of Jesus' critique (Mark 7:1–23)?

If Jesus' charge that the temple had become "a den of robbers" meant that it had become "a den of revolutionaries," why did Jesus drive out the buyers and sellers of sacrificial animals and birds (Mark 11:15–17)? In what way did their activity represent insurrectionism? And if Jesus meant to do away with the temple and its sacrificial worship, why did he tell a cleansed leper to go show himself to the priest and offer the things commanded by Moses (Mark 1:44)? Why did Jesus say to offer your gift at the altar after reconciliation with your brother (Matt 5:23–24)? Why did Jesus clear the outer court of the temple to enable gentiles to pray there (Mark 11:15–17)?

Why should we regard the mountain being cast into the sea as Mount Zion, where the temple was located, when that mountain has not been mentioned in the context, when the Mount of Olives *has* been mentioned recently; when "this mountain" refers more naturally to the Mount of Olives, right where Jesus and his disciples were located, than to Mount Zion in the distance; and when he hardly meant that the destruction of the temple would happen because some disciple of his was actually going to tell Mount Zion to be thrown into the sea (Mark 11:23)?

If in speaking of judgment to come Jesus did not refer to the last judgment but to the destruction in AD 70, what are we to make of the Ninevites' and queen of the south's being raised "in the judgment with the men of this generation" (Matt 12:41–42)? Did Jesus think the Ninevites and queen would rise from the dead at the destruction? And in what sense did the destruction fulfill the judgment of "all the nations," a judgment issuing in "eternal life" for "the sheep" and "eternal punishment" for "the goats," not in temporal survival and death, as in AD 70 (Matt 25:31–46)? Did the destruction of Jerusalem and the temple really exhaust Jesus' warnings of judgment?

Does the accusation that Jesus said he would destroy the temple and in three days build another one form "the rock of history" on which, "ironically enough," we may stand? Is not the irony rather that Wright takes as rock solid a testimony whose wording differs seriously from passage to passage but whose canonical description as "false" he freely admits (Mark 14:56–59)? Solid *and* slippery? How can the house built on the rock be "a clear allusion to the Temple," that is, "the true Temple" built by Jesus, when the wise man who builds that house is a person who "hears and does" Jesus' *words*, not Jesus himself (Matt 7:24–27)?

Can it be that no first-century Jew would take Dan 7:13 as the Son of Man's descent from heaven? What of John 3:13, "And no one has ascended into heaven except the one who descended from heaven, the Son of Man"? Does not Wright's way of saving Jesus from making a mistake about the occurrence of "all these things" within a generation come at the price of subverting the natural meaning of Jesus' other eschatological pronouncements (Mark 13:30)? If Paul agreed with Jesus by equating the Day of the Lord with the coming destruction of Jerusalem rather than with the end, as Wright avers, how is it that Paul made that day an object of watchfulness and source of comfort for Christians living far off in Greece. Further, how is it that he described the day as one in which the Lord himself will descend from heaven, the dead in Christ will rise, and living Christians will be caught up together with them to meet the Lord in the air (1 Thess 4:13—5:11)? How can Wright allow that Paul was describing Jesus' return to earth yet affirm that Paul thought of the Day of the Lord as entailing intermediate destruction rather than the final return?

Wright also avers that later Christians invented the doctrine of Jesus' return because they could not conceive that he was resurrected if not to join those who will yet be resurrected to populate the coming new earth. But where is the evidence for any puzzling over the problem of Jesus' absence from the new earth—till someone hit on the solution of a return? For that matter, why could not Jesus himself have followed the line of reasoning that Wright ascribes to later Christians?

Readers understandably eager to celebrate Wright's demolition of the Jesus Seminar and its anemic Jesus would do well to think twice before accepting the Jesus that Wright has reconstructed as an alternative. They would do even better to put the canonical Jesuses on a higher pedestal than a putatively historical Jesus, whether Wright's or someone else's. The older Jesuses of the New Testament are superior to any Jesus reconstructed by modern scholars.

The Burden of Christ's Passion

IT IS MILDLY AMUSING to see scholars who in their own quests of the historical Jesus pick and choose from among the four Gospels, then criticize Mel Gibson for doing the same in his film *The Passion of the Christ*. It is less amusing to see scholars accuse Gibson of reading the Gospels through the *contra Iudaeos* tradition when these scholars themselves read his film through that same tradition. Of course, they think the film gives them good reason to do so. But Gibson likewise thinks the Gospels give him good reason to read them thus. Is it correct, then, to interpret *The Passion of the Christ* as laying a burden of guilt on the Jewish people?

The persecutions that Jews have endured throughout the centuries make that interpretation of the film understandable, and the interpretation contains an element of truth—but neither the whole truth nor the fundamental truth. Yes, the film portrays Jewish leaders as responsible for Jesus' arrest and as hauling him to Pontius Pilate and demanding Jesus' crucifixion. Yes, the film portrays a Jewish mob as joining in the demand. On the other hand, the rabbis' own Talmud accepts Jewish responsibility for Jesus' death by changing crucifixion into stoning, a Jewish rather than Roman method of execution, followed by a hanging of the corpse (b. Sanh. 43a, 67a; y. Sanh. 7:16). Moreover, the apostle Paul, an outstandingly earnest Jew prior to his Christian conversion, blamed the Jews for Jesus' death (1 Thess 2:14–16, a passage sometimes disputed but usually considered genuinely Pauline); and it is hard to imagine why according to his own account (Gal 1:13, 23; Phil 3:6, passages universally accepted as authentic) Paul persecuted the church "exceedingly" and "zealously," were it not for Jewish complicity in the death of the one in whom Christians believed. Paul's writing before the Jewish rebellion against Rome in

AD 66–73 undercuts the view that to distance themselves from the Jews, Christians started blaming them unhistorically for Jesus' death not till after that rebellion.

Though Satan moves among the jeering Jews in Gibson's film, other Jews—not Simon of Cyrene and Jesus' mother and disciples alone—sympathize with Jesus. And Satan moves not only among Jesus' Jewish enemies but also among the Roman soldiers as they beat Jesus mercilessly. Someone will say, however, that Gibson portrays the Romans and those Jews alike as cardboard characters; that is to say, he caricatures them. Precisely the point! They are Satan's tools, for human beings would not commit such horrors apart from demonic influence. Even disbelievers in Satan must sometimes wonder at the mystery of human evil.

As for Pilate, he is known from outside the New Testament to have been cruel. But we also know from outside the New Testament that he yielded to Jewish pressure on at least one occasion earlier than Jesus' trial (Josephus, *Ant.* 18.55–59; *J.W.* 2.169–74). Pilate's position was precarious; for in the past, complaints by Jewish leaders against a predecessor, Archelaus, had led to Rome's deposing that predecessor (Josephus, *Ant.* 17.342–44; cf. Strabo 16.2.46); and Pilate himself had complaints lodged against him (Philo, *Embassy* 299–305; Josephus, *Ant.* 18.85–89), the latter of which led to his own deposition. So he had reason to get the jitters and cave in. And since he did cave in despite his belief in Jesus' innocence (all the foregoing and following according to the movie and the Gospels, of course), he himself does not look innocent in the least. Rather, he looks all the more guilty for giving Jesus over to crucifixion against his better judgment. Because of his knowing injustice and the Roman soldiers' unspeakable brutality, in other words, gentiles share with Jews an equal burden of guilt.

But in this film neither the gentiles nor the Jews do the fundamental burden-bearing. Jesus does. The quotation of Isa 53 in the opening frame provides the interpretive key to the whole film. This quotation reads in part that the Servant of the Lord "was crushed for our iniquities" and that "by his wounds we are healed." To the contrary, Satan tells Jesus in the opening scene that "one man" cannot "bear the whole burden of sin. . . . It is far too heavy." Will Jesus succeed in doing what Satan told him nobody can do? Here is the question the film seeks to answer. At bottom it is not a question of how much or little blame for Jesus' death rests on the backs of Jews or of gentiles, whether past or present. It is a question of Jesus' ability to bear the sins of all humanity on his own back in order that human beings may be unburdened of their sins.

In this light, the nearly interminable beating of Jesus does not have the look of gratuitous violence in the sadomasochistic mode. Not at all! Its very length and brutality are designed to test the ability of Jesus to carry "the whole burden of sin" and prove Satan wrong. Unbelievers may not like this theology. It may disgust them. But believers or not, reviewers only expose their theological insensitivity to call the violence inflicted on Jesus "gratuitous." *The Passion of the Christ* gives us to understand that it is the *forgiveness of sins* made possible by the violence which is gratuitous, not the violence itself. And the palpable exhaustion of the Romans who beat Jesus stands for the exhaustion of all human guilt on his body. As an old gospel song puts it, "Jesus paid it all."

Right among Jesus' closest disciples there is guilt to be paid for. They forsake him. Three times Peter denies him. Under Satan's influence Judas Iscariot betrays Jesus. Gibson's portrayal of Judas and Satan displays special sophistication. The Gospel of Matthew has Judas throw back to the chief priests the thirty pieces of blood money they had given him for the betrayal but does not have them throw it to him at the time of bargain. But in a fine artistic touch Gibson does have them do so to form bookends out of a throwing *to* and a throwing *back*. In each throwing the coins scatter on the floor; and Judas's scooping them up when they are thrown to him betrays his greed in the betraying of Jesus for a paltry sum. But boyish demons drive Judas to suicide, so that Satan holds aloft the soul of Judas as a trophy in the form of a warty, hairy baby—albino to represent disembodiment and hideous to represent Satan's disfigurement of a human being who had been made in God's image. (Compare and contrast El Greco's portrayal of the departing soul of the godly Count Orgaz.)

Satan has a comeuppance too. When Jesus dies having successfully borne the weight of the whole world's sin, Satan collapses on the site of Jesus' death—and shrieks. Why? Because that is what demons do when exorcised, when cast out. Shortly before his passion Jesus said, "Now is the prince of this world cast out." Exorcistic language if there ever was such! Satan has had his day; but thanks to Jesus' burden-bearing, that day is over.

The treatment of Herod Antipas, to whom Pilate sent Jesus and who sent Jesus back to Pilate, exhibits Gibson's artistry—and homework as well—at its most subtle and thorough. The drunken feast that Jesus' entry interrupts recalls the drunken feast at which the severed head of Jesus' forerunner, John the Baptist, was served to Herod on a platter. Herod's wife, Herodias, is present here as she was present there. But Herod wears a woman's wig and mascara. Why this womanish portrayal of him despite his heterosexual marriage? Well, it was Herodias who manipulated Herod against his will to have John the Baptist beheaded. To represent her dominance over Herod, Gibson makes him effeminate. There is more. On his way to Jerusalem some Pharisees had said to Jesus, "Get away from here, for Herod wants to kill you." But Jesus answered, "Go tell that fox for me, 'Listen, I am casting out demons and performing cures today and tomorrow, and on the third day I finish my work. . . . It is impossible for a prophet to be killed outside Jerusalem'" (Luke 13:31–33). The Greek word behind "fox" is often feminine, so that Jesus may be calling Herod a vixen, a female fox—not an animal to be afraid of or to run away from. Gibson matches Herod to Jesus' slur.

The Passion of the Christ opens with Jesus standing beside a tree in a garden called Gethsemane. Not as in the Gospels, Gibson puts a temptation of Jesus in that garden and by this means recollects for us the original temptation beside a tree in another garden, the one called Eden. A succumbing to that original temptation led to expulsion, debarment from the tree of life, and death. Jesus' resistance of temptation so as to bear the heavy burden of humanity's sin on another tree, the cross, opened the way back to the tree of life—*eternal* life.

Lest theologically superficial reviews of this film, whether critical or supportive, contribute to an anti-Semitic misuse of it, let us all treat it more perceptively than some have thus far been equipped or disposed to do.

Zealot, or Jesus as a Jewish *Jihadist*

IN HIS *NEW YORK Times* #1 best seller for nonfiction, *Zealot: The Life and Times of Jesus of Nazareth*,[1] Reza Aslan—lionized in some quarters for his previous books, *No god but God* and *Beyond Fundamentalism*—portrays the historical Jesus as a zealot who preached sedition against Rome. According to Aslan, Jesus' message of God's kingdom promised the overthrow of Rome, the expulsion of all foreign elements from the Holy Land, and the Jews' worldwide political dominance under Jesus' kingship. Though he himself did not take up arms, he said he came not to bring peace on earth, but the sword; and he told his disciples to arm themselves with swords for the coming conflict. Since the Jewish hierarchs who controlled the temple served as lackeys to the Romans, Jesus' cleansing the temple challenged not only the hierarchs' authority but also that of the Romans. Hence his crucifixion as "The King of the Jews" counted as the execution of a messianic rebel. But the kingdom of God as Jesus envisioned it did not come. In fact, even the nearly successful Jewish rebellion against Rome in AD 66–73 collapsed under the onslaught of Roman power. As a result of these embarrassments and the influx of non-Palestinian Jews and non-Jews into the Jesus movement, the historically human Jesus of zealotic rebellion was transformed into the fictitiously divine Christ of a peaceful, heavenly kingdom.

Aslan works from what he regards as the "only two hard historical facts" known about Jesus, namely, that he was a Jew who led a popular Jewish movement in first-century Palestine and that Rome crucified him

1. New York: Random, 2014.

for doing so. Beyond these, Aslan relies mainly on the first-century Jewish historian Josephus's record of various rebellious movements of Jews from shortly before Jesus' birth through the destruction of Jerusalem and the temple in AD 70 to the rebellion led by Bar Kokhba in the second century. Add a basically Marxist analysis of first-century Palestinian economy, and you have Aslan's thesis in a nutshell: Jesus was a proletarian Jewish jihadist who like present-day jihadists of the militant sort wanted, at the cost of his own life if necessary, to rid sacred territory of the ungodly and impose divine rule the world over. It helps this comparison—mine, not Aslan's—that Aslan was born in Iran, grew up a nominal Muslim at first, converted to evangelical Christianity during his teens in northern California, lost that faith during his higher education, returned to Islam (minus its usual denial of Jesus' crucifixion), and has written also on jihadism.

Despite the dust jacket's claim that this thesis is "entirely new" and "fresh," it dates back in its essentials to Hermann Samuel Reimarus (eighteenth century) and includes the more recent notables S. G. F. Brandon (1967) and John Dominic Crossan (1995). Though Aslan repeatedly appeals to his "two decades of ['rigorous'] scholarly research into the New Testament and early Christian history" and "exhaustively" details this research in notes at the end of his book, he is not a New Testament scholar or ancient historian comparable in learning to a wide variety of heavyweights who over the years have discredited the revolutionary thesis. To his credit, nevertheless, he has read widely in secondary scholarly literature (yet only in English), including some of a conservative evangelical stamp. Also to his credit, he admits that "for every well-attested, heavily researched, and eminently authoritative argument made about the historical Jesus, there is an equally well-attested, equally researched, and equally authoritative argument opposing it." Despite a contrary promise, however, opposite points of view go largely unaddressed even in the supposedly exhaustive ending notes; and the dogmatism, bordering sometimes on bombast, with which Aslan states his own views will unfortunately leave on a popular readership misimpressions of certainty.

One can appreciate a number of Aslan's observations, such as the following (among others): The progressive demotion of John the Baptist in favor of Jesus from early to late New Testament literature. The lack of ancient debate over the actuality of Jesus' exorcisms and miracles. The purpose of the exorcisms and miracles to manifest God's kingdom on earth. The variety of messianic expectations in first-century Judaism(s).

The tracing to Dan 7:13 of Jesus' self-designation "the Son of Man." The gradual easing of Pontius Pilate's guilt in later New Testament literature. The development of the Zealot *Party* not till after Jesus' career. The possibility that Christianity may have influenced pagan mystery religions rather than vice versa.

Among Aslan's pronouncements lacking solid evidence are that David hid from King Saul at Masada. That during the first century "countless prophets, preachers, and messiahs tramped through the Holy Land." (Excluding John the Baptist and Jesus, Aslan identifies only ten.) That John the Baptist taught Jesus the Lord's Prayer. That John Mark was from the Diaspora. That Matthew wrote in Damascus and Luke in Syrian Antioch. That Jesus was born "some time between 4 B.C.E. and 6 C.E." (Most scholars of all stripes say only sometime prior to 4 BC.)[2] That without exception, victims of crucifixion had attached to their cross a plaque inscribed with their crime. That Stephen's martyrdom made permanent a division between Hebraistic and Hellenistic Christians.

Despite doubting the historicity of all but Jesus' leading a popular movement and being crucified for doing so, Aslan bases his reconstruction time after time not only on Mark and a hypothetical Q (the latter a putative sayings-source reflected in Matthew and Luke) as our earliest documents, plus the grid of Jewish revolutionism, but also on other materials, including John's Gospel (strikingly). Sad to say, the reconstruction is riddled with factual errors—some significant, others insignificant:

According to Aslan, Matthew and Luke are "the only two evangelists" who mention Joseph, Jesus' father. (But Joseph is mentioned also in John 1:45; 6:42.) "The building boom in Jerusalem and the completion of the Temple" ended "shortly before Herod's death." (But the sanctuary proper reached completion a whole decade and a half before Herod's death, while construction of the out-buildings and courts and the building boom lasted for more than six decades after the death of Herod.) "Nazareth was just a day's walk from . . . Sepphoris." (Make it about an hour's walk.) The Samaritans worshiped God "in their temple on Mt. Gerizim." (Not during Jesus' time, for their temple had been destroyed in the second century BC.) "Jesus replaced the costly blood and flesh sacrifice mandated by the Temple with his free healings and exorcisms." (Why then did he instruct his disciples to prepare a Passover meal, which included a lamb sacrificed at the temple?)

---

2. Aslan uses the politically correct "B.C.E." and "C.E."

Luke had no idea what we mean by "history." (Why then does he appeal to eyewitnesses?) Crucifixion entailed "the nailing of the hands and feet to a crossbeam." (The feet too? Only in the case of a contortionist.) John's Jesus is "an otherworldly spirit without earthly origins." (But according to John he "became flesh," had a mother named Mary, had his rib cage pierced and his corpse given a sumptuous burial, and upon his resurrection told Mary Magdalene to let go of him and invited doubting Thomas to touch the nail- and spearprints in his body.)

"The earliest manuscripts we have of the gospel of Mark end the first verse at 'Jesus the Christ.'" (Wrong! Most of the earliest manuscripts add "the Son of God.") For lack of interest, Mark writes "nothing at all" about Jesus' resurrection. (But "He's been raised" and "there [in Galilee] you'll see him," spoken at Jesus' empty tomb, trumpet resurrection, as in three passion-and-resurrection predictions earlier in Mark.) "Anyone who reads Mark in the original Greek can tell that a different hand wrote the final eight verses [of Mark 16]." (True only of the twelve verses *following* Mark 16:1–8.)

Greek was "the language of the [Roman] victors." (How about Latin, as on the Arch of Titus, which celebrated their victory over the Jews?) Noncanonical gospels "written mostly in the second and third centuries . . . demonstrate the dramatic divergence of opinion [concerning Jesus] . . . even among those who claimed to walk with him, who shared his bread and ate with him, who heard his words and prayed with him." (They must have lived a long time, then.)

Paul's hometown Tarsus was located "on the Mediterranean Sea." (Actually, twenty-two kilometers inland.) Upon his conversion, Saul of Tarsus "changed his name to Paul," according to Aslan. (But Saul almost certainly bore from birth the Hellenistic name "Paul" as well as the Hebraistic name "Saul.") Luke never refers to Paul as an "apostle." (On the contrary, see Acts 14:14.) Paul "thinks he is the *first* apostle" (emphasis original). (What to do, then, with 1 Cor 15:8: "Last of all . . . to me"?) "The letters of Paul . . . make up the bulk of the New Testament." (Oh? Page-wise, barely more than 22 percent and bookwise thirteen over against fourteen non-Paulines.) Paul did not preach "to his fellow Jews." (Scratch the book of Acts, then—also Paul's saying in 1 Cor 9:20, "To the Jews I became as a Jew, in order to win Jews.") Apart from Jesus' Words of Institution, "Paul seems totally unconcerned with anything 'Jesus-in-the-flesh' may or may not have said." (Yet in 1 Cor 7:10 he explicitly cites Jesus' teaching on divorce.) "Paul's Christ is not even human, though he has taken on the likeness of one (Phil 2:7)." (But according to Paul, Jesus "was descended from David according to the flesh" [Rom 1:3] and "born of a woman" [Gal 4:4].)

There are other errors, but it's time to stop nibbling around the edges. As to the central thesis that Jesus was a revolutionary, Aslan has to admit that in AD 10–36—that is, during Jesus' teens and on through his public ministry and beyond—"the Galileans enjoyed a period of peace and tranquility." This "most stable period in the entire first century" casts doubt on Jesus' supposed anti-Roman revolutionism. So Aslan has to resort to speaking of a "slow burn." To maintain that Jesus "render[ed] irrelevant the entire priestly establishment and their costly, exclusivistic [sacrificial] rituals," Aslan similarly has to say that "Jesus is joking" when telling a healed leper to go offer the Mosaically prescribed sacrificial gift for a testimony to the priests. Jesus' saying to "go also the second mile" when a Roman soldier requisitions you to carry his gear "one mile" ill suits Aslan's speaking of Jesus' "condemnation of the Roman occupation."

Astonishingly, Aslan affirms Jesus' teaching that Caesar should be paid back the tax owed to him, exactly opposite what a revolutionary should or would have said. Then Aslan tries shifting the issue from tax-paying to that of Palestine as "*God's* land" (emphasis original), which should be paid back to him. But nothing in the context speaks of the Holy Land, and Jesus' addressees (Pharisees and Herodians) were in no position vis-à-vis the Romans to give that land back to God. Aslan might have been better off to deny the historicity of that episode, except that doing so would have made more obvious than ever the Procrustean bed he uses to amputate materials unfriendly to his thesis.

Granted, the Jews who acclaimed Jesus at his triumphal entry into Jerusalem may well have thought of him as a messianic king who would overthrow the Romans; but the Jesus who proceeded to cleanse the temple as "a house of prayer for all the nations" and aimed "to give his life a ransom for many" seems to have had in mind something different from a messianic rebellion against Rome. The two swords that he told his disciples were "enough" would hardly have sufficed for such a rebellion, and his repeated predictions of his own and his disciples' violent deaths betray a nonexpectation of God's imminent overthrow of Rome.

Though Jesus wasn't "a violent revolutionary bent on armed rebellion," he "instructs his disciples immediately after the Passover meal" to go sell their cloaks and each buy a sword, as for a violent revolution. So says Aslan, but he fails to mention the context of an evangelistic mission requiring not only a sword for self-protection but also a purse, bag, and sandals for travel, just as he fails to mention that Jesus' bringing a sword has to do, figuratively and contextually, with division in families over whether to follow Jesus, not with revolution against Rome. (Compare Jesus' saying in the different context of violence that "all who take the sword will perish by the sword.") Undoubtedly Jesus was crucified as "The King of the Jews"—that is, as a messianic rebel—but Aslan has to doubt or deny that the Sanhedrin shifted from the religious charge of blasphemy, under which they condemned Jesus, to a false political charge of sedition when arraigning him before Pilate.

Stephen's seeing Jesus at God's right hand is supposed to have launched "a wholly new religion" divorced from "the historical person known as Jesus of Nazareth." Such a dictum requires a denial that Jesus himself predicted he would take a position at God's right hand. "After the Jewish revolt and the destruction of Jerusalem [in AD 70]," according to Aslan, "the early Christian church tried desperately to distance Jesus from the zealous nationalism that had led to that awful war" and consequently "transform[ed] their messiah from a fierce Jewish nationalist into a pacifistic preacher of good works whose kingdom was not of this world." It's strange, then, that Paul wrote already in the AD 50s that "the kingdom of God is . . . righteousness and peace and joy in the Holy Spirit" (Rom 14:16). But Paul and Peter didn't share "the same faith," says Aslan. So it's strange once more that in 1 Corinthians 3:22 Paul included Peter along with himself and Apollos as those belonging in Christ to the Corinthian believers (see also 1 Cor 1:10–17).

Beyond further criticisms, deserving of mention are Aslan's flights of imagination, whether they be true or false: "After his baptism" Jesus "stayed in the wilderness for a while . . . to learn from John [the Baptist] and to commune with his [John's] followers." When Jesus cleanses the temple, "a corps of Roman guards and heavily armed Temple police blitz through the courtyard looking to arrest whoever is responsible for the mayhem." Jesus died "on a bald hill covered in crosses, beset by the cries and moans of agony from hundreds of dying criminals as a murder of crows circled eagerly over his head waiting for him to breathe his last." The assassin "who killed Jonathan son of Ananus as he strode across the Temple Mount in the year 56 C.E." was probably "the first to cry, 'Murder!'" Such lively prose befits an "associate professor of creative writing" who holds "a master of fine arts in fiction" as well as "a Ph.D. in the sociology of religions."

EPILOGUE

Aslan's apostasy from evangelical Christianity stemmed from his discovery of unhistorical elements in the Bible and having been taught that "every word of the Bible is God-breathed and true, literal and inerrant." Teachers whose version of biblical inerrancy lacks enough literary sensitivity to acknowledge in Scripture the presence of genres that mix fact and fiction for more than purely historical purposes—these teachers should take warning from the example of Aslan, and of too many others like him.

Jesus the *Halakic* Jew

THE QUEST OF THE historical Jesus is turning out to be like my wife's search for the perfect coffee maker: unending. Albert Schweitzer traced the quest critically from the eighteenth century up to his own time (the early twentieth century) and added an apocalyptic wrinkle to that quest, now called *the first quest*. Largely because the temporary ascendance of existential theology made historical concerns seem relatively unimportant (what counts is what affects your existence here and now), questing for the historical Jesus lapsed into a partial (but only partial) coma till Ernst Käsemann revived it with an influential lecture in 1953. This second quest fizzled quickly, though. Its historiographical skepticism kept it from producing very much more than a question mark. In reaction, a cadre of scholars said we can do better by concentrating on the Jewishness of Jesus. For we now have an increased understanding of first-century Judaism, against which background we can evaluate the canonical evangelists' portrayals of Jesus. Hence the so-called *third quest*.

Enter John P. Meier into the ranks of third-questers. *Law and Love* makes up volume 4 of his *A Marginal Jew: Rethinking the Historical Jesus*.[1] Meier intended to write only one volume, but two more volumes followed. He then determined to make volume 4 his last by taking up in it the enigmas of Jesus on the Mosaic law, Jesus' parables, Jesus' self-identifications, and the reason(s) for his crucifixion. (Apparently because it would entail the supernatural, a resurrection of Jesus, along with his miracles, lies outside the confines of enigmas open to historical research "using scientific tools," in which case David Hume wins—historiographically speaking—before an examination of testimonial

---

1. New Haven, CT: Yale University Press, 2009.

evidence even starts.) Alas, volume 4 manages to cover only the first enigma; and it's hard to imagine that Jesus' parables, self-identifications, and crucifixion, about each of which others have written voluminously, can be covered in a single fifth volume by so learned and meticulous a scholar as Meier. The perfect coffee maker is turning into an elusive pot of gold at the end of a rainbow.

To his credit, Meier differentiates the historical Jesus, limited to what can be learned about him through accepted criteria of historical research, from the totality of Jesus' words and deeds; and he disavows presenting his historical Jesus as "the new and improved version of Christian faith in Christ." The supposedly accepted criteria of historical research used by Meier have suffered considerable qualification and criticism, however; and his use of those criteria shows some inconsistency. Take, for example, the criterion of dissimilarity, or discontinuity: what "cannot be derived either from the Judaism(s) of Jesus' time or from the early church" is likely historical, because it's unlikely to have been made up. Yet Meier hails as historical several of Jesus' legal pronouncements not only because they *differ* from Judaism (and early Christianity) but also because Jesus' very making of legal pronouncements *characterizes* Judaism: "First-century Palestinian Judaism being what it was, how could a religiously oriented Jew who tried to lead a religious movement . . . among his fellow Jews be anything else [than 'the halakic Jesus,' that is, a Jesus who made pronouncements concerning the Mosaic law]?" So it's dissimilarity that supports historicity for Jesus' halakic pronouncements, but it's similarity that supports historicity for the halakic Jesus himself. Hmmm. Why couldn't someone argue that Jesus' Jewish followers falsely made him appear halakic so as to tone down his off-putting, unfulfilled apocalypticism and thus appeal to a wider audience for whom halakic teachers were acceptable?

Meier trumpets his own dissimilarity by averring that though he may not be right in his positions, "every other book or article on the historical Jesus and the Law has been to a great degree wrong." Yet similarity to majority opinion among current scholars marks Meier when without argument he treats none of the canonical Gospels as written till forty to seventy years after Jesus' death and treats the traditions about Jesus as reworked many times prior to even our earliest records of those traditions in Mark and Q (the latter a putative sayings-source reflected in Matthew and Luke). Never mind the arguments of some scholars that the description of Mark's Gospel given by the very early church father Papias, which portrays it as enshrining Peter's recollections, favors a severe limitation of reworking. And never mind that favoring earlier dates of writing are the lack of any reference in the reports of Jesus' Olivet Discourse to the burning of the Jews' temple in AD 70 and Matthew's repeated insertions of Sadducees into paralleled material though the Sadducees lost their importance (and most of them their very lives) in the destruction of Jerusalem at that time. The dating of our sources affects judgments about historicity, of course.

Let it be said, though, that Meier's book contains a wealth of useful information, acute observations, and penetrating argument, many of which appear in lengthy footnotes. Consider the superb explanation of Old Testament purity laws, buttressed by five hundred lines of bibliography in a single footnote of fine print. What appear to be digressions make sense as comparative backcloth for the purported legal pronouncements of Jesus. Regardless of disagreements, the breadth and depth of Meier's scholarship call for high admiration.

As to the Mosaic law, Meier helpfully notes (1) variant readings in its texts; (2) the later addition of commands to the law as though they originally appeared in it (take Jesus' transforming Moses' *assumption* of a divorce certificate [Deut 24:1-4] into Moses' *commanding* such a certificate to be written and given [Mark 10:2-5; Matt 5:31]); and (3) diverse interpretations of the law in the Dead Sea Scrolls, the Old Testament apocrypha and pseudepigrapha, writings of the first-century Jewish philosopher Philo and the first-century Jewish historian Josephus, and rabbinical literature dating from considerably later—all these for comparison with Jesus' legal pronouncements. As to primitive Christianity, Meier commendably denies that the apocryphal Gospels and the Nag Hammadi materials, including the Gospel of Thomas, provide independent historical sources concerning Jesus; rejects the Jesus Seminar's portrayal of Jesus as "a wandering Cynic philosopher in the Greco-Roman mold"; and speaks of "mainstream Christianity" in the first century as opposed to the notion of a crazy quilt of disparate Jesus-sects.

After discussing the question *What is the Law?* Meier takes up the pronouncements of Jesus on divorce, notes that Jesus' making adultery a consequence of divorce presumes remarriage, and judges that the historical Jesus forbade such divorce totally. Supporting this judgment are (1) the multiple attestation of these pronouncements in various kinds of literature (the Gospels [the Synoptics], a sayings-source [Q], and a Pauline epistle [1 Corinthians]); (2) the pronouncements' dissimilarity to what is said about divorce in all relevant background literature (so that it's unlikely Jesus' pronouncements were read onto his lips from elsewhere); (3) the coherence of such radical pronouncements with the radicality of Jesus' other pronouncements and celibacy; and (4) the embarrassment caused Christians by the stringency of Jesus' pronouncements on divorce—an embarrassment evident in Matthew's redactional addition of "except for immorality" (even if this exception were to apply only to remarriage-less divorce [Matt 5:32; 19:9]) and in Paul's acquiescence to the divorce of a Christian by his or her non-Christian spouse (its remaining unclear whether Paul allows the Christian to remarry [1 Cor 7:15]). I would quibble with Meier over his treating as unhistorical the narrative surrounding Jesus' pronouncements in Mark 10:2–12; Matt 19:3–12, and over his brushing aside the Mishnaic evidence of a first-century debate between Hillelites and Shammaites over sufficient grounds for divorce (there being astounding correspondences between the Mishnaic rules for judging cases of capital blasphemy and Mark's account of Jesus' trial before the Sanhedrin, to take a parallel case). Nevertheless, Meier is justified in his scoring of those who allow their pastorally lenient concerns to lower the bar set by the historical Jesus on the topic of divorce.

Next comes Jesus' absolute prohibition of oaths. Meier traces this prohibition back to the historical Jesus on the ground of its attestation in both a Gospel (Matt 5:34–37) and an epistle (Jas 5:12); on the additional ground of the prohibition's dissimilarity, particularly in its absoluteness, to all relevant background literature (the law allowing and sometimes commanding oaths); and finally on the ground that throughout the church's history most Christians have loosened the prohibition out of embarrassment over its stringency, so that early Christian invention seems unlikely.

If then the absolute prohibitions of divorce and oaths derive from the historical Jesus, he dared to prohibit what the law allowed and commanded even though (it goes almost without saying) he affirmed the law as a whole. How does Meier handle this inconcinnity? A full answer awaits his discussion of Jesus' self-identifications. Already, though, Meier portrays him as a self-consciously eschatological prophet. But would such a prophet have arrogated to himself the authority to abrogate certain elements of God's law given through Moses? Wouldn't an even more exalted self-image have been required?

Yet precisely because Mark 2:28 plays "the Christological trump card" in favor of Jesus' allowing his disciples to violate the Sabbath ("And so the Son of Man is Lord even of the Sabbath"), Meier judges the saying inauthentic. But if the historical Jesus attacked, subverted, or annulled the laws regarding divorce and oaths, as Meier affirms he did, why should Meier judge it "too ludicrous" to think Jesus did the same in regard to Sabbath law? Furthermore, all supposed violations of the Sabbath by Jesus himself take place in stories of miraculous healings. Since miracle-stories are ipso facto historically suspect, those violations are likewise suspect. But Meier judges it historically true that Jesus and his followers *thought* he performed miracles whether or not he *actually* did. So what is to prevent our judging those stories to be dealing with the historical Jesus? Might the failure of all relevant background literature written prior to AD 70—might its failure to prohibit healing on the Sabbath keep us from judging those stories historically authentic? Meier thinks so. To the contrary we might ask why first-generation Christians would have invented stories that made recognizable nonsense regarding contemporary understandings of Sabbath law. And why don't the New Testament stories count as evidence that Jesus' opponents regarded healing on the Sabbath as a violation thereof? It seems as though Meier *would* regard similar stories about others as such evidence if those stories appeared outside the Gospels.

Because of well-known differences between Jesus' appeal to David's action at the house of God (Mark 2:25–26) and the story as it appears in 1 Sam 21:2–10, Meier thinks it impossible that Jesus, halakic as Meier portrays him to have been, would have "proceed[ed] in the presence of those scriptural experts [the Pharisees] to mangle and distort the text of the story" and make "embarrassing mistakes." Take but two of many possible examples, however: since Matthew, no slouch when it came to mining the Old Testament, freely used Hos 11:1's reference to Israel's exodus from Egypt in the distant past as a messianic prediction (Matt 2:15), and since Paul, an ex-Pharisee and scriptural expert, freely applied the rejection and restoration of Israel as God's people according to Hos 2:23; 1:10 to believing gentiles, who had never been God's people (Rom 9:24–27), the historical Jesus could have used Scripture with similar freedom. Meier's argument rests faultily on a modern canon of interpretation.

Mainly because it expresses "creation theology within the context of the end time," as does one of Jesus' authentic pronouncements on divorce, Meier does give the saying that "the Sabbath came into being because of humanity, and not humanity because of the Sabbath" (Mark 2:27) "a good chance of coming from the historical Jesus." Mark 2:27 doesn't negate

Sabbath law, however. Nor does Jesus' asking what man wouldn't pull his son, ox, or sheep out of a well or pit on the Sabbath (Matt 12:11; Luke 14:15; see also Luke 13:15). Instead, these sayings give expression to the historical Jesus' "commonsense approach to Sabbath observance" so as "to shield ordinary pious Jews ['who could hardly afford to stand by when they were in danger of losing one of their livestock, to say nothing of their children'] from the attraction of sectarian rigorism" as taught and practiced by "the Essenes or other sectarians." Oops! I thought radical rigorism is supposed to characterize sayings attributable to the historical Jesus, as in his absolute prohibitions of divorce and oaths. Now relaxed common sense does the trick. Oh the vagaries of the quest!

The topic of Jesus and Jewish laws of purity comes up next, with a focus on Mark 7:1–23, the whole of which Meier considers inauthentic with the possible exception of vv. 10–12 concerning the vow of corban (the dedication of a gift to God). As to this exception, Meier says "the conflict [between the dedication to God and the command to honor your needy parents by letting them use the gift] does not seem to annul the very practice of making a vow." But if the historical Jesus forbade all vows, he had no need to say that honoring your parents overrides the vow of corban. The vow shouldn't have been made in the first place. So either Meier should consider these verses inauthentic along with the rest; or we should regard these verses as simply an exposé of the Pharisees' hypocrisy, in which case historicity not only for vv. 10–12 but also for their narrative framework, where the Pharisees figure, becomes a viable possibility.

Meier lodges a battery of objections to dog that possibility, however: (1) Extrabiblical literature doesn't support that all Jews rinsed their hands before eating. Yet examples of hyperbole occur in Mark 1:5, 33, 39; 6:33 (cf. John 12:19). Why not in 7:3, too, especially since despite a similar lack of literary support the immersions that Mark also mentions in 7:4 are supported by archaeological evidence? If 7:3–4 occurred in pre-AD 70 Jewish literature outside the New Testament, would Meier count the passage as valid evidence? Why would Mark or some Christian before him engage in the hyperbole that all Jews rinsed their hands before eating if not enough of them did so to justify the hyperbole? Surely it would be generally known that they didn't. And the mysterious phrase, "with a fist" (Mark 7:3–4), speaks against unhistorical invention. For wouldn't a fabricator of the story make it culturally understandable?

(2) In vv. 6–7 Mark writes for the most part the Greek text of Isaiah 29:13, which excoriates the *teaching* of merely human commandments,

whereas Jesus would have used the Hebrew text, which excoriates the merely mechanical *practice* of commandments. But it's the practice of *human* commandments according to the Hebrew, so that the shift from practice to teaching simply sharpens the point of the commandments' human origin; and the evangelists often redacted an authentic quotation to suit their own emphases.

(3) The shift from hand-rinsing to food laws is unnatural. Not at all! Shifting from how to eat to what to eat makes for a natural progression.

(4) Though an abrogation of kosher laws satisfies the criteria of "both discontinuity from the Judaism of Jesus' day . . . and a style coherent with those sayings of Jesus that are generally considered authentic,"

> it hardly seems credible that the popular Palestinian Jewish teacher named Jesus should have rejected or annulled in a single logion [the saying in verse 15 that nothing going into the body can defile a person] all the laws on prohibited foods enshrined in Leviticus and Deuteronomy. . . . If Jesus did actually annul the food laws, how did he remain so popular and influential among the common people . . . ?

Well, it seems credible to Meier that Jesus prohibited divorce and oaths absolutely yet remained popular (despite the frequency of divorce and oaths, one might add).

(6) Early Jewish Christians kept kosher, so that Jesus mustn't have abrogated that feature of the law. But why did the table fellowship of Peter, Barnabas, and other Jewish Christians with gentile Christians come under criticism from Judaizers if it wasn't for the eating of non-kosher food (Gal 2:11–13)?

So much for Jesus and the law. Now for Jesus and love. There is much to laud in Meier's discussion of this topic. He argues that the historical Jesus reaffirmed the Old Testament commands to love God and your neighbor. Dissimilarity favors historicity in that neither any Jewish writing prior to Jesus or soon after him nor any New Testament book outside the Synoptics quotes Deut 6:5 and Lev 19:18b word-for-word and back-to-back, ranks them in order of importance, and rates the two of them superior to all other commands, as Jesus does. A kind of multiple attestation likewise favors historicity in that the double love-command in the earliest Gospel (Mark 12:29–31) is joined by the command in a sayings-source (Q as reflected in Matt 5:44; Luke 6:27) to love your enemies. Jesus' welding together widely separated love-commands, ranking them in relation to each other, and rating them superior to all other commands show that he reflected on the totality of the law, possessed halakic competence, and probably knew how to read.

But given Matthew's redaction in 22:40 ("On these two commands hang the whole Law and the Prophets"), Meier observes that the conjoined love-commands do not provide the historical Jesus' key to interpreting the whole law. Nor does "your neighbor" mean anyone near you. For the immediate context in Leviticus distinguishes aliens from neighbors and thereby limits "your neighbor" to a fellow Israelite, and Jesus does not expand this meaning. (The parable of the Good Samaritan in Luke 10:29–37 refuses to define "my neighbor" and challenges me *to be* a neighbor.) In addition, John 13:34 commands only the loving of one another in the Christian community; and 1 John 2:15 prohibits loving the world, that is, the world of unsaved human beings, whom only God (and not even Jesus) is said to have loved (John 3:16). The command to love your enemies has in its favor dissimilarity: it doesn't occur in the Old Testament; and though parallels are found in other early literature, Jesus' command, like many of his commands, is distinctively laconic, whereas the parallels add elements of self-benefit and divine vengeance.

Talking about love, I remember that my beloved teacher Marchant King once said, somewhat dismissively of the quest, that all we have is the biblical Jesus. Naturally, Christians want as much correspondence as possible between the various biblical portraits of Jesus, which we still have in our hands, and the historical Jesus, whom we no longer have in person. Theologically, nonetheless, more stress should fall on the biblical Jesus than on the historical Jesus, so that believing scholars might well beware lest a zeal to establish the historicity of every jot and tittle in the Gospels lead them to harmonize the texts unnaturally and thereby miss the rich variegation of God's love in Christ. And since, grammatically speaking, the quest *of* the historical Jesus can mean a quest *by* Jesus as well as a quest *for* him, the evangelist in me wants to say that as a shepherd, the biblical-historical Jesus is lovingly searching for us, lost sheep that we sinners are.

Kingdom and Power, Love and Violence

THE CANONICAL GOSPELS PACK a lot of material about Jesus between his birth and crucifixion. With the sole exception of an account concerning Jesus at the age of twelve (Luke 2:40–52), this material deals with his public ministry and features, above all and at least in the Synoptics, the theme of God's kingdom as established in that ministry. The classic Christian creeds omit the ministry, however, by skipping from Jesus' birth to his crucifixion. As a result, argues N. T. Wright in his book *How God Became King: The Forgotten Story of the Gospels*,[1] the Christian church has by and large—and for many centuries—missed the message of God's kingdom contained in the Gospels. Not that their individual units (sayings, parables, sermons, accounts of miracles and exorcisms) have suffered wholesale neglect, of course. But Wright sees inattention to what he regards as the metanarrative of how God became king, a narrative that does not exclude Jesus' birth, crucifixion, resurrection, and ascension but that certainly does include the other material missing from the creeds yet present in the Gospels. In view of the many modern studies of God's kingdom (far too many even for a lengthy footnote) and in view not only of Luther's doctrine of two kingdoms but also of Tatian's, Origen's, Augustine's, and surprisingly the emperor Constantine's far earlier distinguishing between divine and human governments,[2] plus historical phenomena such as the

---

1. New York: HarperOne, 2012. Wright wrote this book not only for lay people but also for "theologians as well as biblical scholars" (xvi). Throughout this review mere page numbers will refer to *How God Became King*.

2. Tatian, *Ad. Gr.* 28; Origen, *Cels.* 8.75; Augustine, *Civ.*; Eusebius, *Vit. Const.* 4.8, 13 (Letter to Sapor II). Leading me to these passages were George H. van Kooten,

Holy Roman Empire, the Roman Catholic Church, and Calvin's Geneva, we should probably say that Wright laments the lack heretofore of *his* interpretation of God's kingdom, though the Puritan experiment(s) in New England presaged the interpretation in significant respects.

The key point in Wright's interpretation seems to be that Jesus established God's kingdom through nonviolent means, as opposed to armed rebellion by Jews against their Roman overlords. These nonviolent means started in the healings and exorcisms performed by Jesus, received explanation in his preaching and teaching, reached their acme of nonviolence in his suffering and death on a cross, and gained the impress of power-through-suffering in his resurrection and ascension. Consequently, according to Wright, the Christian church—especially in the West and most especially in the United States—should oppose the use of military force and accompany the preaching of eternal salvation with philanthropic works in society at large, these works being inherent to God's continuing to become king on earth as in heaven right now, not merely utilitarian for the purpose of recommending the gospel of salvation in the age to come.

Underlying Wright's pacifistic-cum-philanthropic emphasis is a corollary emphasis on the story of Jesus and the church as a continuation, in revised form, of the story of Israel and Israel's God. Just as Israel was a theocracy, so Jesus established a theocracy in the church, a theocracy the church is commissioned to extend throughout the world politically as well as theologically. For politics and theology are intertwined (if there is any distinction at all). Away, then, not only with Christian support of bombs and bullets in misguided, futile attempts to suppress evil: "We still seem to think that bombs and bullets can deal with 'evil,' liberating people who, once the 'evil' has been thus obliterated, will turn out to be nice liberal Western democrats after all," and "it has been possible for Christians in our own day to think of bringing 'justice and peace' into the world by the normal, disastrous means of bombs and bullets. Not so" (160 and 203, respectively). Someone is bound to ask whether countering the Axis with bombs and bullets in World War II did a pretty good job of obliterating that evil, an obliteration which has brought justice and peace to Wright and a good many others. That question aside, though,

---

"Ἐκκλησία τοῦ Θεοῦ: The 'Church of God' and the Civic Assemblies (ἐκκλησίαι) of the Greek Cities in the Roman Empire: A Response to Paul Trebilco and Richard A. Horsley," *NTS* 58 (2012) 528, and, in turn, Clifford Ando, *Imperial Ideology in the Roman Empire*, Classics and Contemporary Thought 6 (Berkeley: University of California Press, 2000), 343–48.

theological-philosophical discussions of just war theory and high-level political deliberations over just war call in question his reference to "dangerous naïveté" in the supposed detachment from one another of "theology, philosophy, and politics" (160).[3]

Away too, says Wright, with the separation of church and state and with Christian support of democracy. As Israelite society was to be governed by divine-righted rulers, in an increasingly Christian-laced economy current nations should also be governed by divine-righted rulers, not by representatives chosen in popular elections: "In a genuinely creational monotheism, the world works best when ruled by wise stewards, human beings who are humble before God and hence effective in bringing fruitful order to his world. . . . The Jews didn't, it seems, care very much how rulers became rulers; so much for our modern ideals of 'legitimacy through voting'" (169-70). Hence, Jesus' introduction of a radically new theocracy and its extension throughout the world by the church is creating a "new era of justice, peace, and freedom" (45).

At this point a tension is to be noted in Wright's proposal. To support its theocratically political aspect, he stresses that "the four Gospels present themselves as *the climax of the story of Israel*" (65, emphasis original),[4] so that "Israel had not been abandoned" (196-97), the theory of abandonment being "a gross caricature of the actual biblical story" (85). On the other hand, though Israel "had not been 'replaced,'" "it had been transformed" through the inclusion of "pagan converts" (197). To the extent that this transformation is emphasized, the theocratically political cast of God's Israelitish kingdom recedes as, for example, in Jesus' statement that "God's kingdom will be taken away from you [the leaders of Israel] and given to a nation [called Jesus' 'church' in Matt 16:18] producing its fruits" (Matt 21:43) and in Paul's distinguishing "God's church" from "Jews" as well as "Greeks" (1 Cor 10:32).[5] Are these scriptural statements gross caricatures? Even in the passage where Paul compares gentile believers to wild olive branches grafted into the stock of Israel,

---

3. To take but one example, see Oliver O'Donovan, *The Just War Revisited*, Current Issues in Theology (Cambridge: Cambridge University Press, 2003).

4. To distinguish books from a message, I am changing Wright's "gospel(s)" into "Gospel(s)" even in direct quotations.

5. See also 1 Pet 2:9-10, where the Christian addressees, who as non-Jews were "once not ['God's'] people," are called "a holy nation." Translations of Scripture are my own unless otherwise indicated, and verse-numbering (particularly in the Psalms) follows that of English versions.

a distinction is maintained between ethnic Israel, whose story Wright highlights for its theocratically political relevance to his thesis, and the united body of Jewish and gentile believers: "Salvation has come to the Gentiles for the purpose of provoking them [ethnic Israelites, according to the context] to jealousy.... And those [natural branches that have already been cut off], too, will be grafted in if they do not continue in unbelief" (Rom 11:11, 23).

The Gospels were written long after the gospel had burst Jewish boundaries. So the Gospels' messages were in fact written for the multiethnic church and for the purpose of spelling out "God's answer to the plight of the human race in general."[6] Wright may legitimately take refuge in qualifying with "simply" his denial that the Gospels were written in answer to this plight. Again, however, to the extent that he allows difference between the old, monoethnic Israel and a new, multiethnic "Israel," leverage is lost for a transference of Israelitish political theocracy to the church.[7]

In addition to the transformation of Israel's monoethnic story into the church's multiethnic story, Wright sees a transformation of the kingdom-story of power through violent force into the kingdom-story of power through suffering love, this latter being concentrated in Jesus' crucifixion. Thus Part Three of Wright's book is called "The Kingdom and the Cross," which is to say that God became king by means of Jesus' suffering crucifixion: "Jesus establishes the new kind of power—God's kingdom as opposed to Caesar's, on earth as in heaven—precisely *through* his (scripturally interpreted) death" (119, emphasis added). Again: "When this God finally claims the nations as his own possession, rescuing them from their evil ways, the *means* by which he does it is through the suffering of his people—or ... the suffering of his people's official, divinely appointed representative [Jesus the Messiah]" (183, emphasis added).[8]

---

6. Wright's phraseology in *How God Became King*, 65-67.

7. In a paper unpublished and titled "What Is God's Kingdom?" Daniel C. Fredericks canvasses massive evidence of God's kingship in the Old Testament. To defend his thesis of God's *becoming* king in the life, death, resurrection, and ascension of Jesus, Wright would almost surely counter with an emphasis on the newness of what happened through Jesus. But such an emphasis would exacerbate the break (at most) or the strain (at best) between Israel as a monoethnic, political entity in the Old Testament and the church as a multiethnic, questionably political entity in the New Testament.

8. Cf. N. T. Wright, "Whence and Whither Historical Jesus Studies in the Life of the Church?," in *Jesus, Paul and the People of God: A Theological Dialogue with N. T.*

In the Old Testament, however, God often exercised his kingship violently. Take, for example, his slaying of Egypt's firstborn (Exod 12:29), the divinely ordered slaughter of the Canaanites (Deut 31:3–6), David's divinely enabled killing of Goliath (1 Sam 18:37–49), and the many portrayals of God as a military king for the doing of battle in the most literal sense (Deut 32:34–43; Pss 20:6–9; 44:4–5; 47:2–3, and so on). With only a passing reference to Yahweh's drowning of Pharaoh's army in the Red Sea during the exodus and "cutting . . . down to size" rulers such as Nebuchadnezzar and Belshazzar, Wright skates lightly over this element in God's earlier kingship (153, 169)—and for good reason, because the radicality in a transformation of old, wrathful violence into new, loving nonviolence weakens further the thesis of a transference of Israelitish political theocracy to the church.

Certainly the Gospels juxtapose kingdom and cross. But is it true to say they interpret the cross as the means by which God became king? Wright recognizes that prior to the cross Jesus' preaching, teaching, exorcisms, and miracles of healing were already establishing the kingdom: "What Jesus did between the time of his birth and the time of his death. . . . his kingdom-inaugurating work; the deeds and words that declared that God's kingdom was coming then and there" (11; see esp. Matt 12:28; Luke 11:20; 17:21). Those words and deeds did not entail suffering. So the question remains, *Do the Gospels interpret Jesus' suffering of crucifixion as at least the main means by which God became king, by which his kingdom came on earth as in heaven?* Wright himself raises the question, "How can the suffering and death of Israel's Messiah somehow bring about his worldwide sovereign kingdom?" (176; cf. similar occurrences of "somehow" on 196, 237). But the question *whether* the suffering and death brought about the kingdom—that question takes precedence over Wright's question *how* it might have done so. To answer the question of whether, it is necessary to examine the Gospel texts—plus some other texts in Acts, the Epistles, and Revelation—on which Wright rests his case for kingdom *by means of* cross. For one could think of other possibilities: kingdom *in spite of* and/or *in compensation for* cross, for example. To the texts, then:

Wright appeals to "the key text of Mark 9:1 and parallels, so often read as an unfulfilled prediction of an imminent 'second coming' or even of the 'end of the world'" (223): "And he [Jesus] was saying to them,

---

Wright, ed. Nicholas Perrin and Richard B. Hays (Downers Grove: InterVarsity, 2011), 137–47.

'Amen I tell you that there are some standing here who will by no means taste death till they see God's kingdom as having come in power'" (cf. Matt 16:28; Luke 9:27). According to Wright, "these parallel verses, in the intention of all three evangelists, are best read as indicating a kingdom fulfillment that they, the authors of the Gospels in question, believe *had already come to pass* in the death and resurrection of Jesus" (224, emphasis original). In support of this reading, Wright notes the proximity of Jesus' first passion prediction in Mark 8:31; Matt 16:21; Luke 9:22. But a fair amount of material (Mark 8:32-38; Matt 16:22-27; Luke 9:23-26) intervenes between that prediction and the prediction that some will not taste death till they see the kingdom. By contrast, all three synoptic evangelists link the prediction of not tasting death—they link it immediately and chronologically to their accounts of Jesus' transfiguration: "and after six days" (Mark 9:2; Matt 17:1); "and about eight days after these words" (Luke 7:28). Luke's "after these words [of the prediction]" makes the linkage especially tight. So it looks much more likely that the evangelists understood Jesus' transfiguration to have fulfilled the prediction of not tasting death, an understanding Wright fails even to mention despite its being well-represented in literature on the New Testament.[9]

Moreover, fitting the prediction that "there are some standing here who will by no means taste death till they see (*idōsin*) God's kingdom as having come in power" (Mark 9:1) is a long list of expressions describing what happened at the transfiguration: (1) *kai metemorphōthē emprosthen autōn*, "and he [Jesus] was transfigured *in their presence* [that of Peter, James, and John]" (Mark 9:2; Matt 17:2); (2) *ha eidon* [cf. *idōsin* in the prediction], "the things that they had *seen*" (Mark 9:9); (3) *to horama*, "the *vision*" (Matt 17:9); (4) *to eidos* [cognate to *idōsin* in the prediction] *tou prosōpou autou*, "the *appearance* of his face" (Luke 9:29); (5) *eidon tēn doxan autou*, "they *saw* his glory" (Luke 9:32); and (6) *hōn heōrakan*, "the things that they had *seen*" (Luke 9:36).

Moreover again, "here" (*hōde* [Mark 9:5; Matt 17:4; Luke 9:33]) echoes the same word in Jesus' prediction (Mark 9:1; Matt 16:28); and "by themselves alone" (*kat' idian monous* [Mark 9:2; see also Matt 17:1 for *kat' idian*]) points up that the three disciples are the "*some* (*tines*) who will not taste death till they see . . ." Moreover yet again, since mountains symbolize power and dominion, as in Dan 2:35, 44-45 ("The stone that struck the statue became a great mountain and filled the whole earth. . . .

---

9. See esp. Martin Künzi, *Das Naherwartungslogion Markus 9,1 par.: Geschichte seiner Auslegung*, BGBE 21 (Tübingen: Mohr Siebeck, 1977).

The God of heaven will set up a kingdom that will never be destroyed"),[10] the "high mountain" on which Peter, James, and John see Jesus transfigured symbolizes the *power* of God's kingdom (cf. also the association of "glory" and "power" in Mark 13:27; 2 Pet 1:16-18 as well as in Mark 8:38—9:1; Luke 9:31) just as the transfiguration itself shows these three disciples that in Jesus the kingdom of God has *come*.[11] The adjective "high" adds to the connotation of a powerful coming; the three disciples' terror (Mark 9:6) confirms its power; and Peter's saying, "It's good we are here," naturally reflects on the fulfillment of Jesus' prediction.

It is objected that the transfiguration's occurrence only six days later ill suits Jesus' prediction, because hardly anybody in his audience would have run the risk of dying during the interim. But this objection presumes without evidence that Jesus knew, or that the Synoptists wanted their audiences to think he knew, he would be transfigured six days later. There is no evidence that he went up a mountain to be transfigured. According to Luke 9:28, on the contrary, he went up to pray. Jesus' subsequently taking the same three disciples—Peter, James, and John—farther into Gethsemane to pray suggests retrospectively that also in the other two Synoptics Jesus went up to pray (Mark 14:32-40; Matt 26:36-44). Furthermore, just as Jesus said "this generation" would not pass away till "all these things happen" (Mark 13:30; Matt 24:34; Luke 21:32) but did not know "that day or hour" (Mark 13:32; Matt 24:36), so too he could say that some would not die till they had seen that God's kingdom had come with power but not know exactly how soon they would do so.

---

10. See also Matt 28:16-18; Rev 17:9-10; W. Foerster, "ὄρος," *TDNT* 5:475-78, 480-81, 486-87.

11. For a transfigurational preview of Jesus' second coming in Matthew and Luke, see Robert H. Gundry, *Commentary on the New Testament* (Grand Rapids: Baker, 2010), 74, 269-70; Gundry, *Mark: A Commentary on His Apology for the Cross* (Grand Rapids: Eerdmans, 1993), 466-70. Wright interprets the Son of Man's "coming in his kingdom" (Matt 16:28) and "in clouds with much power and glory" (Mark 13:26; cf. Dan 7:13) as a reference to Jesus' ascension rather than to the second coming (223-24). This interpretation does not necessitate Jesus' suffering as the means of God's becoming king (the point presently at issue), however, and itself suffers a number of weaknesses, among them the wide visibility of Jesus' "coming" and the failure of the abomination of desolation to have taken place before the ascension in accordance with Mark 13:14-27; Matt 24:15-31; Luke 21:20-28. See further Robert H. Gundry, *The Use of the Old Testament in St. Matthew's Gospel with Special Reference to the Messianic Hope*, NovTSup 18 (Leiden: Brill, 1967), 232-33; Gundry, *Matthew: A Commentary on His Handbook for a Mixed Church under Persecution*, 2nd ed. (Grand Rapids: Eerdmans, 1994), 545-46; Gundry, *Mark*, 784.

It is also argued that the Synoptists, and especially Mark, portray Jesus' crucifixion as a Roman triumphal procession, so that God's kingdom comes in the crucifixion rather than at the transfiguration.[12] But the leading theme of mockery in the soldiers' robing Jesus in purple, crowning him with thorns, hailing him as "king of the Jews," striking his head with a reed, spitting on him, and doing him obeisance—this theme of mockery that runs throughout the narrative undermines the notion of an intentional portrayal of the kingdom's coming by way of Jesus' crucifixion.

Wright turns then to Mark 10:35-45, where in connection with giving his life as a ransom for many, "Mark's Jesus explains that the rulers of the nations use ordinary power, but that he will use servant power instead," and where "the kings of the earth exercise power one way, by lording it over their subjects, but Jesus' followers are going to do it the other way, the way of the servant," which as in the case of Jesus entails suffering (206 and 118-19, respectively; cf. Matt 20:24-28). But here Jesus says nothing either about the coming of God's kingdom or about servant *power*. Instead, serving stands *opposite* the exercise of power. So the passage fails to support a powerful coming of God's kingdom by means of servitorial suffering. It could just as well be that such suffering by Jesus and his disciples was, and is, due to the erstwhile failure of that kingdom to have come fully.

Also Col 2:15 comes into play as an argument for Wright's thesis of triumphant kingly power through the suffering of crucifixion: "He [Christ] stripped the rulers and authorities of their armor, and displayed them contemptuously to public view, celebrating his triumph over them in him" (205, translation by Wright). Strikingly, though, the preceding verse does not have Christ nailed to a cross. Instead, it has him nailing the hostile-to-us "certificate of debt" to the cross. Here, in other words, he is the crucifier, not the crucified. And far from displaying the power of his kingship, *his* crucifixion displayed his weakness: "For he was also crucified because of weakness" (2 Cor 13:4a). By contrast, both his power and that of God are associated with Jesus' resurrection: "yet he lives because of God's power" (2 Cor 13:4b); "that I may know . . . the power of his resurrection" (Phil 3:10; see also Rom 1:4; 1 Cor 6:14). So

---

12. Among others, see Thomas E. Schmidt, "Mark 15.16-32: The Crucifixion Narrative and the Roman Triumphal Procession," *NTS* 41 (1995) 1-18; Michael F. Bird, "The Crucifixion of Jesus as the Fulfillment of Mark 9:1," *TJ* 24 (2003) 23-36.

it is in *Paul's* weakness, not Christ's, that the power of Christ is perfected (2 Cor 12:9).[13]

Given his theocratically political thesis, Wright naturally has to deal with Jesus' saying, "Pay Caesar's things back to Caesar, and God's things back to God" (Mark 12:17; Matt 22:21; Luke 20:25). For nowadays this saying is commonly understood in terms of a separation between church and state, or in terms of a Lutheran distinction between two kingdoms, one of human government and the other of divine government. Wright is undeterred, however (see 147–51, 161). He blames the Enlightenment's secularism for that understanding. (I leave it to historians of church and state to argue whether Martin Luther's doctrine of two kingdoms and Tatian's, Origen's, Augustine's, and Constantine's above-cited similar doctrines, all of which antedated the Enlightenment, corresponded to contemporary understanding.) Wright avers that Jesus' "double command has nothing to do ['in context'] with a church–state split and everything to do with the fact that God trumps Caesar" (149). Oh? Just how does Jesus' telling people to pay back to God the things that belong to God "trump" Jesus' telling people equally to pay back to Caesar the things that belong to Caesar?

Astonishingly, Wright appeals to the use of "pay back" (*apodote* in the Synoptics) also in 1 Macc 2:68: "Pay back (*antapodote*) the Gentiles in full (*antapodoma*)." But there old Mattathias is telling his sons to wreak military vengeance on their and their fellows' persecutors: "and avenge the wrong done to your people" (1 Macc 2:67 NRSV; *kai ekdikēsate ekdikēsin tou laou hymōn*). Hardly the meaning Wright wants! For Jesus would then be teaching the very violence that Wright denies has any part in the establishment of God's kingdom. But by playing "a trick," yet "not *just* a trick" (emphasis added), says Wright, "Jesus is refusing to collude either with the pro-Roman party in Jerusalem or with the would-be violent revolutionaries." Apparently, then, Wright accepts the connotation of violence in a payback to Caesar—as implied by Wright's saying that Mattathias "wasn't telling them [his sons] to pay the Gentile taxes"—and thinks that such a payback keeps him (Jesus) from colluding with the pro-Roman party in Jerusalem while at the same time his advocacy of paying God's things back to God keeps him from colluding with the would-be violent revolutionaries.

---

13. N.B.: It is the preached message of the cross, not the cross itself, that according to 1 Cor 1:18 is God's power for those who are being saved.

With no appreciation of this nearly Buddhist-like "koan" (as Wright imagines it to be), however, those revolutionaries and the pro-Roman party would have taken straightforwardly—rather than paradoxically or ironically—Jesus' advocating a violent payback to Caesar; and "Caesar's things," which has no parallel in 1 Macc 2:67, would have ceased to bear any relation to the coin that Jesus asked to see. That is to say, if in "echoing" (Wright's term) Mattathias's statement Jesus was saying to pay back Caesar with violence rather than with coins, he had no reason to ask to see a coin, to inquire whose it was, or to refer to "Caesar's things" in connection with the coin. For under Wright's interpretation the coin becomes extraneous to Jesus' "one-liner." This point holds even if Jesus was speaking ironically and paradoxically; and even if he was speaking thus, the pro-Roman party would have used his seeming advocacy of a violent payback to charge him with insurrectionism. On the other hand, the revolutionaries would have used the seeming advocacy as a battle cry. Jesus would surely have anticipated these unintended reactions and therefore not have spoken in a koan-like vein. Nor did the revolutionaries and pro-Roman party react in such ways. Instead, they were dumbfounded (Mark 12:17; Matt 22:22; Luke 20:26).

As to paying God's things back to God, Wright adds, "Perhaps it's time for God—whose image is on every human being and whose inscription is written across the pages of creation and the story of Israel—to receive his due" (150). Here we have a homiletical flight on Wright's part, but in Jesus' statement there is nothing at all about the image of God on every human being or about his inscription on creation and Israel's story. And if it is time for God to receive his due, as Wright understands Jesus' saying, it is also time for Caesar to receive *his* due—in coin (cf. Rom 13:7; 1 Pet 2:13–16). Jesus does appear, then, to have taught a doctrine of two kingdoms (cf. Caesar's violent but God-ordained power of "the sword," to be exercised for "the good" of human beings [Rom 13:4]).

Finally on "Render unto Caesar" Wright says that "there may be a time for confrontation [with Caesar]; there may be a time for appropriate collaboration. But all is to be done within the bounds of God's kingdom" (150). Well and good; but in this statement we seem to have a capitulation to the doctrine of two kingdoms, God's and Caesar's, so that Christians have to negotiate their way through both.

Against "a clear division between God and Caesar, a split of church and state" so far as Luke-Acts is concerned, Wright appeals further to Acts 28:31, where "we find Paul in Rome, announcing God as king and

Jesus as Lord right under Caesar's nose 'with all boldness and with no one stopping him'" (134, 136-37). But in view of the Roman governor Pilate's multiple declarations of Jesus' innocence according to Luke 23:4, 14-15, 22, Peter's and others' blaming "Israelites" for the crucifixion of Jesus (Acts 2:23; 3:13-15; 4:10-11, 27-28; 5:30; 7:52; 10:39; 13:27-29), and the many favorable portrayals of the centurion Cornelius (Acts 10:1—11:18; cf. 27:43) and Roman officials (Acts 13:7, 12; 18:12-17; 19:31; 21:31-40; 22:28-30; 23:10, 16-35; 24:10; 24: 22-25:27; 28:16, 18), Luke's phraseology in Acts 28:31 could just as well favor that God's and Caesar's kingdoms do not always or necessarily conflict with each other.

To push further his thesis that God became king nonviolently by means of Jesus' suffering, Wright says that "Jesus . . . is the 'green' tree [in Luke 23:28-31], the tree that is not ready for burning. He is innocent. But all around him . . . are the young firebrands who will be only too ready for the fire when the time comes" (234). But the green tree does not refer to Jesus himself. It refers instead to the time of his crucifixion. Similarly, the dry tree does not refer to revolutionary firebrands themselves. It refers instead to the coming time of their revolution, Jerusalem's siege, and destruction. To avoid these contextually determined understandings, Wright translates the two occurrences of *en* in v. 31 as meaning "with" ("Yes, if this is what they do *with* the green tree") and "to" ("what will happen *to* the dry one?" [emphasis added]), respectively, whereas *en* is much more naturally taken as temporal, as in the NRSV and other translations ("*when* the wood is green . . . *when* it is dry"). And the pericope includes not a word about the arrival of God's kingdom or of God's becoming king by means of Jesus' crucifixion.

"For Mark, it is clear that the two brigands on Jesus' right and left [at the crucifixion], as described in 15:27, are the ones to whom 'it's been assigned already' [according to Mark 10:40, where Jesus is quoted as saying, 'But to sit on my right or left (in Jesus' "glory" [10:37]) is not mine to give; rather, (it will be given) to those for whom it has been prepared']." So says Wright, who then adds, "But that means . . . that Jesus' crucifixion is the moment when he becomes king. . . . That is the powerful—if deeply paradoxical!—'coming of the kingdom' as spoken of in Mark 9:1" (227). This interpretation of Mark 9:1 has been dealt with above. As to the interpretation of Mark 15:27, the brigands are not disciples of Jesus; and the brigands' jeering at him contrasts sharply with his disciples' later self-sacrificial proclamation of him as the world's Savior.[14] So we are still waiting to see who have been assigned seats on his right and left in the kingdom.

To support kingship by crucifixion, Wright appeals further to Jesus' statement that "this is what *had* to happen: the Messiah had to suffer, and then come into his glory!" (Luke 24:26 [Wright's translation; emphasis original]; 183–84, 217). But sequence, which Wright emphasizes by inserting "then" without support in the Greek text, is accommodated by kingdom-in-spite-of and/or kingdom-in-compensation-for cross just as well as by kingdom-through-the-means-of a cross.

In regard to Jesus' suffering, Mark minimizes it by noting both that someone else (Simon of Cyrene) carried a cross on behalf of Jesus (Mark 15:21) and that Jesus hung on the cross only six hours before dying (15:25, 33–37), a brevity of time that surprised Pilate (15:44–45). Matthew glosses over Jesus' suffering by using and heightening (in comparison with the other Gospels) Old Testament language to portray it as a fulfillment of ancient prophecy,[15] and in the process he demotes Jesus' crucifixion to a mere participial phrase: *staurōsantes auton*, "having crucified him" (Matt 27:35; contrast the finite verbs in Mark 15:24; Luke 23:33; John 19:18). For his part, Luke diverts attention from Jesus' suffering to Jesus' innocence, indeed righteousness, and does so even more than the other evangelists do (see esp. Luke 23:4, 14–15, 22, 41, 47). No note is taken of physical agony because of violence inflicted on Jesus. In other words, the Synoptists do not emphasize his suffering as such, much less as the means by which God became king.

This lack of emphasis on Jesus' suffering brings us to John's Gospel, where Wright thinks he may have his strongest case: "What, then, about John? There is a whole book to be written on the implicit and sometimes explicit undermining of Caesar's empire in John's Gospel" (140), and "John 18–19 offers an explosion of dense and detailed kingdom theology" (220). But already in John 13:1 Wright sees Jesus' death as "assisting in the enthronement of the one whose bringing of justice to the nations flowed out of his sovereign, healing love" (219; cf. 230). In that passage, however, Jesus' love is mentioned only in regard to the disciples ("his

---

14. See pp. 198–99, 203, 223, 227, 241 for Wright's associating the later suffering of Jesus' disciples with that of Jesus himself for the bringing of the kingdom.

15. See Matt 26:52 (Isa 50:11), 67 (Isa 50:6), 15 and 27:5, 6, 9 (Zech 11:13); 27:24 (Deut 21:6, 9), 34 (Ps 69:21), 35 (Ps 22:18), 39 (Lam 2:15; Ps 22:7), 43 (Ps 22:8), 46 (Ps 22:1), 48 (Ps 69:21), 57 (Isa 53:9), and Gundry, *Use of the Old Testament*, 61–66, 143–46.

Kingdom and Power, Love and Violence

own"); and the passage says nothing at all about the bringing of justice to the nations through Jesus' imminent death. Regrettably, Wright overlooks that in John's Gospel Jesus is not said to have loved the world. Only God is said to have done so (John 3:16). And just as according to 1 John 2:15-17 believers in Jesus are *not* to love the world (i.e., worldlings as opposed to "those who do the will of God"), so in John 17:9 Jesus makes a point of his not even praying for the world. So much for Wright's rejection of Johannine sectarianism and other Christian movements of withdrawal (as, for example, on 165-66, 242)![16]

Wright finds firmer ground in John 18:33-38a. There, indeed, "God's kingdom [represented as that of Jesus] . . . makes its way (as Jesus insists) by nonviolence rather than by violence" (230): "Jesus answered, 'My kingdom is not from this world. If my kingdom were from this world, my officers would have been fighting lest I be given over to the Jews [cf. Jesus' stopping Peter's brief swordplay in vv. 10-11]. But now my kingdom is not from here'" (v. 36). It is also true that in John the crucifixion of Jesus is portrayed as his glorification, his elevation, the first step in his exaltation (John 3:14; 6:62; 7:39; 8:28; 12:23, 28, 32-34; 13:31-32; 17:1, 5) as opposed to two earlier attempts to knock him down by stoning him (8:58-59; 10:30-31, 39; 11:8; 18:31-32). But according to the Fourth Gospel, does his royal exaltation through being lifted up on a cross entail suffering—in particular, suffering as the nonviolent *means* of exaltation to kingship? Hardly, for John downplays Jesus' suffering.

To be sure, the scourging and slapping of Jesus stay, also his being crowned with thorns and clothed with purple (John 19:1-3), but not to call attention to his suffering. For "therefore" (v. 1) indicates that the Jewish authorities' shouting for the release of Barabbas rather than Jesus provoked Pilate to have Jesus scourged as a form of physical mockery added to Pilate's verbal mockery of the Jewish authorities by calling Jesus their king (18:39). Pilate uses Jesus to mock the Jewish authorities. Similarly, the soldiers join Pilate's mockery of those authorities by coronating, robing, and acclaiming

---

16. See further Robert H. Gundry, *Jesus the Word according to John the Sectarian* (Grand Rapids: Eerdmans, 2002), 51-70; and for a critique of Miroslav Volf's attempt to soften John's sectarianism ("Johannine Dualism and Contemporary Pluralism," in *The Gospel of John and Christian Theology*, ed. Richard Bauckham and Carl Mosser [Grand Rapids: Eerdmans, 2008], 19-50, esp. 39-48), see Robert H. Gundry, *The Old Is Better*, WUNT 178 (Eugene, OR: Wipf & Stock, 2010), 315-23.

him as "king of the Jews" (19:2–3). John's point does not lie in Jesus' suffering—rather, in the shaming of the Jewish authorities.[17]

On the other hand, gone from John are the spitting on Jesus, his being blindfolded, fisticuffed, taunted to prophesy, beaten on the head with a reed (see Mark 14:65; 15:15, 19 and synoptic parallels). Gone too is his Cry of Dereliction, "My God, my God, why have you forsaken me?" (Mark 15:34; Matt 27:46). Instead, Jesus calmly takes care of his personal affairs ("Woman, behold your son," he says to his mother concerning the beloved disciple, and vice versa to him [John 19:25–27]), just as he calmly prayed for his disciples in chapter 17 rather than throwing himself on the ground in a sweat of emotional turmoil and praying about his own fate. He did not pray repeatedly for a removal of "this cup" from him (Mark 14:36–42; Matt 26:36–46; Luke 22:39–46). Instead, he asked, "The cup that the Father has given me—by all means should I not drink it?" (John 18:11); and earlier he had firmly refused to ask his Father for deliverance "from this hour" and declared to the contrary that he had come precisely for "this hour" (12:27).

According to John, Jesus even carried his cross "by himself" (19:17)—no help from Simon of Cyrene being needed or requested (contrast Mark 15:21 and synoptic parallels)—and, for the fulfillment of Scripture, said "I thirst" and thereby got the soldiers (19:23–25a)—or was it the just-mentioned beloved disciple and women (John 19:25b–27)?—to serve him vinegary wine for the slaking of his thirst (19:28–30a). Then he victoriously declared, "They [his 'works,' 'signs,' and 'words'] are finished!" (19:30b),[18] bowed his head, and with all deliberation started giving over the Spirit (*paredōken to pneuma* [19:30]) because he had started being glorified in his elevation on a cross. (See 7:39 for his glorification as a condition of the Spirit's being given over, and 20:17, 22 for the completions of Jesus' glorification and giving over of the Spirit.) Jesus had not been seized in the garden but had presented himself voluntarily, with the effect that his would-be arresters recoiled and fell to the ground. And after presenting himself a second time he allowed them to "take [him] along" only on the condition that his disciples be let go (18:1–9, 12). Even the scurrilous accusations against Jesus disappear from John. Replacing

---

17. See Gundry, *Commentary on the New Testament*, 449.

18. For this translation instead of "It is finished!" see Robert H. Gundry, "New Wine in Old Wineskins: Bursting Traditional Interpretations in John's Gospel (Part Two)," *BBR* 17 (2007) 292–96.

them are the true statements that Jesus made himself out to be the Son of God and a king (18:33–39; 19:3, 7, 12–15, 19–22).

So Jesus' kingship is not predicated on suffering. Not in the Fourth Gospel. For John does his best to eliminate the element of suffering inflicted by outside force. That is to say, though Jesus' nonviolent kingship contrasts with Caesar's violent kingship, the thesis of kingship by means of servitorial suffering fails to receive support. Not a victim, Jesus imperiously took charge, as we would expect the Word who was God (John 1:1) to do and as he himself said he would do by laying down his life of his own accord rather than because of anyone's taking it away from him violently (10:18).[19]

Beyond the story of Jesus' death, resurrection, and ascension is a further story to be told. It is that his second coming and the last judgment feature a lot of violence on his and God's part. Vivid portrayals of this violence appear in 2 Thess 1:6–9; Rev 19:11–21; 20:11–15, and sayings of Jesus himself do not lag behind in this respect. (Among many such sayings, see Mark 9:42–43, 45, 47–48; Matt 5:22, 29–30; 13:40–42, 49–50; 18:6–9, 34–35; 22:13; Luke 12:45–48.) Wright's emphasis on nonviolence leads him to soft-pedal this element in the New Testament theology of God's kingdom: "The 'last judgment' will be the moment when the powers of the world are overthrown by the power of God, the power that was displayed fully in the crucifixion of the Lamb," that is, "the violent death of the Lamb," which "has won the decisive victory" (270 and 204, respectively). By Wright's lights, that power was the power of suffering love; and if according to him it was displayed "fully" at the cross, what room is left for Jesus' coming again in flaming fire to wreak vengeance on those who do not know God and do not obey the gospel and to cast them into hell?

Surely the violence of divine judgment needs to be incorporated into a comprehensive New Testament theology of God's kingdom. Yet Wright writes, "The establishment of God's kingdom means the dethroning of the world's kingdoms, not in order to replace them with another one of basically the same sort (one that makes its way through superior force of arms), but in order to replace it with one whose power is the power of the servant and whose strength is the strength of love" (205). Yes indeed, so far as present-day evangelism is concerned. But the story of God's

---

19. Unfortunately, the particulars of John's suppression of Jesus' suffering do not figure in Tord Larsson's essay "Glory or Persecution: The God of the Gospel of John in the History of Interpretation," in *The Gospel of John and Christian Theology*, ed. Richard Bauckham and Carl Mosser (Grand Rapids: Eerdmans, 2008), 82–88.

kingdom does not end with the present power of love. For the ungodly, according to the New Testament, that story will end with their being "slice[d] in two" (Luke 12:46) and "cast into a furnace of [unquenchable] fire" where there is "weeping and gnashing of teeth" (Matt 13:42; 22:13). That is to say, the story will end with the power of divine violence, with the superior force of heavenly armies of powerful angels when the returning Lamb "makes war" by "stomping the winepress of the wine of the rage of the wrath of God Almighty" (Rev 19:11–16, excerpts). Moreover, the saints will take pleasure in this violence; for it will avenge their suffering for the gospel's sake (Rev 19:1–8; cf. 2 Thess 1:6–9). Nor does the violence in Jesus' cleansing of the temple already during his first coming comport very well with kingdom-through-peace (Mark 11:15–17; Matt 21:12–13; Luke 19:45–46; John 2:13–17; cf. Jesus' saying he did not come to bring peace on the earth; rather, a sword [Matt 10:34–36; Luke 12:49–53]).

Wright, however, seems to think that because of successful evangelism, divinely judgmental violence will not occur: "when the people of God are renewed . . . [they] will take over the world not with the love of power but with the power of love" (239). Again, "[the Gospels] are the central means by which those who read and pray them can help make that kingdom [of God] a reality in tomorrow's world" (176). These statements look very like postmillennialists' expectation of a coming Christian conversion and utopian transformation of the whole of human society, an expectation popular in the nineteenth century but moribund ever since for lack of good exegetical support. Whether we like it or not, whether we take it literally or figuratively, New Testament language of final judgment bespeaks violence—violence of an extreme sort, in fact.[20]

The cross, then, is not the means by which God became king. It is, simply, the reason why God transformed his kingdom into one that is now church-centered instead of Israel-centered, as it had been before the Jews rejected Jesus by and large and as it will yet be when the redeemer has come out of Zion, all Israel has been saved, and the twelve apostles have sat on twelve thrones to judge the twelve tribes of Israel (Matt 19:28; Luke 22:30; Rom 11:25–27; cf. Acts 1:6–7; 3:19–21). Hence the Great

20. I take it for granted that Wright wants to stick true to the New Testament text regardless of both moral and higher critical questions (cf. his comments on pages xii–xv). In this respect, if I am correct, he differs from Miroslav Volf, who refers (approvingly, it seems) to "Gilles Deleuze's unmasking of the violence of John of Patmos" ("Johannine Dualism and Contemporary Pluralism," 20). Consistency would demand a like unmasking of the violence of Jesus of Nazareth, if not a refusal to accept his violent sayings as authentic.

Commission, according to which Jesus' followers are to go in the meantime *from* Jerusalem throughout the world discipling all the nations, in contrast with those nations' coming *to* Jerusalem to worship the Lord according to what Wright calls "Israel's story" in the Old Testament.[21] Acts 28:23–38, a passage highlighted by Wright in an effort to make another point, puts the matter plainly:

> And after setting a day to meet with him [Paul], more of them [the Jews in Rome] than before came to him at his lodging, to whom by way of solemnly testifying and trying to persuade them concerning Jesus from both the law of Moses and the prophets from morning till evening *he was expounding God's kingdom*. And some were being persuaded by the things being said [by Paul], but others were disbelieving. And being in disagreement with one another, they started leaving after Paul had said one word [i.e., had issued a final statement]: "Beautifully [to be taken as sarcasm] did the Holy Spirit speak through Isaiah the prophet to your [fore]fathers, saying, 'Go to this people and say, "By hearing you will hear and never understand [what you hear], and though seeing you will see and never perceive [what you see]." For the heart of this people has become impenetrable, and with [their] ears they have heard ponderously [i.e., they have heard hardly at all], and they have closed their eyes lest they perceive with their eyes and hear with their ears and understand with their heart and convert and I heal them [Isa 6:9–10]." *Therefore* be it known to you that this salvation from God *has been sent to the Gentiles*. They too will hear (see also Acts 1:3–8; 13:44–47; 18:6; 22:17–21; 23:11 and, of course, Rom 9–11).[22]

In summary, then, God's kingdom continued *despite* the cross; God's kingdom underwent revision *because of* the cross; and this revision consisted in the internationalizing of God's people and the delay of his

---

21. For the nations' streaming to Jerusalem to worship the Lord, see Isa 2:1–5; 60:1–22; Micah 4:1–2; Zech 8:20–23. "The rejection of Jesus' message by national Israel meant the end of the possibility of a centripetal attraction by the nations. The inversion of eschatological hope meant the inversion of the direction of mission" (Michael Bird, "Mission as an Apocalyptic Event: Reflections on Luke 10:18 and Mark 13:10," *EvQ* 76 [2004] 133).

22. For more along this line, see Barry Smith, *Jesus' Twofold Teaching about the Kingdom of God*, New Testament Monographs 24 (Sheffield: Sheffield Phoenix, 2009); and cf. in this respect the offer of God's kingdom to Israel, its rejection, and the consequent churchward turn according to the dispensational school of thought, discussed measuredly by David L. Turner, "Matthew among the Dispensationalists," *JETS* 53 (2010) 697–716.

political rule over the world till the second coming of Christ in resurrected, judgmental power.

"You Can*not* Be Serious!"

THE EXISTENTIAL JESUS,[1] AUTHORED by John Carroll, feeds mainly on the Gospel of Mark, chews especially hard on Jesus' statement, "I am," when he's walking on the water, and treats John's Gospel as a side dish. The menu features some surprises:

Did you know, for example, that Mark opens his Gospel with the words, "In the beginning was the Story"? (Never mind that it is *John's* Gospel which opens with those words—that is, if you allow "Story" to be a legitimate translation of *logos*.)

Did you know that since Mark's Story, which supposedly was in the beginning, has to do with the purely human Jesus rather than with God and that therefore the Hebrew Bible's account of creation by God has to be scrapped because "Jesus replaces God"? (Never mind that Jesus—yes, *Mark's* Jesus—says, "But from the beginning of creation, God made them male and female," and attributes knowledge of the day and hour of his return exclusively to God the Father, so that not even Jesus himself knows.)

Did you know that Mark's Jesus wasn't interested in morals? (Never mind that he said fornications, thefts, murders, adulteries, covetings, deceit, and sensuality, among other things, defile a human being.)

Did you know that up on a mountain after feeding the five thousand Jesus met himself, not God? (Never mind that he went up the mountain "to pray," presumably to God.)

Did you know that the Markan Jesus' mission ended with a focus on himself alone? (Never mind his saying on the eve of crucifixion, "This is my blood of the covenant which is being shed on behalf of *many*.")

---

1. Berkeley: Counterpoint, 2007.

Did you know that in Gethsemane Mark's Jesus did not pray to God above—for no longer did he *trust* his god—but groaningly uttered a curse in anticipation of his nonexistence? (Never mind "Abba! Father! . . . not what I will; rather, what you [will].")

Did you know that according to Mark's Gospel Jesus never claimed to be the Christ? (Never mind his answer, "I am," when asked, "Are you the Christ, the Son of the Blessed One?")

Did you know that in this Gospel Jesus' using "the son of man" as a self-designation meant he was no more than an ordinary human being? (Never mind that he told his judges they would see him as the son of man "sitting at the right hand of the Power [God] and coming with the clouds of heaven [the Deity's mode of transport]" and told his disciples he will come as the son of man "with great power and glory," "send out angels," and "gather together his chosen ones" from everywhere.)

Did you know that in Mark's Gospel Jesus' cry of dereliction was not a direct and personal call "to some power up above"—for Jesus had finally come to disbelieve there *is* a god—but was "a cry against existence"? (Never mind "*My* God, *my* God . . .")

Did you know that the Gospel of Mark closes with "no resurrection from the dead" on Jesus' part? (Never mind that the women at the empty tomb were told, "He has risen.")

Well, now you know, thanks to John Carroll. According to him this Jesus, existentially baked and basted by the evangelist Mark, is supposed to appeal to the palates of contemporary non-churchgoers and thereby recapture Jesus' importance for Western culture, an importance frittered away by the increasingly irrelevant church in her maintenance of tired old Christian doctrines, the denial of which "Mark's existential Jesus would approve." One might think to the contrary that churches have lost their relevance, where they *have* lost it, because of jettisoning those doctrines. But Mark's purportedly existential Jesus is the Jesus that Carroll owns for himself, a Jesus who is "solitary," "individual-centered," and "antitribal," a noncommunitarian example of "free[dom] . . . from the yoke of human collectivity." Ironically, Carroll is a sociologist at La Trobe University in Australia. His very profession deals with the human collectivity he decries.

Drawing on a knowledge of classical Greek (as evident, incidentally, in his spelling a Greek verb for "I know" *gignōskō* instead of *ginōskō*, its spelling in the New Testament), Carroll provides his own translations of much of Mark—and also of John, which he considers a profoundly perceptive reworking of Mark. Interspersed with the translations are Carroll's interpretations. He doesn't concern himself with the historical Jesus, about whom he thinks "we ['of course'] know virtually nothing." He concerns himself rather with Mark's and John's mythic Jesuses—that is, their timeless, archetypal stories about Jesus—and repeatedly draws comparisons with Greek myths (Homer's *The Iliad*, for example). Somewhat oddly, he interlaces Greek mythology with the Jewish midrashic technique of reconfiguring a text, especially a narrative, to make it currently relevant. Yet other literature, such as Shakespeare's *Hamlet* and Melville's *Billy Budd*, and famous paintings also come in for comparison. Though uncited by name, the movie *Dead Man Walking* and Albert Schweitzer's portrayal of Jesus as a mysterious stranger seem to hover in the background.

Oh how Carroll himself reconfigures Mark's and John's stories to make them what is currently tasteworthy in his opinion! But he presents his reconfigurations as midrashes on Mark's and John's midrashes, and as midrashes that carry forward the intentions of Mark and John in their own midrashes. To take but one example, the reconfiguring of the centurion's exclamation at the foot of the cross, "Truly this man was the Son of God," to read, "Truly this man was the *mystery*," counts as Carroll's midrash on Mark's midrash. But Carroll presents this and other such reconfigurations of his as true to Mark's intention, to Mark's portrayal of an existential Jesus.

Carroll also offers some interesting though curious readings. For instance, on the Mount of Transfiguration Peter "misreads" divinity in the cloud "profanely" as "looming rain" and therefore wants to build shelters from the rain; and this misreading anticipates the misdirection of his future into "building churches," which as ethical institutions, "symbolized by the black cloud of dirty, drenching water from above," serve no good end. For "the divinity in the black cloud is a dying god." It might occur to someone that a cloud doesn't drop dirty water. Or maybe Carroll has in mind acid rain. In any case, he has no use for churches or for the dying god of the Jews, whom he derisively calls their "external God," or for their history and culture, which he declares "obsolete." Regardless of intention, the anti-Semitic undertone is disturbing.

At times Carroll's imagination takes off, as when he says that in Gethsemane Jesus lapsed into unconsciousness, describes Golgotha as a "rocky waste where nothing grows," and equates Legion, the unclean spirits exorcised by Jesus, with the young man inside Jesus' tomb. After all, Legion had dwelt among tombs and displayed prodigious strength such as would be required for the young man to roll away the stone (if he did). The power that went out of Jesus when the woman with a flow of blood touched his robe—this power lodged in Legion and reappeared as the young man in the tomb and as Mark, the young man who fled naked from Gethsemane and later wrote the Gospel that we call his.

As for John's Gospel, Carroll springs a surprise, given his unorthodoxy, by ascribing that Gospel to John the beloved disciple and son of Zebedee. But there is no surprise in Carroll's subscribing to the distinction between *agapē* as sacred love and *philia* as friendly or brotherly love, for this distinction has attained wide popularity. How sacred, though, is the *agapē*-loving of darkness rather than light (John 3:19) and the *agapē*-loving of men's approval rather than God's (John 12:43)? For that matter, how *un*sacredly friendly and brotherly is the Father's *philia*-loving of the Son (John 5:20) and the Father's *philia*-loving of believers in his Son (John 16:27)? Since in John's account of the Last Supper only Judas Iscariot is given a morsel of bread, Carroll says "the story mocks the idea of a sacred community." What then does he do with Jesus' proceeding to tell the disciples to love one another as he has loved them? Carroll does nothing with it, because a community of reciprocal love mocks his notion of existential isolation.

According to him, the import of the Johannine Jesus' telling Magdalene not to touch him is that "it's time for [her] to find [her] own way, on [her] own," that "she must summon up from within herself an *I* that suffices unto itself" (emphasis original). So does this same Jesus' saying that he himself is "the way" and that "no one comes to the Father except through [him]" (John 14:6) not apply to her? Space won't allow further consideration of Carroll's interpretation of the women who figure prominently in the Gospels, though it does bear mention that since Legion is many, he affirms that Magdalene too—like the young man in Jesus' tomb—"is Legion sitting calmly clothed" (as though the legion of unclean spirits hadn't left their host, entered a herd of swine, and accompanied them into the Sea of Galilee by the time their former host was sitting calm and clothed).

For Carroll the existential truth that I am means this: the I that I am doesn't have to undergo any change, not even by way of moral reform. It suffices to know that I am, for this is all that's to be known. Consequently, Carroll dislikes all those who assert, "I am *x*," rather than a simple, "I *am*." For as noted, the latter affirms the only truth you can be sure of, your own individual existence, whereas the former affirms an illusory identity. No wonder then that despite liking John's midrash of Mark, as when Carroll happily cites the Johannine Jesus' saying, "Before Abraham came into being, I am," he skirts that same Jesus' saying, "I am the bread of life," "I am the bread that came down from heaven," "I am the light of the world," "I am the resurrection and the life," "I am the way and the truth and the life" (and so on). And since atheistic existentialism like Carroll's normally pits individual existence against objective essence, you wonder whether he isn't confused when calling his existential Jesus "*essential* humanity" and "the quint*essence* of humanity, in its Platonic form or ideal" (emphasis added).

To Carroll: You've cherry-picked elements of Mark's Gospel for your portrayal of an existential Jesus. But by flying in the face of many obviously contrary elements in this Gospel and shielding your readers from them, you have passed off your existential Jesus as Mark's too. So the best I can do in defense of your scholarly integrity is to borrow from tennis star John McEnroe a statement he directed incredulously to 1981 Wimbledon umpire Edward James: "You can*not* be serious!"

Bible and Tradition

On *The Mind Behind the Gospels: A Commentary on Matthew 1–14*[1]

FOR AUTHOR HERBERT BASSER the mind behind the Gospels doesn't consist either in the mind of Matthew (despite a suggestion in the subtitle) or of the other evangelists—or particularly even of Jesus, about whom they wrote. It consists, instead, of the "collective 'mind' shared by Jewish teachers from the first century (if not earlier) until the present: a mind of which early Jewish-(Christian) raconteurs [who 'spread stories of Jesus . . . before the earliest written Gospels were composed'] were still a part." This mind deals in Jewish rhetoric—having to do with interpretive methods more than with content—such as is found in rabbinic tradition dating at least from Jesus' time up through the fifteenth century.

Basser's stress falls therefore on continuity so as to blunt the criticism that he freely uses rabbinic sources too late to be of service for the interpretation of Matthew. It then becomes a question whether the generally late rabbinic rhetoric really does correspond more closely to the pre-Matthean rhetoric embedded in the first Gospel than does the rhetoric appearing elsewhere in that Gospel, in other early Christian literature, and in the nonrabbinic Jewish literature of the Second Temple period. But Basser often neglects to establish dissimilarity between the latter literature and the supposedly pre-Matthean elements in Matthew. In fact, to keep these elements purely as well as rhetorically rabbinic, Basser regularly assigns nonrabbinic elements to later Christian revisions, especially

1. Boston: Academic Studies, 2009.

to Matthean revisions—so much so that he pronounces Matthew himself a non-Jew in all likelihood or, if a Jew, one who loathed his Jewishness, inveighed against the unwritten traditions of the Jews, and, so as to favor the gentiles, excluded the Jews from God's kingdom. Thus the rabbinic hypothesis determines Basser's method, which works out to produce a sharp cleavage in Matthew between pro-Jewish, rabbinic-like material and anti-Jewish, nonrabbinic-like material.

On the one hand, furthermore, the evangelist Matthew becomes diabolically clever by at first commandeering mainly the original traditions that reflect a thorough Jewishness on Jesus' part, and then by increasingly overlaying those traditions with a false ascription to Jesus of virulently anti-Jewish sentiments. *Ex hypothesi*, for example, a Jesus who speaks of gentiles' inclusion in and Jews' exclusion from the kingdom of heaven (Matt 8:11–12) is almost certainly unhistorical, whereas a Jesus who affirms each jot and tittle of the Torah (5:17–19) is likely historical. For Matthew, then, a parting of the ways between church and synagogue has already occurred. (An early date for this parting need not depend on Basser's hypothesis, of course.)

On the other hand, says Basser, as a gentile or (less probably) as a Jew-turned-gentile, Matthew often did not even understand the Jewish rhetoric represented in the Jesuanic traditions at his disposal. Sometimes, nevertheless, he followed them to the letter; and at other times he interpolated his own anti-Jewish and especially anti-Pharisaic point of view. "To the letter" includes not only his following those traditions exactly but includes also the traditions themselves in that the rabbis, Jesus, and his original tradents found hyperliteral meanings even in the discrete words and letters of an Old Testament passage—that is, quite apart from an overarching, contextually determined meaning. So in regard to pre-Matthean materials, Basser challenges the currently popular effort to discover echoes of a context, be it an Old Testament context or a historical context in Jesus' life, and consequently challenges any "conceptual paradigm," say, of Matthew's Jesus as a new Moses. "The images and the words" are "no more than evocative of biblical vocabulary."

Undergirding Basser's interpretation of Matthew is an extremely wide-ranging treatment of comparable rabbinic tradition; but the consideration of modern secondary literature on Matthew, the other Gospels, and the rest of the New Testament is lamentably spotty. Such consideration might have saved Basser from a number of missteps. Confusingly, he speaks of his own translations of the Hebrew Bible,

Greek Matthew, and the Hebrew/Aramaic writings of rabbis yet speaks also of utilizing a translation of Matthew by Peter Zaas and various internet translations of biblical passages. In any case, some unusual and even provocative translations appear: "students" instead of "disciples," "impersonators" instead of "hypocrites," "houseboy" instead of "servant," and "blather" instead of "babble" or "heap up empty phrases." Numerous references to Dale Allison arise out of private communication indicating a fair amount of friendly disagreement between him and Basser. The usual questions of historicity and synoptic interrelations go largely ignored, and the failure to discuss synoptic interrelations sometimes leads to a neglect of Matthew's redaction of Mark and Q (the latter a putative sayings-source reflected in Matthew and Luke).

Despite Basser's resolve to avoid saying what earlier commentators have said, he often does just that, as in his comments on betrothal and marriage and on the eye as the body's lamp. But against the grain of most other commentaries, he detects a surprising amount of gnostic thought in what he judges to be Matthew's later, non-Jesuanic elements. Though reserving most of his criticisms for the secondary Jesus of Matthew's anti-Jewish making, Basser is not above criticizing the original, Jewish Jesus too, as when he scores that Jesus for asking poor fishermen to leave their families destitute by following him and for following "the pattern of all populist leaders" by mocking the current leadership of his day and treating its members as enemies, "while at the same time [according to Basser] espousing most of their values." Here are several of Basser's interpretations worth considering:

- "The Prophets" (Matt 2:23) and "the Writings" (21:43) refer to the second and third sections of the Hebrew Bible.

- Unworthiness to carry the shoes of the coming one (3:11) makes the Baptist unfit to become his disciple rather than unfit to become his slave.

- Except for being homiletic rather than exegetical, the Antitheses (5:21–48) compare well with the rabbis' building a fence around the law.

- Cross-taking (10:38) was a known idiom (Gen. Rab. 56 to Gen 22:6) and therefore did not necessarily allude in advance to Jesus' crucifixion.

Here are some of Basser's eyebrow-raising interpretations:

- The genealogy of Jesus (Matt 1:1–17) corresponds to the phases of the moon.
- In Jesus' teaching, as distinct from Matthew's understanding, the persecuted (5:10) were almost certainly the children of Israel in general.
- The Pharisees are puzzled rather than critical when asking why Jesus eats with tax collectors and sinners (9:11), and informative rather than confrontational when telling him that his disciples are breaking the Sabbath (12:2), because the story of Jesus *underlying* the Synoptics presents him as aligned to and in sympathy with Pharisaic teaching.
- The twelveness of the apostles (10:1) is not symbolic of Israel's twelve tribes and therefore is only historical.
- God is the treasure- and pearl-finder (13:44–46), and the treasure and pearl represent—in Matthew's view—gentiles as opposed to the Jews.
- In Matthew's view, the tares sown among wheat (13:24–30, 36–43) represent the Pharisees or, more widely, the Jews as the devil's tools who must be eradicated—hence the representation's "toxic effect on Christendom's treatment of Jews from early times through the twentieth century." In this connection Basser does not document any Christian equation of the tares with the Pharisees or Jews; does not take account that the parable *prohibits* an uprooting of the tares during the present age; does not distinguish between Christians and the angels who will do the uprooting; and does not relate the tares to the theme of false discipleship that runs throughout Matthew.

All in all, the alleged mind behind the Gospels looks closer to that of the evangelist Matthew than Basser's view admits.

Smithereens!

The Bible Made Impossible: Why Biblicism Is Not a Truly Evangelical Reading of Scripture[1] is sure to sizzle before it fizzles; and fizzle it will, at least among the readers to whom it is primarily addressed, namely, evangelical Christians. The author, Christian Smith, is a well-known sociologist who converted from evangelical Protestantism to Roman Catholicism but maintains the moniker *evangelical* and disclaims that the reasons for his conversion had very much to do with why he thinks biblicism isn't a truly evangelical reading of Scripture. But what does he mean by *biblicism* and by its making the Bible "impossible"? Biblicism makes the Bible impossible to put into practice, according to Smith; and as used by him, biblicism means an emphasis on the Bible's "exclusive authority, infallibility [or 'inerrancy'], perspicuity, self-sufficiency, internal consistency, self-evident meaning, and universal applicability," though not every version of biblicism contains all these ingredients—at least not all in equal measure.

How then does the foregoing constellation of emphases make the Bible impossible to put into practice? It does so by producing "pervasive interpretive pluralism," so that evangelical Christians differ widely on what they should believe and how they should behave; and their differences include important as well as unimportant matters. Thus "practice" includes belief as well as behavior, and "impossible" has to do with *shared* practices. For example, biblicists differ over human free will and divine sovereignty; penal satisfaction and Christus Victor; creation and evolution; sprinkling and immersion; divorce and remarriage; complementarianism and egalitarianism; just war theory and pacifism;

[1]. Grand Rapids: Brazos, 2011.

pretribulationism and posttribulationism; amillennialism, premillennialism, and postmillennialism; everlasting torment and annihilation; soteriological exclusivism, inclusivisim, and universalism; and on and on. In other words, biblicism fails to produce the theological and behavioral unity that Smith thinks necessary to validate it. Furthermore, biblicism fosters using the Bible as a handbook for matters of diet, dating, gardening, good sex, alternative medicine, psychological counseling, business practices, and so on—all matters of little or no importance in the Bible, he avers.

Why then do biblicists go wrong? Because they mistakenly assume that the Bible contains no errors in whatever it says, always speaks clearly, and therefore can be understood correctly by any able- and fair-minded individual who reads it inductively. Giving rise to these assumptions have been the culture of American democratic individualism; the influence of Scottish commonsense realism and Baconian inductivism on and through Charles Hodge (1797-1878) and Benjamin Warfield (1851-1921) at Princeton Theological Seminary (as though belief in the Bible's exclusive authority, infallibility, perspicuity, and other ingredients of biblicism don't date back at least to the Protestant Reformation!); the early twentieth-century battle against theological liberalism on the part of Christian fundamentalists, who fathered (or grandfathered) current evangelicals; and the failure of early evangelicals (then called neo-evangelicals) to appropriate Karl Barth's nonbiblicist but antiliberal way of reading Scripture.

Undermining the biblicists' assumptions, according to Smith, are biblical texts that almost no reader, biblicists included, actually lives by, such as "Greet one another with a holy kiss"; that need explaining away by arbitrary appeals to cultural relativism, such as Paul's prohibiting women from braiding their hair; that seem so strange as to merit neglect, such as the statement, "Cretans are always liars, bad beasts, lazy bellies"; and that disagree with other biblical texts, such as the disallowing of women's speech in church meetings over against such an allowance if their heads are covered.

How then does Smith propose to solve the problem of pervasive interpretive pluralism while maintaining a belief in the Bible's divine inspiration and avoiding a lapse into theological liberalism? His main answers: (1) by accepting the presence in the Bible of ambiguity, complexity, errors, contradictions, and thus the legitimacy of at least some different and even opposing interpretations of Scripture; (2) by importing extrabiblical theological concepts, such as that of the Trinity with its ontological categories of person and nature; (3) by submitting to "a stronger ... ecclesial teaching office than biblicism has ever provided" (which answer, along with his book *How to Go from Being a Good Evangelical to a Committed Catholic in Ninety-Five Difficult Steps* calls in question Smith's aforementioned claim that his conversion to Roman Catholicism had little to do with his rejection of biblicism); and, most importantly, (4) by reading Scripture christologically, à la Barth, so that its problematic passages and the different interpretations thereof recede in importance before the main message of salvation in Christ, the incarnate second person of the Trinity.

But will these maneuvers work to solve the problem of pervasive interpretive pluralism? Smith himself admits that "various parts of scripture [such as the 'nasty things' said about Cretans in Titus 1:12–13] ... do not clearly fit its gospel message centered on Jesus Christ." So he backtracks from reading in Scripture "*every* narrative, *every* prayer, *every* proverb, *every* law, *every* Epistle ... *always* and *only* in light of Jesus Christ and God reconciling the world to himself through him" and says that the christological thread runs "more *or less* explicitly" through the Bible's "sometimes-*meandering* story" (emphasis added). To resist universalizing certain passages on the ground that they "do not clearly fit" the gospel doesn't solve the problem of pervasive interpretive pluralism, however, so long as opinions differ on what fits and what doesn't fit. Furthermore, though wanting to rein in the pluralism by interpreting Scripture always and only in the light of the gospel concerning salvation through Jesus Christ, Smith lists this very salvation among the topics plagued by pervasive interpretive pluralism because of what he sees as Scripture's multivocality. You also have to ask whether a christological reading doesn't produce its own such pluralism in attempts to relate somehow to Christ the Cretan passage, the "grab-the-hot-looking woman" passage (Deut 21:10–14), imprecatory passages (e.g., Ps 137:7–9), and other passages also cited by Smith as problematic for biblicism. And will whatever relations to Christ might be drawn seem any less strained than biblicists' using Scripture for guidelines on dating (to cite one of the many examples that Smith describes as kitschy)?

Why shouldn't Scripture be mined for Christian behavioral guidelines relevant to this and that? No less a personage than Carl F. H. Henry, hardly a kitschmonger, once asked me face-to-face how I thought Christian young people should and should not behave on dates; and though

Smith declares that the commands to greet one another with a holy kiss are "much more overt" than scriptural teachings against premarital sex (but what about the multiple prohibitions of fornication, a general term for extramarital sex?), Smith himself gives ground:

> That is not to say that evangelical Christians will never have theologically informed moral and practical views of dating and romance [exemplary of "further insights and implications of what the gospel means for belief and life in the world" for "every new generation of believers"].... But the significance and content of all such views will be defined completely in terms of thinking about them in view of the larger facts of Jesus Christ and the gospel—not primarily by gathering and arranging pieces of scriptural texts that seem to be relevant to such topics.

Well and good, yet do the larger facts ever erase the pieces of scriptural texts ("pieces of" being pejorative, because Smith doesn't like proof texting except when the texts feature God's reconciliation of the world to himself through Christ)? If not, those pieces retain every ounce of applicability. But if so, we're back to the plurality of differing opinions on applicability, as when—despite admittedly specific biblical statements to the contrary—Smith declares that larger scriptural implications "clearly favor" egalitarianism over complementarianism. Why doesn't he ascribe egalitarianism along with biblicism to American democratic individualism instead, unless his own individualism leads him to ascribe only his dislikes to American democratic individualism?

Nor does this failure of a christological reading stop at "strange" texts in the Bible's margins. For early on, Smith emphasizes that "on most matters of significance ['essentials'] concerning Christian doctrine, salvation, church life, practice, and morality, different Christians—including [but not limited to] different biblicist Christians—insist that the Bible teaches positions that are divergent and often incompatible with one another." In the early church, Christology itself fell prey to pervasive interpretive pluralism—and increasingly does so again among nonbiblicist Christians. When it comes to such pluralism, then, reliance on a christological reading of the Bible proves just as "self-defeating" as biblicism does according to Smith.

Nor does Smith's appeal to the late Barth's christological reading of Scripture cut ice. At least not with me. For in Basel during the fall of 1960 I regularly climbed out of the basement of biblical studies to attend the theological seminars held by Barth upstairs, only to hear him repeatedly engage in subjective judgments on what in the Bible carries authority and what therein does not. Dismissively, for example: "Oh, that's just a bit of Jewish apocalyptic that crept into Scripture." As I wrote shortly afterward to an acquaintance, "For all Barth's likeableness I must think that [Cornelius] Van Til's harsh judgment on his theology is more *grundlich* and closer to the truth than the sympathetic attitude which has appeared even in some American evangelical circles. . . . So far as I can see, Barth is the sole judge of what in the Bible is authoritative for him." Others disagree, I know; but that was my take.

Perhaps feeling some inadequacy in a christological reading of Scripture to solve sufficiently well the problem of pervasive interpretive pluralism, Smith reaches behind the New Testament to the early church's "rule of faith," which existed prior to the canonizing of New Testament books and allegedly helped regulate the process of canonization. This rule of faith consists, it is said, in the gospel of Jesus Christ, so that books containing it got canonized—hence, a canon *behind* the canon as well as *within* the canon. What then of Christian books that didn't make it into the New Testament even though they too present the gospel of Jesus Christ? More importantly, how is it that those books which did get canonized can be legitimately interpreted, according to Smith, as disagreeing on the essentials of Christ's gospel, that is, on the rule of faith? And why are my suspicions aroused when Smith repeatedly cites the fate of the unevangelized as an open question, and refers again and again to the gospel of God's reconciling the world to himself through Christ, but says nary a word about divine judgment and the lostness of unbelievers despite the apostle Paul's declaring that for their salvation people have to believe in Christ; that to believe in him they have to hear about him; that to hear about him preaching is necessary; and that the preaching requires a sending of preachers (Rom 10:9-17)? Paul also qualifies "the ministry of reconciliation" by describing himself as "an odor deriving from death, resulting in death" through the preaching of this very gospel to those who are perishing (2 Cor 2:15-16; 5:19).

As to the ancient Christian creeds, they were forged in response to pervasive interpretive pluralism; and to date they haven't put a stop to pluralism outside biblicist circles any more than inside them. Nor has a strong teaching office. Not even pronouncements of the Roman Catholic Magisterium have stopped it among theologians, clergy, and lay people of that communion, not to detail disagreements among Roman Catholics on the Magisterium itself. If both Scripture and tradition are unalterably ambiguous, then, how can "a stronger hermeneutical guide" be judged "consistent with, if not directly derived from, Christian scripture and tradition"? "The larger, longer Christian tradition" with which Smith wants American evangelicals to interact is itself shot through with interpretive pluralism, as he himself says: "church history is replete with multiple credible understandings, interpretations, and conclusions about the Bible's teachings."

Toward the same end of wider interaction, Smith distinguishes between dogmas (beliefs nonnegotiable for any Christian), doctrines (beliefs firmly held but not considered crucial to the faith), and opinions (less sure beliefs). And then he urges evangelical Christians to decrease the number of their dogmas in favor of increasing the number of their doctrines and mere opinions: "For example, many evangelicals have the tendency to push the 'penal satisfaction doctrine of atonement' up to the level of dogma." To the contrary, Smith wants to make this doctrine negotiable because some Christians prefer, say, the Christus Victor theory of atonement. Never mind that the apostle Paul included Christ's having died "for our sins" among "the *foremost* things" in the gospel (1 Cor 15:3). Sorry, but victory without the penal is pyrrhic.

Smith also wants evangelicals to expand the number of interpretations they regard as *adiaphora*, matters of indifference—such as baptism by immersion versus baptism by sprinkling (as though *baptizein* in the Greek New Testament could mean merely "to sprinkle"). Expansion of *adiaphora* should be accompanied, he says, by "further insights and implications of what the gospel means for belief and life in the world," as in the matter of slavery, for instance. Despite explicitly negative biblical statements concerning homosexual intercourse, does his including it among christianly disputable issues tend to put it on a theological trajectory similar to the one traveled by slavery? (This is a question, not an accusation.) In any event, the charge that "biblicism lacks the imagination and categories to understand the dynamic nature of the gospel and the church's understanding of truth under the guidance of the Holy Spirit" masks with the happy face of doctrinal advance a lot of *non*biblicist interpretive pluralism in the questionable twists and turns of church dogma. The charge of interpretive unimaginativeness also rings somewhat hollow, given the echo of Smith's cannonades aimed against biblicists' imaginatively using the Bible as a handbook for "perfect and explicit instructions on every imaginable topic it seems to address, as well as indirectly to literally every possible topic."

How might further insights and implications come to light? Smith confesses the Bible to be "the primary testifying, mediating witness to Jesus Christ," but he adds that "Jesus Christ is present to his people in the church in the bread and the wine," also "in baptism," "in the Holy Spirit," "in prayer," and "in the form of his or her [a Christian's] needy neighbor." The question of sacramentalism aside, are these extrabiblical presences of Christ any less subject to pervasive interpretive pluralism than is biblicism? May not the reverse be true? For that matter, must we assume that the validity of interpretive principles, such as those in biblicism, requires uniformity of interpretive results?

Smith argues that "scriptural multivocality is a fact that profoundly challenges evangelical biblicism." As already noted, however, multivocality characterizes also the rule of faith, the gospel contained within Scripture, and the early and ongoing creeds and extrabiblical traditions on which he wants evangelicals to draw and to which may be added the title "Smithereens!" (Who is blowing what to smithereens? Biblicists, the Bible? Smith, biblicism? I, his book?) To the extent that *scriptural* multivocality entails seeming contradictions, it may be better to speak of diverse literary genres and the suiting of different messages to different situations, so that given a postbiblical *like* situation, the suited message carries full, unvarnished authority.

"Biblicists . . . tend to assume the single, univocal meaning of biblical texts," says Smith. Not true, as he unconsciously admits when scoring biblicists for seeing no fewer than seventeen meanings in the story of Jesus and a Samaritan woman at Jacob's well, to take but one example. Or take biblicists' affirming double fulfillments of prophecy and relishing typological, especially *christologically* typological, as well as historical meanings in the Old Testament—also salvific symbolism in Jesus' miraculous signs, particularly those recorded in John's Gospel.

I believe Smith makes a mistake in lumping together theological issues such as Calvinism versus Arminianism and kitschy books such as *Cooking with the Bible: Recipes for Biblical Meals*. The latter arises out of the popular secular fad of writing cookbooks, not out of Scripture, whereas the issue of Calvinism versus Arminianism does arise out of Scripture—specifically, out of passages that highlight divine sovereignty and out of other passages that highlight human responsibility.

Smith outlines the combination of Scottish commonsense realism and Baconian inductivism that's used by biblicists as a gathering of biblical facts, which are considered self-evidently intelligible; an arranging of them in logical order; and an inferring from them general truths. This method is outdated, says Smith, because the impossibility of complete objectivity makes the meaning of facts at least somewhat less than self-evidently intelligible. Granted this impossibility, but how does *he* operate? He gathers a host of facts in the form of biblical passages, interpretations thereof, doctrinal confessions, book titles, slogans on bumper stickers and T-shirts, internet pronouncements, and sociological surveys. He treats these facts as self-evidently intelligible. He arranges them in a logical order, from the popular to the institutional to the scholarly. He infers from them a general truth that interpretive pluralism pervades biblicism and concludes that this pluralism undermines biblicism. Welcome to Scottish commonsense realism and Baconian inductivism redux! Thanks to Smith they've made a comeback. To say so is neither to deny nor to affirm his thesis. It is only to say that he uses the very method he purportedly rejects, as did also John Calvin and others in their individualistic interpretations of Scripture long before the Scotsman Thomas Reid ever lived, even before Sir Francis Bacon lived, and long before the rise of American democratic individualism. Moreover, Bacon promoted inductive reasoning particularly in regard to the *material* sciences, which kind of reasoning seems at best only distantly pertinent to textual interpretation, as Smith himself seems to recognize in saying that "language operates as a different dimension of reality than most *material* and mental objects" (emphasis added).

There's more: Not only does Smith ascribe biblicism in large part to Scottish commonsense realism and Baconian inductivism. He also ascribes biblicism in large part to a *presupposition* that Scripture speaks authoritatively on many more topics than salvation in Christ. Hence biblicism looks presuppositional as well as commonsensically inductive. As for his own presupposition, it's that Scripture speaks authoritatively only on salvation in Christ and topics related to that salvation. Under this presupposition, Smith appears to use just as much commonsensical inductivism as biblicists do under their presupposition.

I applaud Smith's opposition to forced harmonizations of differing scriptural passages—harmonizations that grow out of many biblicists' excessive fear of narrative that may be less than purely historical. He rightly derides, for instance, Harold Lindsell's argument that since the parallel biblical accounts of Peter's denials of Jesus differ in their circumstantial details, Peter must have denied him six times. During a telephone conversation long ago, I told Lindsell, "Harold, the Bible says that Peter denied Jesus three times, not six." He answered, "Well, if Peter denied Jesus six times, he must have denied him three times," an answer that harms rather than helps the view of Scripture held by biblicists.

Though Smith has justifiably brought to the fore a problem in pervasive interpretive pluralism, then, this problem plagues all literature, not just the Bible as perceived by biblicists. In regard to the latter, I find his arguments incoherent and his solutions inadequate. He cites Don Carson to the effect that solving the problem requires "better scriptural exegesis." Indeed. So maybe someone should write a book arguing that pervasive pluralism in biblical interpretation is due to the lingering deleterious effects, even on biblicists, of *non*biblicism in the past. But what do I know? I'm neither a sociologist nor a theologian. Just a biblicist.

Corrigenda: "The author of 2 Timothy's specific teaching about eating meat sacrificed to pagan idols" (70) should be corrected to *1 Corinthians'* teaching on that topic. The statement, "*All* of scripture is not clear" (132, emphasis original), which means that none of Scripture is clear, should read, "Not all Scripture is clear," which means that some Scripture is unclear (the same kind of correction being needed in the sentence that bridges 115 and 116). Robert K. Johnston should have "t" restored to his last name (xiv, 17, 18 [4x], 21 [2x], 22, 186 [2x], 190, 216); and "Greg Bashan" (87, 213) should be corrected to "Greg Bahnsen," as twice on page 198, though when a college student of mine and others, Greg wrote a weekly column in our students' newspaper under the pen name "Balaam's Ass."

POSTSCRIPT

Christian Smith responded to my critical review of his book *The Bible Made Impossible* with various complaints. His response prompted me to issue the following reply:

In my review of *The Bible Made Impossible* I stated outright, "Smith has justifiably brought to the fore a problem in pervasive interpretive pluralism [from here on PIP]." Does that statement look as though I "don't even believe the problem exists," as Smith complains? I followed up by observing—against Smith's treatment of PIP as a distinctively fatal flaw in biblicism—that "this problem plagues all literature, not just the Bible as perceived by biblicists." Supported earlier in some detail, does that observation (among others) look as though I "reject[ed]" Smith's "critical case literally without explaining what is wrong with it"?

Smith rejects biblicists' belief in biblical clarity but refers to the "clarity" of his book. So are we to believe in the clarity of *The Bible Made Impossible* but not in that of the Bible itself? If Smith thinks I and others have variously misinterpreted his book, then PIP plagues the book and by his own standard renders *it* "Impossible" along with the Bible. Doubtless he would nuance what he means by the clarity of his book, but so too do biblicists in regard to the Bible's clarity.

If biblicism has failed to "produce . . . a largely shared understanding of what scripture teaches," how can Smith speak as he does of "American evangelicalism"? Doesn't the phenomenon of American evangelicalism, which is just as "patently obvious" as is PIP, imply a largely shared understanding of what Scripture teaches, despite numerous disagreements? If Smith won't give that much ground, he'll have to denude American evangelicalism even of its doctrinal underwear and treat the phenomenon in nondoctrinal terms alone. What then makes evangelicals *evangelicals*?

Smith complains that I paid a disproportionately small amount of attention to the evidence he cited for PIP in American evangelicalism and a disproportionately large amount of attention to his proposed solutions to the problem of PIP. Guilty as charged! But unrepentant, because I accept the problem's actuality (and said so). Other biblicists accept it, too. Smith even cites some of them to that effect. Besides, what's there to say about his long inventories of slogans on automobile bumper stickers and T-shirts, titles of both popular and serious Christian books, evangelical institutions, quotations of their doctrinal statements, doctrinal disagreements, multiple interpretations of the same scriptural passage? Evidence of PIP? Yes, of course. So I was, and am, more interested in Smith's proposed *solutions* to the problem of PIP.

True, Smith proposes solutions "tentative[ly]" and for the sake of a long-running discussion. So given my stated acknowledgment of PIP, I expected that my criticisms of those solutions would be taken as part of the discussion rather than as evasions of the problem. And the heaviness of my criticisms should have kept Smith from thinking I wrongly suggested he agrees with Don Carson that better scriptural exegesis is needed to solve the problem. If those criticisms weren't enough, my suggestion, "Maybe someone should write a book arguing that pervasive pluralism in biblical interpretation is due to the lingering deleterious effects, even on biblicists, of *non*biblicism in the past"—this suggestion should have ensured that the immediately preceding "Indeed" declared *my* agreement with Carson rather than Smith's agreement with him.

As to "multivocality and pluralism . . . everywhere in the Christian tradition," Smith says that "we are not talking about the entire Christian tradition. We are talking about biblicism." But despite acknowledging PIP in the entire Christian tradition, he *does* call on that tradition to help solve the problem of PIP as regards the Bible.

Incidentally, I did not rely "on recollections of [Karl Barth's] *lectures* from five decades ago" (emphasis added). As stated in my review, I sat in the late Barth's "seminars," which consisted in free-flowing discussions of *Church Dogmatics* (what Smith calls Barth's "mature, published work"); and I wrote up an evaluation, quoted only partially in my review, the very next academic term (in early 1961, Barth's death coming not long afterward in 1968). In my rejection of Barthianism I wasn't "running down" the idea as *such* of a christocentric reading of Scripture. Instead, and given the plurality of Christologies proffered throughout church history, I was running down the adequacy of a christocentric reading as a *solution* to the problem of PIP. I even emphasized biblicists' liking of a christocentric reading, as in their "relishing typological, especially *christologically* typological, . . . meanings of the Old Testament" (emphasis original).

Finally, Smith needs to tell how the method he used to construct his critique of biblicism differs from the Scottish commonsense realism which, he argues, contributed mightily to the error of biblicism.

In Response to Rich Mouw, Mark Noll, and Chris Smith

IN 2001 EERDMANS PUBLISHED *my book* Jesus the Word according to John the Sectarian: A Paleofundamentalist Manifesto for Contemporary Evangelicalism, Especially Its Elites, in North America. *In it I cited the characteristics of sectarianism as described by contemporary sociologists, interpreted the Fourth Gospel as accordingly sectarian, and assessed the state of American evangelicalism at the time as in need of a Johannine sectarianism similar to what characterized American evangelicalism in the early twentieth century. The* Evangelical Studies Bulletin *19 (2002) 1–9 carried a Review Forum on the book. Well-known scholars Richard Mouw, Mark Noll, and Christian Smith contributed to the forum. Their criticisms can be inferred from my following responses.*

Rich, by contrasting your, Randy Balmer's, and Philip Yancey's reliance "on the personal memoir style" with my offering "no solid personal clues" to my "own actual experience of fundamentalism," you seem to imply that if I'd had an experience of it like yours and theirs, I'd "pay much attention to fundamentalism's defects," as the three of you do. Well, let me tell you about my experience of fundamentalism:

Early conversion through *The Old Fashioned Revival Hour*. Regular listening not only to that radio broadcast but also to *Back to the Bible Hour, The Biola Hour*, and similar broadcasts by M. R. DeHaan and Percy Crawford. Repeated sitting under the preaching of Louis T. Talbot, John G. Mitchell, Robert T. Ketcham, Carl T. McIntire, and—on occasion—evangelists Merv Rosell, Hyman Appleman, and John R. Rice, not to name many lesser lights. Frequent attendance at Youth for Christ rallies in downtown Los Angeles, Torrey Memorial Bible Conferences, national conferences of the Regular Baptists, Quaker and Nazarene camp meetings, and revival meetings of all sorts, including those of Pentecostalists ranging from O. L. Jaggers to Oral Roberts.

Evangelists from the Southern Baptist Convention and the Independent Fundamental Churches of America held two-week revivals twice a year in my father's Regular Baptist church. He himself wore the badge of fundamentalism proudly and with my mother, who grew up an evangelical Quaker, had attended Biola around 1930 and—with me in tow—done missionary work in Nigeria under the Sudan Interior Mission and, informally, with the American Sunday School Union in southwestern Idaho, so that our personal associations in fundamentalism were interdenominationally widespread. Dad preached at least monthly against smoking, drinking, gambling, movies, and lipstick and had as his favorite book after the Bible John R. Rice's *Bobbed Hair, Bossy Wives, and Women Preachers*.

For years I avidly read Rice's *Sword of the Lord*, McIntire's *Christian Beacon*, the *Baptist Bulletin*, *Moody Monthly*, the *Sunday School Times*, and countless Bible studies and books of sermons by fundamentalist teachers and pulpiteers. You wouldn't have found me "sitting in a theater while worrying that the Lord might return during the movie." I didn't see one till my mid-20s and the middle of my doctoral work. (The movie I saw? A travelogue.) My college and seminary education took place in a fundamentalist school of such high separatism that Bob Jones University seemed a bit leftist. And even before attending my first class in college I started preaching on a street corner (4th and San Pedro) in Los Angeles's Skid Row and in a nearby rescue mission.

As for the possibility "that fundamentalism might have wounded some of its own," my discarding of pretribulationism caused my denomination's two main mission boards (Baptist Mid Missions and the Association of Baptists for World Evangelism) to reject my application for missionary work among tribespeople in the mountains of the Philippines; and the Evangelical Theological Society gave me the boot for my redaction-critical commentary on Matthew, which some fundamentalists have taken as evidence that I'm not saved. But they're still my people; and I love them, not for disowning me, to be sure, but for the very concern that led them to disown me, their concern for the purity and distinctiveness of the gospel.

I hope to have convinced you, Rich, that I do know fundamentalism up close and personal. But your criticism that I fail to pay much attention to its defects fails itself to note the distinction my book makes between fundamentalism of the mid-twentieth century, to whose defects you refer, and paleofundamentalism of the early twentieth century, which I invoked. This failure shows itself in your reference to "the situation" that existed "in 1947," that is, "the actual conditions that led a generation of evangelicals [such as Carl Henry] to move away from paleofundamentalist patterns." But these neoevangelicals weren't moving away from the patterns of early twentieth-century paleofundamentalism so much as from those of mid-twentieth-century fundamentalism: its isolationism, anti-intellectualism, and such like. These characteristics were hardly those of the paleofundamentalists I put forward: W. H. Griffith Thomas, Melvin Grove Kyle, E. Y. Mullins, James Orr, Robert Speer, B. B. Warfield, J. Gresham Machen, and others. I'm not even sure you have mid-twentieth-century fundamentalism entirely right. At least my experience of it didn't include "superpatriotism" and "militarism," which seem to me more characteristic of *late* twentieth-century, Falwell-type fundamentalism.

Your "typically slipping in some nostalgia whenever we [you, Balmer, and Yancey] venture to highlight whatever strengths in fundamentalism we are willing to acknowledge" and the follow-up, "We go out of our way to send signals to the liberal and secularist types that we really have abandoned most, if not all, of what we learned from fundamentalists," strike me as minimalistic, even craven. How long can such minimalism and cravenness *Stand Up for Jesus*? ('Tisn't Fanny Crosby's, but it'll do.)

As to your theological concern for "the whole Bible" rather than my "range of canonical options to be kept discrete": (1) The Bible isn't a single book but a collection of books, each one geared to the needs of a particular historical moment, so that it's only biblical to gear our use of the Bible to the respective needs of various historical moments. (2) Since these moments vary, we honor "the whole counsel of God" by varying our choices of canonical options from one moment to another, in accord with cultural as well as biblical exegesis. (3) A homogenizing failure to keep these options discrete dulls their cutting and therefore useful edge. (4) A "canon within the canon" is a fixed canon by which the rest of the canon is qualified or judged, so that it's wrong to put in that category my advocacy of shifting from one canonical option to another in accord with changing circumstances. (5) I don't worry about adaptation as such, but about present-day evangelicalism's accommodating itself to worldly culture so that behavioral and convictional distinctions between the church and the world are dangerously blurred. (6) If issues of race, poverty, and militarism remain problematic today, by all means my "situation-sensitive" approach should help us address these issues scripturally; but if the pendulum has swung too far away from preaching about the eternal destinies of human beings, I want to reverse the pendulum's swing.

I'm grateful to you, Mark, for your agreements—though their having to do mainly with the sociology of contemporary evangelicalism makes me wonder why you find that sociology only "semi-persuasive." On the other hand, you think my citations of nonsectarian scholarship contradict my "paleofundamentalist injunction to be wary as a general principle of the world's responsible scholarship." But wariness doesn't equate with nonuse; and the early twentieth-century paleofundamentalists whom I invoked certainly interacted with the world's responsible scholarship. Israelites can still "spoil the Egyptians."

If I'm mistaken in my view that the world looks wholly negative in John's Gospel and that therefore sacramentalism and Christians' so-called *cultural mandate* have no basis in the Word's incarnation, then it's passing strange that John sets out no program for redeeming or reforming worldly culture, much less appreciating it or contributing to it; that in contrast with Gen 1, John has nothing good to say about the world; that the Johannine Jesus goes out of his way to say he doesn't even pray for the world; that the institution of the Lord's Supper makes no appearance in John; and so on. "Incarnation-thinking" will not do the sacramental and cultural jobs you want it to do until you deal with these and other textual phenomena in John's Gospel.

Your line of thinking rests largely on a confusion of "the world," which in John normally and perhaps exclusively means the society of unbelievers, with the physical creation. This confusion comes out dramatically in the opposition between your statement "God acted to redeem this world by becoming part of the world" and Jesus' repeated statement in John, "I am *not* of this world" (8:23; 17:14, 16).

Jesus' "glory," manifested in the "sign" of water-turned-wine, was the glory of his "grace and truth" (see John 2:11 with 1:14). To infer from the text "the goodness of the fruits of the earth, the goodness of social institutions like marriage, and the goodness of human pleasure at a feast" smacks of eisegesis. Would you want to infer the goodness of getting drunk? That's there, too (2:10).

What you describe as my "over-against strategy" may seem to you, a church historian, like "a strangely fissiparous view of divine revelation"; but it won't seem so to biblical scholars, who constantly have to work with often snaggy differences in the biblical text. You say that "calling for a balance among scriptural emphases seems . . . a much better strategy than calling for following one scriptural emphasis over against other scriptural emphases." Over the long haul—yes. But in a situation of imbalance, it takes ballast to restore balance. Important though it is, determining how "John's sectarian message . . . fits in with other messages from Scripture" simply fell outside my authorial purpose, just as it fell outside John's.

Chris, you ask, "Why, in the absence of an institutional church authority, should I believe in Gundry's exegetical story over any of the myriad others?" and therefore find "the logic behind a Roman Magisterium . . . all the more compelling." I couldn't have imagined a better individual example of evangelical elites' migration from sectarianism to institutionalism. With you and others I can appreciate the attraction of "rich liturgy and sacrament," and indeed yielded to that attraction for a while myself. In the end, however, the disconnect between that roted richness and the accompanying sermonettes deficient in gospel, scriptural exposition, and exhortation proved intolerable to me.

But, Chris, you've put your finger on what seems to me most debatable: my assessment of the current trajectory of North American evangelicalism. For an assessment of that trajectory, however, I trust my own observations and those of others over the last sixty years—whether the observers be secularists, nonevangelical Christians, evangelical ones, or fundamentalists—more than I trust your point-in-time surveys (fifteen months in 1995–96 for *American Evangelicalism*).

State-of-the-art methods of sociological surveying that are used nowadays weren't in use fifty to sixty years ago, so that the kind of data you demand for "(better) evidence" of declension over time is largely unattainable. Therefore we have to depend on the testimonial evidence of those who've observed evangelicalism closely over the past half century and more. I hope to have persuaded you as well as Rich of my own qualifications as a witness, to which I add my having taught ten to twelve thousand college students, almost all of them from evangelical homes and churches, during the period 1962–2000. But I welcome others' testimonies, because only by comparing notes can we arrive at accurate assessments.

A number of your criticisms have gone wrong, I think. You downgrade my anecdotal evidence but add a bit of your own (with the caveat, "If anecdotes count") and neglect to note that your work is chock-full of anecdotes gleaned from interviews and offered as evidence.

As to Barna's statistics on divorce among born-agains, 90 percent of those divorces occurred after one or both spouses' Christian conversion. The statistics rest on random sample telephone interviews of an equal geographical spread (forty-eight continental states) and an equal response rate (70 percent) to the statistics that underlie a good part of your *American Evangelicalism*. Moreover, the number of Barna's interviews (3,854) exceeded yours (2,591) by nearly fifty percent. Anyone who has lived with evangelicals through the past half century knows that among them divorce has become more frequent and more acceptable for a burgeoning variety of reasons at ever higher levels of leadership. I've only to look at my own circle of friends, former students, and other acquaintances and hear students' tales about the breakup of their Christian parents to confirm that observation.

Deans of students with long experience at evangelical colleges will join in testifying to a remarkable deterioration in students' behavioral standards—not just in regard to the legalistic taboos of yore, either. The president of a major evangelical seminary has told me of his concern over the extent to which his seminarians were "sleeping around." (He is well-known to all three of you.) A gnostic-like gulf is widening between spirituality and morality.

True, "we just don't know" whether earlier evangelicals would have behaved better than today's if they'd had our present supply of porn. But that unknown doesn't erase computer-related evidence that pornography has become much more of a problem among evangelicals than it used to be.

You say that I offer "no evidence about the extent of seeker-church influence" on the promotion of "subjectivistic, psychologized faith." But I didn't need to, because seeker-churches have no corner on that kind of faith. Indeed, psychologizing the faith started prior to and apart from the Willow Creek movement.

On annihilationism and other questions of eternal destiny, you disparage my citation of only four books and ask why I didn't notice from your book that "96 percent of self-identified evangelicals reported that faith in Christ is the only hope for salvation." What then do you make of Barna's finding that thirty-four percent of born-agains believe that generally good people will go to heaven? Your statistic didn't make it into my book because it's irrelevant to the ways and means by which an ever-increasing number of evangelicals mitigate the doctrine of damnation. Annihilationists, inclusivists, universalists—they all believe that faith in Christ is the only hope of salvation. They just don't think that the penalty for unbelief is everlastingly conscious, or they think that if people don't get a fair chance at Christian belief in this life they'll get it later, at least if they've lived up to general revelation. My fellow teachers tell me that most evangelicals of college age find exclusivism, which used to be standard, almost impossible to stomach, and even inclusivism a little too strict. Inclusivism is fast becoming standard among evangelical teachers themselves. And your readers would never guess that my citation of four books includes a pointer to further bibliography (79n22; compare the extensive bibliography on exclusivism, inclusivism, and universalism on 108–10).

In saying that I provide no evidence for a cooling of missionary ardor among evangelicals, you ignore the evidence I cited from Michael S. Hamilton for "the proportional decrease in expenditures on saving souls for eternity" (85–86). I've also observed personally this cooling among evangelical college students.

I never wrote that sects evolve into institutionalized churches "inevitably"; rather, I called attention to exceptions. And you'd have to refute a vast body of sociological literature to deny the usualness of such an evolution. That the majority (but not all) of this literature is somewhat dated doesn't undermine the historical truth of sociologists' observations, and the recent decline of interest in the evolution is probably due to a case proved.

You call my attack on liturgy and sacrament "simply ludicrous" as well as "individualistic, subjectivistic, and ahistorical." But your fellow sociologists have long noted that sectarians typically distrust ritual and rite; and a vast body of sociological research has shown that sectarians form tighter communities, conduct themselves more carefully according to communitarian standards, and pay more attention to primal history than do nonsectarians—exactly the opposite of what you say.

Since I wrote that mid-twentieth-century fundamentalism needed revision, you can hardly accuse me of assigning it to a "Golden Age." Nor do I suppose that everything was peachy perfect in paleofundamentalism earlier on; but in my opinion it had strengths that presently need rehabilitation. You scoff at "returning to early 20th Century Fundamentalism," but have you forgotten that the Bible—from the prophets onward—calls on God's people to return (see, e.g., Rev 2:5)? So maybe it's time for some Johannine sectarianism.

Theological Seitz in Paul's Letter to the Colossians

The series Brazos Theological Commentary on the Bible has as its goal an interpretation of the Old and New Testaments according to an overall theological understanding, as opposed to piecemeal exegesis based on supposedly unprejudiced historical criticism and philology. Where is this understanding, this "rule of faith," to be found? Primarily in the Nicene Creed. And where are examples of biblical interpretation based on the rule of faith to be found? Primarily in what the series preface calls "the great cloud of pre-modern interpreters," though the series aims to add to their number.

It is said that the need for a rule of faith to guide interpretation arises out of the Bible as "vast, heterogeneous, full of confusing passages and obscure words, and difficult to understand." So absent a rule of faith, the doctrine of Scripture's clarity suffers deeper-than-usual qualification. Yet not only is the content of this rule of faith admittedly a subject of debate. Even one-and-the-same early church father Irenaeus used "terms and formulations" that "shift[ed]" from time to time and from circumstance to circumstance. Also questionable is the legitimacy of equating a "rule of faith" with a "creed."[1] Nevertheless, says the series editor R. R. Reno, historical figures so diverse as Gregory the Great, Bonaventure, John Calvin, and Hans Urs von Balthasar (among many others) agree that the rule of faith includes at least "the covenant with Israel, the coming of Christ, [and] the gathering of the nations into the church." Put more

---

1. See Everett Ferguson, *Church History* (Grand Rapids: Zondervan, 2005), 1:109–12.

specifically, "God the Father ... sends his only begotten Son to die for us and for our salvation" and "raises the crucified Son in the power of the Holy Spirit so that the baptized may be joined in one body." Despite disagreements over details, then, and against the view that doctrine has encrusted the biblical text and thereby obscured its meaning, the Brazos series regards the doctrine represented by the rule of faith/Nicene tradition as clarifying the Bible's meaning.

The question then has to be asked, *To what extent has the rule of faith/Nicene tradition affected the comments of Christopher R. Seitz on the apostle Paul's letter to the Colossians in ways that differentiate this commentary from typically* modern *commentaries on Colossians?* And of course the further question, harder to answer: *Whatever the extent of differentiation, has the differentiation helped or hurt our understanding of Colossians?*[2] I leave to philosophers the question, *How can we recognize help* and *hurt?*

Though most commentators in the Brazos series are theologians, Seitz is a biblical scholar, but not in the field of New Testament studies—rather, in that of Old Testament studies. His theological interests shine brightly, however, as evident for example in his frequent citations of early church fathers, Thomas Aquinas, John Calvin, and other theologically attuned premoderns (though not to the exclusion of modern commentators), and also in his devotion to canonical interpretation, that is, to relating the message of Colossians to other sectors of Scripture, and vice versa. Because of an overarching rule of faith, the tendency is (admittedly on Seitz's part) to minimize distinctiveness in a letter such as Colossians and to amalgamate Colossians with the rest of Scripture—in this case especially with Paul's other letters, most especially with his other letters written from prison: Ephesians (above all), Philemon, and Philippians (somewhat).

Naturally, such an amalgamation inclines Seitz toward Pauline authorship of Colossians and Ephesians (disputed in higher critical circles because of differences from undisputed Paulines such as Romans, 1–2 Corinthians, and Galatians) as well as of Philemon and Philippians (likewise undisputed). Yet Seitz supports his inclination with standard higher-critical arguments. And good ones they are, beginning with what is meant by *authorship* in reference to ancient practices of writing. Those who doubt Paul's authorship of Colossians should consider carefully and

---

2. *Colossians* (Grand Rapids: Brazos, 2014).

Theological Seitz in Paul's Letter to the Colossians

especially Seitz's setting out the problems of harmonizing a theory of pseudepigraphy with the thick interpersonal elements in Colossians 4.

In line with his devotion to canon criticism, Seitz discusses the present canonical order of Paul's letters; but it's difficult to see how this order materially affects his interpretation of Paul's text. Chronology, common authorship, and identical or similar circumstances seem much more decisive, just as in noncanonical but conservative higher-critical interpretations.

Against the opinion of many scholars, however, Seitz deemphasizes Paul's authorial intention to correct the so-called *Colossian heresy* of which Epaphras is thought to have informed him. This deemphasis could be credited to Seitz's rule-of-faith and canon-critical tendency toward amalgamation, so that the specificity of a Colossian heresy recedes. But Seitz argues more exegetically within the letter's confines than on the larger canvas of the canon, and he does so by appealing to Paul's starting the letter with autobiographical and christological notes before mentioning any possible elements in a Colossian heresy. The highly christological passage in Col 1:15–20 can be taken, nevertheless, as a deft, preliminary counterblow against a heretical demotion of Christ; and the introductory autobiographical notes can be taken as Paul's portraying himself as an authoritative and reliable corrector of a heresy about which he has been informed. After all, he had neither founded nor visited the church in Colossae and therefore needed to establish his bona fides.

Seitz goes so far as to propose that "Paul is writing a letter whose occasion is borne of his own self-reflection and a new understanding of his apostleship in Christ, the result of prayer and companionship in prison, in the later years of his life." That is to say, Paul reflects on the change in his apostleship from itinerant evangelism to prayer and letter-writing. But he had been in prison before and written letters during itineration, and in another prison epistle he looks forward to further itineration (see Phil 2:24).

Undeterred, though, Seitz proposes additionally that Paul had come to the surprising realization that his letters would be collected and enjoy a scriptural afterlife for the whole church. Apparently, then, the expectation of a soon return of Christ had waned (contrast Phil 4:5b). Seitz also compares the collection with that of the twelve minor prophets and compares the respective locations of these collections within the larger divisions of Old and New Testaments.

One can wholeheartedly agree that we should not read Paul's letters in isolation from each other or from the rest of Scripture; but resistance to their individual peculiarities threatens to take away theological particulars in favor of theological generalities. If it so happens, the result will be a head-in-the-clouds rule of faith rather than the down-to-earth practicalities of belief and behavior. Think here of the difference between expository preaching, which ties itself to the specifics of the biblical text *seriatim*, and topical preaching, which even at its best tends to limit itself to the high points of the rule of faith as crystallized in the Nicene Creed, which, as N. T. Wright likes to point out, omits the entirety of Jesus' teaching about the kingdom of God. To be fair, Seitz does not want such a heady, impractical result; but his emphasis tends in the direction of a relatively minimal though robust rule of faith.

Back to the collection of Paul's letters, including Colossians: Seitz writes in an appendix a lengthy paraphrase in Paul's own words—not his actual words but words as Seitz imagines them to be in a supposed cover letter accompanying both Colossians and a letter coming to Colossae from Laodicea (Col 4:16). In the paraphrase Paul references his memorization of the earlier Scriptures both in the original Hebrew and in Greek translation (the Septuagint); compares his letters to the twelve minor prophets; casts the letters as ecclesiologically inclusive rather than limited to the local churches addressed; takes responsibility for ordering the letters in a collection so as to give Romans pride of place as a prologue to his remaining letters; and even intimates that he urged Peter, James, and John to take up a ministry of letter-writing just as he has done.

As an Old Testament scholar and devotee of canon criticism after the pattern of his teacher Brevard Childs, Seitz wrestles repeatedly with the absence from Colossians of explicit quotations of the Old Testament. Naturally, this absence poses something of a problem in a view that wants to amalgamate the books of the Bible with each other. By way of contrast, the Greek for "the Bible," *ta biblia*, means "the books" and by means of a plural underlines Scriptural variety. So Seitz has to satisfy himself with saying that "the [Old Testament] scriptures are declaring their own christological purpose . . . in a way that Paul may only partly comprehend but not fully track or encompass." Yet "through careful study" we can surpass Paul in comprehension.

To this explanation Seitz adds that Paul's audience in Colossae, consisting at least mainly of non-Jews, did not know the Old Testament and therefore would not have resonated with quotations therefrom. But

Paul quotes the Old Testament extensively and argues from it repeatedly in Romans and Galatians, both of which were addressed to largely non-Jewish audiences. One may therefore be excused for thinking it still a problem that Colossians does not contain so much as one explicit quotation of the Old Testament.

Surprisingly, given his expertise in the Old Testament and devotion to canon criticism, Seitz does not take up C. F. Burney's article "Christ as the Ἀρχή of Creation" in comments on the so-called *Christ Hymn* of Col 1:15–20. Seitz does describe the article as "astonishingly fresh and full of insight" but does not tell what that insight is. According to Burney, Paul played on the multiple meanings—"beginning," "firstborn," and "head"—of the very first Hebrew word (a noun) in Gen 1:1 and on the multiple meanings—"through," "in," and "for"—of the Hebrew preposition prefixed to that noun.[3]

On the whole, though, Seitz offers a wealth of canonical and theological commentary on the text of Colossians. One may disagree with him at points: for example, in his surprising denial that "bodily" in Col 2:9 refers to the specifics of the incarnation and in his affirmation of the cruciality of baptism as the means by which the Holy Spirit transforms us (including babies?). But such disagreements pale before a vast array of wide-ranging, perceptive comments. By and large, readers will be enriched by those comments both theologically and historically.

For Seitz, then, has the rule of faith clarified the meaning of Paul's text? Whatever Seitz might say, I would say that for him as well as for me, Paul's text clarifies the meaning of the rule of faith and along with the rest of Scripture stands in judgment over the many rules of faith that now exist. For the manifold creedal statements of innumerable Christian institutions amount to rules of faith. If it be objected that the meaning of the biblical text is subject to disagreements that call for adjudication by a rule of faith, it may be answered that the meaning of a rule of faith, including the earliest such rule (whatever that was), is likewise subject to disagreements that call for adjudication by Scripture. So the question boils down to one of priority: Scripture versus a rule of faith, whether in respect to chronology or in respect to importance. Here you see the

---

3. Burney's article was published in *JTS* 27 (1926) 160–77. When moving into a semidetached house in Manchester, England, to start doctoral work, I found on a desk in the living room a penholder inscribed with the name "C. F. Burney." Ignorantly, I trashed it, only to discover later the significance of that name in New Testament scholarship.

difference between an Episcopalian, like Seitz, and Reno, an Episcopalian-turned-Roman Catholic, on the one hand, and a Baptist, like me, on the other hand. But happily for me, Seitz's commentary, while paying due attention to the history and importance of theological interpretation as represented in the Nicene tradition, seems to prioritize the scriptural text. Well done!

To Plato or Not to Plato? Questions Theopsychological and Theopolitical

HEBREWS: A COMMENTARY, BY Luke Timothy Johnson.[1] *The Letter to the Hebrews*, by Peter T. O'Brien.[2] How best to review two exegetical commentaries on the New Testament epistle to the Hebrews (if it is indeed an epistle rather than a homily onto which an epistolary ending has been tacked)? That is a question. For modern readers of Hebrews find it difficult to understand. At least they say so. Despite their scholarly expertise, even the authors of the commentaries under review—one a Roman Catholic (Johnson) and the other an evangelical Anglican (O'Brien)—describe Hebrews as filled with difficulties and then proceed to resolve them in great detail.

O'Brien attributes the difficulties mainly to Hebrews' method of argumentation, a mixture of typology and exhortation; Johnson mainly to the strangeness of Hebrews' worldview as compared with that of most moderns. So O'Brien pays a lot of attention to structural analyses, while Johnson waxes genuinely eloquent in his description of Hebrews as contradicting most moderns' practical atheism, moral tolerance, and wimpy intolerance of pain and suffering, all of which contradictions make it hard

---

1. Louisville: Westminster John Knox, 2006.

2. Grand Rapids: Eerdmans, 2010. Since publication, Eerdmans has dropped O'Brien's commentary because charges of plagiarism were judged true, though the plagiarism itself was judged unintentional. Since the commentary represents a widely held interpretive tradition, however (perhaps even in consequence of plagiarism), I have chosen to include my review of it alongside that of Johnson's.

for them to understand—and even harder for them to accept—the truth or relevance of Hebrews' unseen realm of spirits, moral stringency, and discussion of religious sacrifice. At times Johnson himself seems cagey on these matters, though, as when he writes that "the devil stands for the cosmic forces opposed to the righteous" (only *stands* for?), ascribes immortality to the angels "in the tradition" (but not in *fact*?), treats God's wrath as "anthropomorphic" (therefore not *actually* divine?), and calls the "mystery" of Christian faith "enchanting" (rather than *objectively* true?).

While such language leaves a reader uncertain of Johnson's belief or unbelief in the reality of a personal devil, of angelic creatures, of divine wrath, and in the historical solidity of Christian faith, the reader must laud the acuity with which Johnson pinpoints contrasts between the worldviews of Hebrews and moderns, including many professing Christians. It needs saying, though, that the majority of Christians, who now live in the Two-Thirds World and elsewhere in evangelicaldom (including Pentecostalism) have their worldview shaped in significant measure by Hebrews and the rest of the New Testament. When it comes to numbers, then, perhaps a social location outside these circles has led Johnson to overstate the contrasts.

Out of these commentaries' welter of exegetical details, buttressed by both text-critical notes and (especially in O'Brien's commentary) documentary footnotes, I've chosen to highlight three overarching questions: the first one theologically philosophical, the second one theologically psychological, the third one theologically political:

Question #1 (theologically philosophical): *Does the theology of Hebrews rest on Platonism, as do the writings of the first-century Alexandrian Jewish philosopher Philo?* Though allowing for Platonic "terminology" in Heb 8:5; 9:23–24; 10:1; 12:27–28, O'Brien pronounces Hebrews "not Philonic or Platonic." Quite the reverse in the case of Johnson. Though allowing for a christianizing of Platonic philosophy in Hebrews, he pronounces that philosophy foundational to Hebrews' theology. How so? Well, Hebrews describes the Mosaic tabernacle and the sacrifices offered there as earthly copies and shadows of God's heavenly sanctuary, where he took satisfaction in Christ's sacrificial death. According to Johnson, this description rests on Plato's contrast between the phenomenal world of material objects and the noumenal world of ideal forms. More particularly, "the one" of each ideal form (for example, that of a chair) is expressed in "the many" of material objects corresponding to the ideal form (for example, dining chairs, lounging chairs, rocking chairs, et al.). Just as multiplicity, change, and perishability characterize Plato's phenomenal world, so multiplicity, change, and perishability are seen according to Hebrews not only in the line of many prophets who spoke the word of the Lord to Israel but also in the succession of many priests who officiated at the Mosaic tabernacle and in the many sacrifices offered there. And just as singularity, immutability, and eternality characterize Plato's noumenal world, so too in Hebrews' portrayal of God, his heaven, and the once-for-all sacrificial death of Christ. But since the immaterial world of Platonic ideal forms is nonspatial, nondimensional, and nontemporal, Hebrews' heaven is, according to Johnson, the nonspatial, nondimensional, and nontemporal presence of God. "Salvation, therefore, is . . . transtemporal because also transmaterial," and "the [inhabited] world to come" is to be taken "not in the sense of the empirical cosmos, but in the sense of the realm of the divine presence." One thinks of Gertrude Stein's observation concerning Oakland, California: "There's no there there."

To be sure, Johnson tempers Hebrews' Platonism by calling it "a hybrid of Platonic metaphysics [ideal forms as distinct from their material expressions] and Semitic cosmology [heaven as distinct from earth]," so that "Hebrews appreciates rather than deprecates the physical" because of God's having created it. Similarly, in Hebrews "the contrast between type [the noumenal] and antitype [the phenomenal] is spelled out in terms of the past and present, with the present being the more perfect expression." That is to say, Hebrews presents an eschatology. Well, then, this eschatology must stop short at the end of present time; for in Johnson's view the coming world of Hebrews belongs to God's timeless eternity, in which there are no material objects. So does "Jesus Christ, the same yesterday and today and forever [literally, 'unto the ages']" (Heb 13:8) confine "forever" within the bounds of present time? But "unto the ages" seems to rule out any such confinement; and in the Greek of Heb 2:5 the feminine gender of "the inhabited . . . that's coming" (usually translated "the world to come" despite the masculine gender of "world" in Greek) calls for supplying the feminine noun "earth." So Hebrews adds terra firma to endless temporality for what obtains in eternity. Only thus do "the resurrection of the dead" (6:2) and "a better resurrection" (11:35) have purpose. For the very word "resurrection" means a live "standing up" of formerly supine corpses and therefore requires a spatial and timeful new heavens and new earth for their environment.[3] Moreover, though

---

3. The "spiritual body" of which Paul speaks in his discussion of resurrection (1 Cor 15:42–46) isn't an ethereal body. It's a physical body reanimated by the Spirit of

the Mosaic law featured an earthly "shadow" and "copy" of "good" and "heavenly things," these heavenly things were "to come" (see 10:1 with 8:5; 9:23–24). So the earthly shadow was a *fore*shadow, and the earthly copy wasn't of an already existing heavenly reality—rather, the pattern for a *future* heavenly reality, the translation "copy" being misleading therefore. So the palm goes to O'Brien for his denial of Platonism in Hebrews, though he falls somewhat short of a convincing argument to support the denial and adopts the misleading translation "copy."

Question #2 (theologically psychological): *Does Hebrews warn Christian believers against the possibility of forfeiting their salvation, so that they can have no assurance of it?* In the first place, and as noted by both O'Brien and Johnson, the recipients of Hebrews are addressed as true Christians: "holy brothers and sisters," "sharers of a heavenly calling," "those who have once been enlightened and tasted of the heavenly gift and become partakers of the Holy Spirit and tasted the good word of God and the powers of the age to come." (*Tasting* and *partaking* are to be weakened in meaning no more than in the case of Jesus' "tast[ing] death" and "partak[ing] of blood and flesh.")

In the second place, and again as noted by both O'Brien and Johnson, Hebrews repeatedly warns these Christians against apostatizing, which Johnson correctly defines as "a deliberate choice not to participate in the gift once given" and therefore as distinct from Christians' sins which don't reach that level of intentionality. Thirdly, the contrast with "things containing salvation" indicates damnation as the consequence of apostasy; and both of our commentators recognize that Hebrews announces the impossibility of apostates' restoration through a second repentance—an impossibility that has "often troubled earnest Christians, apparently raising doubts about their assurance of salvation, an assurance that appears to be so clearly affirmed in Romans 5, the 'golden chain' of 8:29–30, and the unqualified promise of John 6:39–40, 44" (so O'Brien), and an impossibility that "the Novatians ['in third-century North Africa'] cited . . . as a basis for the refusal to readmit those who had caved in under persecution" (so Johnson).

> Here is one more way in which the author's perspective—and that of a considerable part of the ancient church—seems far away from that of present-day readers, for whom the very concept of

---

Christ. And the "flesh and blood" that "can't inherit God's kingdom" (1 Cor 15:50) is the present perishable body, not the imperishable resurrected body.

To Plato or Not to Plato? Questions Theopsychological and Theopolitical 165

"apostasy" appears strange, and who consider themselves to live in a world in which everything can be forgiven. When the very reality of sin has been reduced to a form of sickness or inadequacy [so Johnson again].

On the other hand, the author of Hebrews is "convinced of better things" concerning his audience, because "God is not unjust so as to forget [their] work, even the love that [they] have exhibited for his name by having served the saints and continuing to serve them" (6:9–10). So Hebrews' combination of fearsome warning and confident encouragement presents a psychological conundrum. Johnson refers to "this hypothetical apostasy." Does "hypothetical" then emasculate the warning in favor of the encouragement, perhaps out of an underlying belief in universal salvation ("Distinctively . . . , Hebrews extends 'the others,' in behalf of whom Jesus died, to 'everyone'"; and "God's intention . . . is to draw all other humans into that same transcendent sphere [of his presence]")? This possibility crossed my mind; but I refrain from making an assertion, because Johnson's statements can be read nonuniversalistically so far as the actuality of salvation is concerned.

To his credit, O'Brien distinguishes between "genuine faith," which "perseveres," and "false faith," which "regardless of its early signs of life, does not [persevere]." I just wish he had pressed the point that given the limitation of human observation to outward appearance (1 Sam 16:7) and the outward Christian appearance of Hebrews' addressees at the time of writing, the epistle's author had to treat them as faithful Christians but at the same time take into account the danger of a faith not yet discernible as false. Under this consideration careless Christians should *lose* their assurance of salvation while conscientious ones should *retain* it.

Question #3 (theologically political): *Does Hebrews teach that the church has superseded Israel, so that from a Christian standpoint Israel deserves no preferential treatment in current global politics?* O'Brien stresses that according to Hebrews "the law of Moses," and hence "the law-covenant," has been abrogated "in its entirety" because "the Aaronic priesthood has been superseded." Now an abrogation of the Mosaic covenant can be understood, and has been understood, to entail not only a permanent replacement of the Mosaic law but also a permanent replacement of ethnic Israel as God's people with the multiethnic church. O'Brien doesn't explicitly affirm such an expanded supersessionism. Much less does he draw from it a political implication. But many *do* affirm it and *have* drawn from it the political implication that ethnic Israel does not deserve preferential treatment in the field of international politics. For this theological reason as well as for what is considered just and right, support goes to the cause of Palestinians over against the Israelis' cause. Amillennialists, who regard the millennium in Rev 20:1–6 as figurative of the present age featuring the church as Israel's permanent replacement, can easily take this position. Historical premillennialists, too, may take it; for though believing in a future millennium, they don't see ethnic Israel as restored during it.

Dispensational premillennialists do see such a restoration during the millennium, however, and consequently oppose supersessionism in the long run. If they also believe in a rapture of the church to heaven prior to a future period of special tribulation, they think that God, during the tribulation, will renew his dealings with ethnic Israel and therefore even before a future millennium. And despite an abrogation of Mosaic sacrifices according to Hebrews, many of these dispensational premillennialists limit the abrogation to the present church age and see a rebuilding of the Jewish temple and a reinstitution there of Mosaic sacrifices during the coming tribulation and millennium. So while supersessionist in regard to the present, because they believe the church has replaced Israel for the time being, dispensational premillennialists are antisupersessionist in regard to the future, as to a lesser degree are those seemingly few amillennialists who see a future salvation of ethnic Israel in accordance with Rom 11:25–27. Naturally, then, and building on the establishment of the Jewish state in 1948, dispensational premillennialists press their version of antisupersessionism into the service of Christian Zionism.

In another vein and apart from millennial views, feelings of Christian guilt over the Holocaust and over prior pogroms of the Jews lead even some supersessionists to give Israelis the benefit of doubt in relation to Palestinians and lead others to renounce supersessionism, whatever the political implications. Johnson feels such guilt so deeply that with an emphasis on Hebrews' nonabrogation of the *Abrahamic* covenant (note the difference from O'Brien's emphasis on Hebrews' abrogation of the *Mosaic* covenant), he (Johnson) mounts a full-scale assault on supersessionism. But he doesn't relate his antisupersessionism to current Middle Eastern politics any more than O'Brien does with his supersessionism. Politics aside, then, the theological issue of supersessionism gives Johnson an occasion, consistent with his emphasis on religious experience (as in "the impact of the resurrection experience, by which Jesus' followers experienced him after his death as the powerful and life-giving spirit

[1 Cor 15:45]"), to declare that "a Jew standing outside the experience of Jesus as exalted Lord . . . might with equal legitimacy [to that of those blessed with this experience] reject that redefinition [by Hebrews of the Mosaic covenant]." For Johnson, in other words, experience outranks theology, so that his version of antisupersessionism opens the door to a religious legitimizing of unbelief in Jesus. (Compare two-covenant theology, according to which Jews needn't become Christians to attain salvation or, more generally, favor with God.) No such theological backpedaling for O'Brien, though. He lets Scripture both determine theology and interpret experience. Hurrah for O'Brien!

People and Scripture

Josephus as a Pre-Raphaelite

NEITHER JOSEPHUS NOR THE author of his biography, *A Jew Among Romans: The Life and Legacy of Flavius Josephus*,[1] was/is a painter, poet, or critic like the pre-Raphaelites of the nineteenth century. So I've cheated a little in giving to this review the title, "Josephus as a Pre-Raphaelite." The title makes a point, though—namely, that the biographer, Frederic Raphael, portrays Josephus, a first-century Jewish historian, as the first in a long line of Jewish intellectual misfits in settings dominated by non-Jews. Since Raphael sees himself mirrored to a large extent in Josephus, that line has culminated, so far as Raphael is concerned, in himself. But since it goes back to Josephus, we can count Josephus as a pre-Raphaelite or, perhaps more accurately, the ur-Raphaelite.

First to consider is Raphael, whom the biography's dust jacket and interior notices justly herald as "a Fellow of The Royal Society of Literature since 1964," "a regular contributor to the *Times Literary Supplement*," and the "acclaimed" author of "more than twenty novels, five volumes of short stories [though only four volumes are listed], biographies of Byron and W. Somerset Maugham, and five volumes of his personal notebooks and journals"—plus translations of several Greek and Latin classics, numerous further books of nonfiction, and a dozen screenplays (among them *Darling*, for which he won an Oscar, *Two for the Road*, which garnered an Oscar nomination, and *Eyes Wide Shut*, his memoir of which raised a ruckus). In volume and variety, then, Raphael's published work compares well with that of Josephus, to whose histories, apology for Judaism, and autobiography the Loeb Classical Library devotes ten volumes—what Raphael calls "Josephus's enormous literary output."

1. New York: Pantheon, 2013.

More importantly, what does Raphael say about himself that can be related more or less to Josephus? He identifies himself as a Jew but says he has "never subscribed, except for politeness's sake, to any God, including that of the Jews," and therefore "neither pray[s] nor abstain[s] from [Mosaically] forbidden foods" nor "go[es] to synagogue; nor . . . adhere[s] to any kind of codified morality [as in the Torah]" nor "believe[s] that the Jews (or anyone else) have some privileged connection with any kind of supernatural power." Along with the foregoing negatives, his "neither seek[ing] nor shun[ning] Jewish company" links him with other Jews who have been "pitched," as he has been and as Josephus was, into non-Jewish settings. Though Raphael and other Jews have traveled farther into apostasy from Judaism, Josephus's "errant footsteps" set the direction. Raphael himself subscribes to such an analysis when saying, "Yet this book reflects on me and I on it, to a degree that others will judge" and "No one—especially, no Jew—can read Josephus without a certain apprehension that Josephus is also reading him."

As Raphael recognizes, Josephus never apostatized from Judaism, never debunked the biblical and subsequent history of the Jews, and advertised "their intimate association with the Creator of the world," whose moral judgments he did not question. Why then does Raphael call Josephus "the archetypal turncoat"? We might have expected a classicist such as Raphael to think of Brutus that way. A Christian would have fingered Judas Iscariot as the archetypal turncoat. But Raphael is no Christian—is anti-Christian, in fact—and references the progression of Judas from turncoat to "victim of undeserved malice" in "the recently discovered manuscript of the so-called Gospel of Judas." This progression reverses that of Josephus from a would-be protector of his fellow Jews to a "guilt-laden pariah" for having defected to the Romans, gone to Rome after the Jewish War of AD 66–73, and spent the rest of his life there under the largesse of Roman emperors. Representing this latter progression is the change of his name from the Semitic Joseph ben Mattathias (or simply Joseph) to the Latinized Titus Flavius Josephus (or simply Flavius Josephus or, more simply, Josephus), between which names Raphael alternates in accordance with Jewish or non-Jewish contexts.

In what looks like a justification of his own and other Jews' apostasies, Raphael seeks to justify Josephus the turncoat by stressing his brilliance and bravery as a leader in the Jewish revolt against Rome; his realism and reasonableness (over against the fantasies and fanaticism—not to say, internecine conflicts—of the rebels) in urging fellow Jews to yield to Rome's overwhelming force; and his finesse in writing the revolt's history so as to highlight the Romans' cruelty without incurring his own elimination or that of his books. Thus "Joseph was able to smuggle brutal truths about the conduct of the [Roman] legions into his history only by appearing to excuse those who commanded them. . . . To call him a traitorous collaborator underrates his subtlety and simplifies his practice. He was more devious than a turncoat—and more consistent."

By now, readers of this review will have noticed my penchant for quoting Raphael copiously. I do so part to give them a taste of his style and in part to nod ever so slightly in the direction of Walter Benjamin's idea of a collage of quotations; and those readers who were previously unacquainted with Josephus (as Raphael was largely unacquainted with him till a few years prior to writing his book) will have picked up something of his role in the Jewish revolt and of his subsequent surrender to the Romans and ensconcement in Rome, where he finished out his life as a writer. *The Jewish War* gives a detailed account of the revolt. Much of *Jewish Antiquities* paraphrases historical portions of the Old Testament. *Against Apion* defends Judaism. And Josephus's *Life* presents us with world literature's first extant autobiography, according to Raphael, who provides many more details than this review can include.

Despite Raphael's criticism of Josephus's interpretation of history as "sorry" because of a "determination to see God's hand in the affairs of men," Raphael lauds Josephus to the skies and portrays him in terms that—given what we know of Raphael's credits as listed on the biography—look and sound like something of a self-portrayal. As Josephus's books were "apologies for himself," then, you gain the impression that this book by Raphael is an apology not only for Josephus (against the attacks on Josephus by other Jews, such as Uriel Rappaport) but also for Raphael himself and for other similarly disaffected Jews. Thus as Raphael cites Josephus's "precociousness," "quick mind," "inventive panache," "mental agility," "ingenuity," and "intellectual and diplomatic education," so in many, many asides Raphael broadcasts his own such abilities (as exampled below). Similarly, the abundantly evident and varied breadth of Raphael's learning puts you in mind of his observations that "Joseph entertained many ideas, and they entertained him, but the breadth of his intelligence worked against single-mindedness" and because of his "cosmopolitan tastes" would have made him "much more at home as a citizen of Alexandria" than of Jerusalem. The equally evident rhetorical skill of Raphael also smacks of Josephus's "rhetorical elegance" and "skillful verbosity."

Most apparent of all, when we recall Raphael's career as a writer of screenplays, is the way he casts Josephus as a thespian, a showman with a flair for the dramatic. In talking about Josephus's ability at "springing surprises," Raphael comments, like the screenwriter he is, that "Joseph both cued and confused his listeners . . . he was able to control the show . . . he became their master of ceremonies," "relying on surprise and showmanship" as an "actor." "Sacerdotal solemnity and theatrical flair surely modulated Joseph's diction." Again: "From the moment when he crossed the lines [to the Roman side], he'd committed himself to being a *performer* [emphasis original]. No longer a Jew among Jews, he was conditioned by his alien audience: it played with him; he played to it. He was, in a literal and theatrical sense, cast among strangers." Thus he had to be "his own writer [read 'screenwriter'?] and his own producer," "his performance" comparable to that of "a method actor." Raphael even imagines an actor's pregnant pause in Josephus's predicting that general Vespasian would become emperor.

Finally along this line, Josephus came to have "no furious commitment to Jewish exclusivity." As a result he depicted himself as "dispassionate and humane," without "political or religious zeal," and thus as "the first Jew to offer an overview of the world's history and evolution that was not Judeocentric"—a man who valued "common sense" and "decency" over "fanaticism" (and over metanarratives, Raphael might add in his own case). If Josephus was "a traitor, it was to a reckless nationalism he never favored," just as Raphael deplores "the aberrations of Zionism and its lobbyists" while at the same time defending the right of Israel's existence against both Jewish and other anti-Zionists. Is it that Raphael sees himself *in* Josephus, or that he projects himself *onto* Josephus? Maybe both. This much is sure: What Raphael calls the "gossipy detail" in Josephus's *Jewish Antiquities* finds its match in *A Jew Among Romans*; and Josephus's elaborations of the Old Testament text find their match in Raphael's elaborations of his subject's works, as when, to take but one example, he dons his classicist's hat to compare Josephus with Odysseus in regard to "the attributes of charm, durability and double-dealing." The two authors are of a kind.

Raphael's elaborations sometimes take the form of speculations: the possibilities, for example, that Josephus became a strong swimmer as a result of "workouts with Bannus [a hermit]" in "a survival course" that was "based on a Greco-Roman curriculum, including marathon swimming"; that the Joseph of the Old Testament inspired Joseph ben Mattathias "to keep calm in the face of important aliens"; that the knives of fanatic Jewish assassins "brought them kudos on the street and, no doubt, allowed unscrupulous *capi* to exact 'protection' from prosperous targets"; that "Felix [a Roman governor] is likely to have arrested appropriate suspects to avoid being accused of fomenting [some] riots himself"; and that there is "small likelihood" some of the Roman legionaries did not "hold out their arms and loll their heads in mimic crucifixion" after taking custody of Josephus.

Other elaborations by Raphael consist in a dizzying array of references that put on exhibit his polymathy. As a reader you learn, if you didn't know it before, that the photographer Leo Friedlander "broke precedent by allowing his shadow to fall into the frame of his photographs." As expected of a classicist (who by the way makes his own translations of Josephus's Greek), you get the usual regarding Homer, Polybius, Plutarch, Cicero, and other well-known historical figures. But you also learn of an ancient belief, recorded by an incredulous Herodotus, that a race of "Hyperboreans" (meaning "Extreme Northerners") wore their heads below their shoulders and of the Greek medical pundit Galen's recommending a diet of figs and nuts. (*Plus ça change, plus c'est la même chose.*) Did you know that when still an aedile responsible for keeping the Roman streets clean, Vespasian happened to meet up with Caligula the emperor on a filthy stretch of road, so that Caligula "had his bodyguard shovel the shit into the folds of the aedile's toga"?

As for Vespasian after his becoming emperor, he was affronted by the smell of perfume on a young man, told him, "You should have smelt of garlic," and retracted the young man's appointment to a prefecture. When Vespasian slapped a tax on urinals, whose contents were used by tanners for ammonia, his son objected that it was inappropriate to get revenue from piss. But Vespasian replied, "Nothing smelly about money," so that in the 1800s Parisian *pissotiers* became known as *vespasiennes*. Or take Nero's empress, Poppaea Sabina. She kept a stable of five hundred she-asses to provide milk for her bathtub; and Seneca, "that elastic moralist," thought glumly of his mortality every time he went through the seven hundred yards of tunnel between Pozzuoli and Naples.

Raphael's knowledge of poetry also comes into play, starts with Archilochos, a Parian soldier of fortune who wrote poems in the first person in the seventh century BC, proceeds with anecdotes about Lord Byron, Percy Bysshe Shelley, and John Keats, and takes in a 1918 poem by Constantine Cavafy. Nor are philosophers exempt from Raphael's purview. So not only do Socrates, Plato, and Aristotle make appearances. So too do Descartes, Nietzsche, Heidegger, Steiner, and Wittgenstein, among others. We learn of André Malraux's observation that eroticism is "a way of escaping one's era" and of Raphael's own view that "the ecologists' quasi-deification of Gaia is a metastasis of monotheism." Other examples of semi-philosophical reflections appear in references to Stanley Kubrick's definition of paranoia as "understanding what's going on" and Dryden's calling Augustus a man who "kills and keeps his temper."

Also coming into view are historical trivia: In seventeenth-century Amsterdam, Spinoza's father traded olive oil along with other commodities. The palmetto occupies a privileged place on South Carolina's state flag because in 1776 the soldiers of Charleston defended their walls against British cannon balls with sacks full of palmetto branches. "Poor von Thoma! I too have dined with Montgomery," said Churchill, who lived by the bottle, when told that the British general, who banned the bottle from his table, had invited the German Panzer general to dinner after defeating him at El Alamein. Michel Foucault defended the French Revolution's Reign of Terror as well as that of the Iranian ayatollahs. Similarly, Eric Hobsbawn justified the Communist experiments in the USSR and China that resulted in the famine-caused deaths of sixty million people.

We learn of a phone call that Stalin made to Pasternak; of two Rothschild sisters' becoming a duchess and a princess, respectively; of the nineteenth-century French politician Ledru-Rollin's saying about a militant mob on the march, "I am their leader, I must follow them" (contemporized as leading from behind); of a comparison between a seventeenth-century Spanish belief that male Jews menstruate and Arnold Schwarzenegger's "girlie men"; of an Argentine soccer tycoon's saying that no Jew should referee a game, because Jews don't like hard work; of Prince Sihanouk's founding an annual film festival in Cambodia, at which the prince received the Grand Prix every year; of George Walden's having heard Henry Kissinger say, when asked what he thought about the Iran–Iraq war, "Pity only one side can lose"; and of "the willful illegibility and esoteric terminology of medical prescriptions" as carrying "a vestige of medieval abracadabra." There is more, a lot more. In their numbers, Auden, Shaw, Racine, Proust, Pound, Trotsky, Dreyfus, Gorbachev, Marcuse, and many others of their likes crawl in and out of Raphael's text like ants in and out of an anthill. And what do all these fellows and factoids have to do with the life and legacy of Josephus? Not much. But like a peacock in full train, Raphael dazzles with the many-colored splendor of his vast learning; and therein lie the delights of his book, especially for those who already know the basics about Josephus and his writings.

Dazzling and delightful, too, is Raphael's ability to turn a phrase. In regard to Sabbath law, "It is nice to think that everybody's weekend owes something to the Torah." "The High Priest Jonathan . . . was only the most distinguished cadaver done to death by the Sicarii." "Roman political tactics were close to those of the Mafia. The domestic scene was littered with excellent cadavers." "Prophets were to the ancient Jews what economists are to the modern world: they dealt in futures." (You could add a comparison of the "dismal science" with scriptural prophecies of doom.) Nero "was the first ruler for whom the X factor of showbiz trumped statesmanship." (Who of more recent vintage might Raphael have in mind?) "Under a jealous autocrat [such as Nero], nothing failed like conspicuous success."

"Jotapata [a town under attack] was a small nut, but not easy to crack." "The Romans advanced . . . crouched under their shields, like a rectangular, articulated tortoise." When scalded with outpoured boiling oil, "the tortoise disintegrated." "Fadus had him [a popular Jewish rebel] arrested and beheaded, which reduced his charisma." "Joseph's tears at the heartlessness of the Zealot leaders were those of a sincere crocodile: he wept for a fate he now stood every chance of escaping." "If he was now in a lonely limbo [ensconced in Rome], it was a limbo with cushions." "Alien intellectuals . . . provided great families [in Rome] with their academic house pets." "Sub/versions [as in irony] are the catacombs in which writers can embalm secret sentiments." "Freud put his patients on the couch; modern philosophers [such as the hedonists A. J. Ayer and Bertrand Russell] have shown an aptitude for joining their pupils there."

In a way Raphael, too, puts people on the couch, namely, his aforementioned fellow Jewish misfits throughout history, whom he usually praises but sometimes pillories in accordance with an intra-Jewish practice that he documents critically without explicitly confessing his own engagement in the pillorying. Josephus's legacy of living as a Jew among Romans provides the couch or, perhaps better, the Procrustean bed by which those Jews ("who, in one way or another, resemble him in having been alienated") are judged.

Raphael pillories Hannah Arendt for her "sentimental moralizing," as opposed to Josephus's "practical politics," which she attributed to Josephan Jews whom she described as "oily" and "adroit." (Compare the "similar moral zealots," Noam Chomsky, Jacqueline Rose, and Harold Pinter, who according to Raphael "tend to regard Israel, in particular, in the light of universal virtues that have nothing to do with the contingent circumstances of their advocates.") Likewise, Heinrich Heine and Benjamin Disraeli get pilloried because unlike Josephus, who did a balancing act, they capitulated to their non-Jewish surroundings. Disraeli, in fact, capitalized on his capitulation—flamboyantly. On the other hand, Walter "Benjamin too [in addition to David Bergelson] furnishes a [different kind of] counter-Josephus, a man incapable of renouncing what was no longer ever going to be available to him, the old country. He lacked the nerve . . . to remake himself [as Josephus did]." And Yigael Yadin's "assertion [that Josephus was 'a great historian and a bad Jew'] tells us more about the do-or-die ethos with which the Israeli general hoped to inculcate his paratroopers than about Joseph ben Mattathias/Titus Flavius Josephus."

On the commendatory side, Michel de Montaigne, who descended on his mother's side from Sephardic Jews, earns praise because like Josephus he wrote in his second language, "took a dispassionate and dismayed attitude to the sectarian violence of his times," and "has been regarded, by severe critics, as a trimmer and even as a coward." Trimming can take the form of ambiguation, so that "in a mutation of Josephan ambiguity [presumably in reference to Roman treatment of the Jewish rebels in AD 66–73], Maimonides offers a cryptic version of the cryptic" in taking "the [Old Testament] text's disjunctions" as "purposeful irregularities, intended to hide and betray deeper order, nay, divine meaning." As Josephus indicted the ruthlessness of Roman emperors only in passing, so "Freud indicted the dominant form of Christianity only en passant"; and "it could be said that Freud's emphasis on the neurotic consequences of, roughly speaking, *sexual* repression was a Josephan ruse" (emphasis original). The Vienna Circle of the 1920s and 1930s "also had a Josephan aspect" in that "it, too, attacked the dominant religion by indirection." In its reticence and lack of overt declaration, the famous concluding line of Ludwig Wittgenstein's *Tractatus Logico Philosophicus*, "Whereof one cannot speak, thereof one should keep silent," could similarly "be said to acquire a Josephan ring."

"Like Joseph ben Mattathias, [Karl] Kraus thought his countrymen [Austrians] mad, and bad, to go to war [a reference to World War I]." Julien Benda's "call for the educated to tell the truth, rather than to bend to ideological cant, echoes Titus Josephus, who claimed to rise above partisanship in his account of *The Jewish War* and of himself." Like Josephus, "he neither denied his origins nor, in his social and intellectual stance, attached importance to them." Raul Hilberg's *The Destruction of the European Jews* (1961) "resembled *The Jewish War* in that it mounted no explicit polemic.... Hilberg chose to work as if he were [like Josephus] under an embargo imposed by Gentiles"; and Claude Lanzmann, who made the monumental film *Shoah*, was "a modernized mutation of Flavius Josephus" in his unflaggingly persistent "retrieval and recording of painful memories." Somewhat as Josephus was "an objective ally of the Romans, if only in the hope of saving Jewish lives," Rudolf Kasztner "negotiated with Adolf Eichmann in Budapest in 1944" to work "a deal that saved a number of Jews" (almost seventeen hundred).

Though Raphael does not make the comparison explicit, Walter Lippman resembled Josephus to a degree through "effac[ing] his Jewishness by a show of urbane righteousness" during "his long heyday as the leading thinker at *The New York Times*." "Leo Strauss . . . was another modern mutation of Joseph ben Mattathias" in that "Strauss made duplicity the emblem of integrity." The two were "men not quite at home, albeit formally enfranchised." "If he [Josephus] was safe in Rome, he had no future there, only his past." Likewise Isaiah Berlin "turn[ed] his rootlessness into the kind of Archimedean point outside all the world, the better to assess them from" (so Raphael's quotation of Michael Ignatieff).

On and on go Raphael's comparisons of Jews—Theodor Adorno, Marc Chagal, Yehuda Halevi, Arthur Koestler, Primo Levi, Romek Marber, Irène Némirovsky, Karl Popper, Joseph Roth, Arthur Schnitzler, Gershom Scholem, Otto Weininger, and still others—with Josephus. But Raphael's Josephan hero of all Josephan heroes is obviously Spinoza. Of course Spinoza apostatized outright, as Josephus did not. But Raphael notes that like Josephus, Spinoza displayed precocity at a young age; that as Joseph ben Mattathias became the Romanized Titus Flavius Josephus, Baruch Spinoza became the Romanized Benedict Spinoza; that Spinoza lived solitarily, "somewhat as Joseph did in Rome—in a ghetto of one," and consequently adopted Josephus's rubric of *caute*, "be careful"; and that as Josephus failed to return to Israel, though the emperor had given him estates there, Spinoza failed to emigrate from the Dutch republic to Israel with other Jews "as a result of the messianic pretensions of Shabbetai Zevi in 1666." Finally, and apart from any parallel with Josephus, Raphael likes Spinoza because in his opinion Spinoza's disdain for his fellow Jews who believed in miracles and resurrection applies "with even greater force" to believing Christians. Though Spinoza said nothing against Christians, Raphael says a great deal against them, and against their beliefs and practices.

In particular and with painful accuracy, Raphael details Christians' verbal, social, and physical persecution of Jews. No contest there; and he dutifully records the occasional sheltering of Jews by Christians, though he might have highlighted both the significantly large amount of current support for Jews and the Jewish state among evangelical Christians and the apostle Paul's having wished himself accursed if it would do any good for the salvation of his fellow Jews (Rom 9:1–5). What needs contesting, however, is his explanation that persecution of the Jews grows out of Christian theology almost necessarily. Though he usually prefers an economic over a theological explanation, his theological explanation of Christians' persecution of the Jews goes like this: Christians believe that Jesus was God's one and only Son; that the Jews had Jesus killed (hence deicide); that as punishment for the killing, God had the Romans destroy Jerusalem in AD 70; and that it is therefore incumbent on Christians to continue the visitation of divine retribution on the Jewish people. To undermine the foregoing set of Christian beliefs, Raphael avers that Jesus made no claim to divine sonship; that his first followers did not consider him God's one and only Son; that the belief in Jesus' divine sonship arose later under the influence of Greco-Roman mythology and oriental mystery religions; that the Jews had nothing to do with the killing of Jesus— rather, the Romans, particularly in the person of Pontius Pilate, bore sole responsibility; and that the modern Israelis' recapture of Jerusalem disproves divine retribution on the Jews in AD 70.

Missing from Raphael's discussion is the New Testament record of massive Christian efforts to evangelize Jews and to weld Jewish and gentile believers into loving, peaceful unity, efforts that disprove any incumbency of persecution. Also missing from Raphael's discussion is the non-Christian Jews' early persecution of Christians, not only well-documented in the book of Acts (which he might take as unhistorically biased) but also suffered by the apostle Paul according to an undisputed letter of his (2 Cor 11:24–26; cf. 1 Thess 2:14–16, though this latter passage is sometimes disputed). Prior to his conversion, of course, Paul persecuted Christians, as he confesses in other undisputed letters of his (1 Cor 15:9; Gal 1:13, 23; Phil 3:6). Raphael does accept this activity of the pre-Christian Paul as historical; but instead of treating it as a fly in the ointment of his argument, he passes it off as the "revolutionary zeal" of an infiltrative "double agent" who "becomes half-infatuated with the cause he has been commissioned to sap." Taken seriously, Paul's early persecution of Christians and later suffering of persecution at the hands of non-Christian Jews should have made it less easy for Raphael to wave away as an unhistorical accretion the strongly Jewish element in the Gospels' accounts of Jesus' crucifixion. For Jewish persecution of Christians most naturally grew out of Jewish persecution (to the death) of Jesus himself, the object of their faith. Uncited by Raphael, moreover, that repository of rabbinic tradition called the Babylonian Talmud—more particularly, *Sanhedrin* 43ab—even exacerbates some first-century Jews' responsibility for Jesus' death by having him stoned (a Jewish rather than Roman mode of execution) under the charge that he had seduced Israel into idolatry (a matter of no concern to the Romans, since they themselves were idolaters).

Raphael's attribution of belief in Jesus' divine lordship to late borrowing from Greco-Roman mythology and oriental mystery religions recalls the old view, now largely discredited, of Wilhelm Bousset and needs correction from the early Christian and Semitic "Maranatha" ("O [our] Lord, come!" [1 Cor 16:22]), not to mention other considerations, such as Jesus' exercising the divine prerogative of forgiving sins; the weaving of Old Testament language (often differing from its intertestamental translation into Greek) into the warp and woof of accounts of Jesus' virgin birth and later public ministry; and the differences between a virginal conception and conception by means of a god's having carnal intercourse with a human female, and between a full bodily resurrection and a slain god's revival in the underworld. By not going into detail in these regards, Raphael lets himself off easy. Suffice it, then, to quote Daniel Boyarin, an orthodox Jew and internationally renowned Talmudic-cum-New Testament scholar who teaches at the University of California, Berkeley: "It won't be possible any longer to think of some ethical religious teacher [Jesus] who was later promoted to divinity under the influence of alien Greek notions, with his so-called original message being distorted and lost; the idea of Jesus as divine-human Messiah goes back to the very beginning of the Christian moment, to Jesus himself."[2]

As for Paul, could it be that Raphael's dislike of Christianity led him to omit the apostle from his inventory of Jewish misfits? After all, Paul's counting for nothing both circumcision and uncircumcision is reminiscent of Josephus's maintaining his Jewishness but putting little stock in it; and both men were tarred as turncoats. Paul's inclusivism might even be

---

2. Daniel Boyarin, *The Jewish Gospels: The Story of the Jewish Christ* (New York: New, 2012), 7.

compared to Josephus's cosmopolitanism. But Paul preceded Josephus, so that a Josephan legacy would not work in his case.[3]

A number of other questions could be raised concerning Raphael's treatment of the New Testament. For example, should the reputedly answered prayers of Hanina ben Dosa and Choni the Circle-Drawer qualify them as miracle-workers on the order of Jesus, who is not said to have worked miracles through prayer? But Raphael does not devote his biography to Jesus. Back to Josephus, then. Given the hellenization of many Jews long before his lifetime—as, for example, at the time of the Maccabean revolt in the second century BC—the question arises whether Josephus started or only continued a trend of turncoating. As Raphael well knows, some Jewish men went so far as to undo their circumcision by means of epispasm. On this point, though, we should cut him some slack, because he is concerned with Jewish intellectuals, not with brainless young jocks ashamed to have their glans exposed when exercising Greek-fashion in the nude. (Never mind the contradiction between "jocks" and complete nudity.)

Given also Raphael's aforementioned, longtime ignorance of Josephus, the further question naturally arises whether the many Jews whom Raphael canvasses were consciously carrying on or, in some cases, consciously casting off a Josephan legacy of behavior. Whatever the answer (and it might determine the appropriateness or inappropriateness of "Legacy" in Raphael's subtitle), the comparisons between Josephus and later Jews who as he did found themselves in societies dominated by non-Jews—these comparisons remain valid, though arguably strained at times. So let Raphael have the last word on his subject, with a fine allusion to an earlier Joseph: "Josephus, the exile, the traitor, the witness, the reasonable patriot, the pious Jew, the alienated solitary, the sponsored propagandist, melts into and disappears into his textual persona as if it were an alibi. Words supply his coat of many colors."

---

3. I owe the comparison between Josephus and Paul to my daughter Judith Gundry.

Everything You Should Know about the Samaritans (Even If You Don't Want To)

IN AUGUST OF 1975, after meeting at the University of Aberdeen, Scotland, members of the Society of New Testament Studies made an excursion to a country house in the Scottish Highlands. As a guide droned on and on about the history and features of the relatively insignificant house, the famous and normally genial Roman Catholic scholar Raymond E. Brown was heard to complain, "I'm learning more about this house than I ever wanted to know." In the course of reading *The Samaritans*,[1] it would be easy to complain similarly, "I'm learning more about these Samaritans, relatively insignificant as they are, than I ever wanted to know." I confess to saying so myself. The innumerable historical, archaeological, political, social, and religious details delineated concerning Samaritans from time immemorial—those details bored me at first. But gradually my boredom turned into admiration of the deep and wide scholarship of the author, Reinhard Pummer. Ultimately, my admiration graduated to fascination with his subject matter.

Pummer has pursued study of the Samaritans for half a century and ranks as probably the world's most knowledgeable student of them. His study has included face-to-face interaction with present-day Samaritans, participation in their religious rites, examination of their own literature and of literature about them from antiquity till now, and on-site investigation of archaeological remains.

---

1. Grand Rapids: Eerdmans, 2016.

The subtitle of Pummer's book, *A Profile*, reflects that a modern explosion of information concerning the Samaritans, both past and present, forestalls an exhaustive presentation. Generally literate readers will already know Jesus' parable of the Good Samaritan and the story of Jesus' encounter and conversation with a Samaritan woman at Jacob's well. Avid Bible-readers will likely know also about the Samaritans' supposed origin in northern Israel after its inhabitants' deportation into Assyrian exile; about the failed opposition by "the army of Samaria" to Nehemiah's rebuilding the walls of Jerusalem following the Judeans' Babylonian exile; about the Samaritan leper who alone out of a group of ten lepers thanked Jesus for healing; about Jesus' being falsely derided as "a Samaritan" by some of his opponents; about a Samaritan village that failed to show him and his disciples hospitality; and about Philip's evangelizing "the city of Samaria." Today's visitors to the Holy Land will likely be aware of a few (about eight hundred) Samaritans who still live there and sacrifice Passover lambs annually on Mount Gerizim.

So what more than the foregoing can be gained from Pummer's book about the Samaritans? For a start, arguments have developed over their ethnic and religious origins. According to the Samaritans' own account, a high priest named Uzzi, who had descended from Moses' elder brother Aaron through Eleazar and then Phinehas, was officiating at a sanctuary on Mount Gerizim in north central Palestine. Eli, another priest who had descended from Aaron (but through Ithamar) and become a kind of godfather to the prophet Samuel, tried to arrogate to himself the high priesthood. Failing in the attempt, he settled for his own, illegitimate high priesthood at a sanctuary in Shiloh, a little south of Mount Gerizim. Later, the sanctuary at Shiloh shifted farther south to Jerusalem in Judea, whereas Mount Gerizim remained, and still remains, the focal point of Samaritan religion. Thus the worshipers at Mount Gerizim, that is, the Samaritans, have always constituted the true and legitimate people of Israel, especially as concentrated in the tribe of Levi and the tribes of Joseph, namely, Ephraim and Manasseh, from which the Samaritans claim to have descended.

According to a traditional Jewish and sometime Christian view, the Samaritans came about much later than the time of Eli and Uzzi, as follows: After taking the northern Israelites captive into exile, the Assyrians replaced them with imported pagan captives, who then converted to the worship of Yahweh and thus became the Samaritans but remained ethnically gentile. Alternatively, these pagans intermarried with some northern Israelites left behind by the Assyrians and then, as in the foregoing version of this view, converted to the worship of Yahweh. Their half-breed offspring became the Samaritans.

Another view starts with the assumption that the Pentateuch is a fundamentally Judean and therefore Jewish document. Nevertheless, Samaritans accept the Pentateuch as Holy Scripture. Their version of it differs in some respects from the Jewish version, though, especially as regards the proper location of worship: Mount Gerizim instead of Mount Zion in Jerusalem. Given the above-stated assumption of the Pentateuch as Judean and therefore Jewish, such differences suggest that the Samaritans, being non-Judeans, revised the Pentateuch to justify their differences from Judaism. They were, in other words, a northern, sectarian offshoot from southern Judaism. This view turns upside down the Samaritan belief that Judaism branched off from an original Yahwism represented faithfully by Samaritanism.

Along with some other scholars, Pummer strongly supports a still different view. It is that the Samaritans descended from northern Israelites who worshiped Yahweh and did not go into Assyrian exile or intermarry with pagans imported by the Assyrians. The Pentateuch (even the Jewish version) contains the Israelites' northern traditions as well as the Judeans' southern traditions. At first, the Israelites exceeded the Judeans in population and prosperity. Only later, during the intertestamental period, did the Judeans gain political, military, and religious dominance over the north. Thus it almost looks as though the Jews who returned to Jerusalem from the Babylonian Exile, not the people we now know as Samaritans, might better be considered sectarian offshoots (though much later than in the Samaritans' account) from an original Yahwism preserved without interruption in the north.

Prior to the successive Assyrian and Babylonian exiles, King Solomon built a temple for Yahweh in Jerusalem. The Babylonians destroyed that temple, but Judean returnees from exile rebuilt it. Not long afterward the Samaritans—or Samarians, as Pummer prefers to call them at this point in history—built a temple on Mount Gerizim. Though recognizing the rivalry and contentiousness between Samaritans/Samarians and Jews/Judeans that we read about in the Old Testament, Pummer tends to play down that rivalry and contentiousness by treating their outbreaks as episodic rather than continuous and by treating the two sides' religious beliefs and practices as largely the same. Even though worshiping Yahweh at their own temple on Mount Gerizim, for example, the inhabitants of Samaria were not yet separate from Yahweh-worshipers in Judea. Pummer has to admit, however, that the destruction of the Samaritans' temple in 111/110 BC by John Hyrcanus, a Jewish Hasmonean ruler, brought relations to a new and lasting low. Pummer therefore dates the start of Samaritanism as a religion separate from Judaism to the second century BC but highlights continuing contacts and enduring similarities between the two religions.

As to the Samaritans in the New Testament, Matthew's Jesus prohibits the Twelve from entering any town of the Samaritans. By making this prohibition reflect the lack of a systematic mission to "the Samaritans *as a group*" (following the New Testament scholar John P. Meier, emphasis original), Pummer skirts the possibility of Jesuanic antagonism against them as individuals. (Does he think this prohibition stems from Matthew more than from Jesus?)

Christian preachers often make the sermonic point that despite the supposed detour around Samaria that Galilean Jewish pilgrims regularly made because of the Samaritans' hostility to Jews, John's Jesus "*had* to go through Samaria" to fulfill his Father's will that he convert the Samaritan woman at Jacob's well and her fellow townspeople (John 4:4). Pummer points out, however, that according to the first-century Jewish historian Josephus, it was the "custom" of Galilean pilgrims to pass through Samaria. Pummer does not discuss the possibility that mention of the woman's five ex-husbands alludes either to the Samaritans' accepting as Holy Scripture only the five books of Moses (the Pentateuch) or to the five locations (Babylon, Cuthah, Avva, Hamath, and Sepharvaim) from which the king of Assyria imported pagans into the cities of Samaria.

The fellow townspeople of the woman at Jacob's well gave hospitality to Jesus and the Twelve for two days. Despite citing the refusal of a Samaritan village to give like hospitality, as already noted, Luke-Acts also tells of a parabolic good Samaritan, of a distinctively thankful healed Samaritan leper, and of a Samaritan city that converted to the Christian gospel. So Luke gives the Samaritans a mixed but usually favorable review, as you might expect both from Jesus' inclusion of "Samaria" in Luke's version of the Great Commission (Acts 1:8) and from Luke's overall theme of the gospel's unstoppable progress throughout the world among all classes of people.

So far as early Jewish references to the Samaritans are concerned, Pummer continues to downplay as much as possible—even in the writings of Josephus—the antagonism that has traditionally and popularly been thought to characterize the relations between Samaritans and Jews. Exceptionally, though, Pummer's brief treatment of rabbinic literature does not display this tendency.

Archaeological excavations give evidence of a Samaritan temple on Mount Gerizim. So too do various literary sources, including the Samaritans' own chronicles. Yet current Samaritans deny that at any time did a legitimate temple of Yahweh stand on that mountain. Why this surprising denial? Could it be to avoid admitting that the Jews' temple antedated a temple of the Samaritans' own? For the older would have been better. Pummer doesn't venture an opinion.

It may also surprise us that like Jews, the Samaritans had—and continue to have—synagogues. In olden times, Samaritan synagogues were to be found not only at various locations in Samaria but also elsewhere in Palestine and, perhaps most surprisingly, throughout the Mediterranean world—as in Damascus, Delos, Tarsus, Thessalonica, Carthage, Rome, Sicily—from as early as the second century BC and on into Christian centuries. Today the Samaritans have synagogues only on Mount Gerizim, in nearby Nablus, and in Holon near Tel Aviv.

The wide geographical distribution of Samaritan synagogues tells you immediately that, again like the Jews, the Samaritans had a sizable diaspora. If you expected this diaspora to be accompanied by a division of Samaritanism into different sects, you'd be correct. We don't know very much about their various peculiarities. But the members of one of them are said to have prayed standing in water, avoided taking their hands out of their sleeves on the Sabbath, and buried their dead with staff in hand and shoes on feet so as to enable speedy resurrection. Did they get their doctrine of resurrection from the Pentateuch in an exegesis like that of Jesus (Mark 12:24-27; Matt 22:29-32; Luke 20:34-38)?

Peaceful relations with non-Samaritans did not always accompany the Samaritans. Under Emperor Justinian I (AD 527-65), to cite but one instance, Samaritans attacked Christians and Jews during an uprising in Scythopolis and burned their estates and churches. But the Samaritans suffered mistreatment in turn. Threats of mistreatment also led many Samaritans to convert to Christianity and, during the Muslim period, to Islam. The crusader period brought them an interim of some relief. Their total number began to fall precipitously, however, ultimately reaching a low of about 150 between 1806 and 1931. At the same time, not a few Samaritans attained positions of considerable authority even in the Ottoman government. Yet a decree issued in the middle of the Ottoman period (in 1772, to be exact) prohibited Samaritans from wearing garments made of superior materials such as silk or even fine cotton; from riding on horses (rather, only on asses, and then only for urgent business out of town); and from building their houses high or near a Muslim's house (among other prohibitions).

Exacerbating the problem of declining population was the disproportion between males and females among the Samaritans. Males outnumbered females by almost two to one. Consequently, according to a Samaritan high priest nearly all the girls were promised in marriage before they could speak and were married off at the age of eleven or twelve. By now the disproportion has been erased almost entirely. Also, Samaritan men are presently marrying non-Samaritan women willing to adopt the Samaritan religion. Given the Samaritan practice of patrilineality, the future of Samaritanism therefore looks more promising than it did when observers were predicting its total demise.

As Pummer warns, however, the allurements of contemporary popular culture constitute a threat. Since unlike Jews the Samaritans classify sexual intercourse as "work" and therefore prohibit it on Sabbath days, for example, you wonder whether Samaritans who have grown up in our heavily sexualized culture will maintain fidelity to their religion. Or take the case of twin boys whom the Samaritan Pentateuch required to be circumcised on the eighth day after birth but who needed longer incubation to stay alive. Upon consultation with one another the high priest and his counselors declared the boys' incubator to be an extension of the mother's womb, so that circumcision could be delayed till the eighth day after extraction from the artificial womb. You wonder whether such pilpulism will lead to young Samaritans' disenchantment. But maybe they will revise certain elements of their religion instead of forsaking it altogether.

You may now know more about the Samaritans than you ever wanted to, but there's much more of genetic, demographic, economic, linguistic, artistic, and musical interest both in Pummer's book and in the rich bibliography that he has amassed.

Trimming the Debate between Craig and Lüdemann

LATE LAST CENTURY WILLIAM Lane Craig and Gerd Lüdemann engaged each other in an oral debate over whether Jesus rose from the dead. A transcript of the debate was then published.[1] We do not expect precision in the give-and-take of an oral debate; so it is hardly surprising that this debate exhibits some imprecision. But a transcript gives us opportunity to trim the debate by pruning away overgrowth of exaggerations, non sequiturs, and the like. At the same time we may trim the debate also by decorating it with additions to the arguments presented by Craig and Lüdemann.

Craig's argument grows out of what he regards as "four established facts": (1) Jesus' burial in a tomb by Joseph of Arimathea, (2) the discovery of Jesus' tomb to be empty, (3) postmortem appearances of Jesus as risen, and (4) the original disciples' coming to believe that he was physically risen from the dead despite their having every reason not to believe so. Craig then argues that God's resurrecting the dead body of Jesus offers the best explanation of these facts.

It would have been more precise for Craig to say that Jesus *is reported* to have been buried in a tomb by Joseph of Arimathea, that Jesus' tomb *is reported* to have been empty, and so on. Of course, Craig can say—and does say—that whatever their own belief or disbelief in a physical resurrection of Jesus, the majority of New Testament scholars join Craig in regarding those four listed events as historically established. But such widespread agreement does not erase the facts (if I may use the word

1. *Jesus' Resurrection: Fact or Figment?*, ed. Paul Copan and Ronald K. Tacelli (Downers Grove: InterVarsity, 2000).

myself) that what we have are reports and that reports are spongier than whatever hard facts may underlie them. So Craig might have worded his argument with greater precision and therefore with a caution that would ultimately carry greater conviction.

For the sake of argument, though, let us agree with Craig and the majority of scholars on the factual truth of those reports. Let us also agree with him that nonresurrectional explanations are fatally flawed. What conclusion is to be drawn? That God raised Jesus from the dead, as Craig says? No, at least not from a strictly historical standpoint. For from this standpoint the most we can validly conclude is that Jesus rose from the dead. Whether or not God made him rise is another question, a theological and philosophical one that by themselves historical facts do not answer. Jesus' rising from the dead may explain Craig's four reported facts, but to add that God made Jesus rise requires theological and philosophical argumentation, which Craig scarcely supplies in the present debate. The problem lies in his failure to distinguish clearly enough two questions: (1) Did Jesus rise from the dead? (2) If he did, who or what effected the event? Precision of argument would again have led to caution, in this case to the more limited conclusion that Jesus rose from the dead however it came about that he did. Despite its limitation, this conclusion would have been quite enough for Lüdemann to try refuting.

In discussing the report of Jesus' burial, Craig asserts that the story "lacks any traces of legendary development." The assertion may hold true for Mark's version of the story, generally considered the earliest. But as Lüdemann correctly points out, Joseph of Arimathea progresses from a distinguished councilman who was awaiting God's kingdom in Mark, where "all" the councilmen joined in condemning Jesus (Mark 14:55, 64; 15:43); then to a disciple of Jesus in Matthew (Matt 27:57); to a good and just man who not only was awaiting God's kingdom but also was not consenting to his fellow councilmen's condemnation of Jesus in Luke (Luke 23:50–51); and finally to a secret disciple of Jesus in John (John 19:38). These progressions are often seen as legendary developments.

But there are more such progressions, unmentioned here by Lüdemann, much less by Craig. Matthew adds to Mark's version that Joseph was rich and that the tomb was new and his own (Matt 27:57, 60). Luke adds that no one had been laid in the tomb before (Luke 23:53). John adds not only those two descriptions but also that Nicodemus helped Joseph bury Jesus and that the two of them wrapped him not in a linen sheet, as in the other Gospels, but in linen cloths along with an astonishingly large amount of spices—seventy-five pounds of them (John 19:38–42)! In John, then, women do not come to anoint Jesus' corpse on Easter Sunday morning as they do in Mark and Luke. Joseph and Nicodemus have already done the job quite lavishly, thank you (contrast John 20:1 with Mark 16:1 and Luke 23:56—24:1). Nor do the women come to anoint Jesus' corpse in Matthew, for there—alone among the Gospels—the tomb is sealed and guarded. As a result, the women can hardly hope to anoint the corpse inside (Matt 27:62—28:1). To many, these differences from Mark suggest some legendary development, so that Craig might advantageously limit his denial of such development precisely to Mark rather than seeming to make the denial cover Matthew, Luke, and John as well.

Craig makes a similarly broad denial of legendary development in regard to the report that some women found Jesus' tomb empty. It would be wrong, however, to assume that a majority of the scholars to whose opinions Craig appeals agree with this denial. Here is why: The young man who according to Mark's report was sitting inside the tomb, wearing a white robe, and terrifyingly announcing to the women Jesus' resurrection (Mark 16:5–7) appears to have been an angel in human guise; and many of those scholars do not believe in angels or angelic appearances to human beings. So in their opinion Mark's account is already infected with legend.

Matthew adds a monster earthquake to the occasion and replaces Mark's young man inside the tomb with a lightning-like angel of the Lord who descends from heaven, rolls away the stone, sits on it *outside* the tomb, and immobilizes the guards with fear before announcing Jesus' resurrection to the women (Matt 28:2–7). The earthquake recalls an earlier earthquake that Matthew added to his version of the crucifixion. He said that the earthquake split the rocks so that tombs were opened and many bodies of the saints who had previously died were raised, came out of their tombs, entered Jerusalem, and appeared to many people there (Matt 27:51b–53). It remains somewhat unclear whether his text means that these resurrected saints came out at Jesus' crucifixion, wandered about the countryside incognito, and only after Jesus' resurrection entered Jerusalem to make their appearances, or that though resurrected they stayed in their tombs till Jesus' resurrection and only then came out to enter Jerusalem and make their appearances. In either event, this episode and its corollary in Matthew's report concerning the empty tomb look legendary to many scholars or, if "legendary" carries a wrong connotation, unhistorical, though making the eschatological point that Jesus' resurrection ensures the saints' resurrection.

In Luke's report, two adult men who suddenly come upon the women replace Mark's one young man already sitting in the tomb; and the two adult men are standing, not sitting (Luke 24:4).[2] Luke may mean for us to identify them with Moses and Elijah; for he used the very same phrase, "and behold, two adult men," to introduce Moses and Elijah into his report of Jesus' transfiguration (Luke 9:30). He will use it also in his report of Jesus' ascension (Acts 1:10). In John's report concerning the empty tomb, two angels replace Luke's two adult men. But the angels are sitting in the tomb, as was the young man in Mark, not standing, as were the two adult men in Luke. And John's two angels seem to have arrived on the scene later than their counterparts in the other Gospels; for according to John's report Mary Magdalene, the beloved disciple, and Peter have all visited the tomb earlier without seeing the angels (John 20:1-13). To many scholars these differences (not to mention others) resist historical harmonization and therefore spell some sort of unhistorical if not legendary embellishment. Craig's argument could therefore stand pruning without loss of the essential point that Jesus' tomb was found empty. In fact, Craig could strengthen his argument by not claiming too much.

According to a further argument of his, the report that Jesus' tomb was empty and the failure of Jewish authorities to point it out as still containing the corpse require Lüdemann to assume that they "suffered a sort of collective amnesia about what they did with the body of Jesus." Probably so, but the argument is not airtight. For to the extent that in burying Jesus, Joseph of Arimathea acted on his own, or only in partnership with Nicodemus, Lüdemann might say that the rest of the council did not know who had buried Jesus, or where he had been buried, and that Joseph feared to incur their wrath by telling them of his service to Jesus' corpse.

Craig might then respond that the Jewish authorities could not have persuaded Pilate to allow a sealing and guarding of the tomb unless they knew its location. But because of widespread scholarly doubt concerning the historicity of that episode, reported only in Matt 27:62-66, Craig does not appeal to it. He wants to argue only from items widely accepted in circles of New Testament scholarship. Whether historical or not, however, Matthew's story includes an element which implies that non-Christian

---

2. See in the Greek lexicons that Luke's word *andres* connotes adulthood as opposed to youth.

Jews accepted the emptiness of Jesus' tomb. That element is the rumor circulating among them that the disciples of Jesus stole his corpse (Matt 28:11-15).

Lüdemann explains appearances of the risen Jesus in terms of subjective visions comparable to dreams rather than in terms of visions as objective sightings of a physically resurrected Jesus. Craig objects that this explanation fails to account for the emptiness of Jesus' tomb. Quite so, but Craig's objection does not take into account Lüdemann's contention that the stories of Jesus' empty tomb arose by unhistorical inference out of subjective visions. Therefore Craig needs to extend his argument by showing the unlikelihood that such visions generated those stories. For starters, and without judging between subjectivity and objectivity, he might call attention to the many visions of deceased people—visions reported both in the Bible and elsewhere—that prompted no inference of a physical resurrection resulting in an empty tomb. King Saul asked the witch of Endor to call up the spirit of Samuel, but neither Saul nor the witch nor the biblical storyteller inferred that Samuel had been physically resurrected just because the witch saw him in the appearance of an old man wrapped in a robe (1 Sam 28:3-25). John the author of Revelation saw in a vision the souls of martyrs—they were even given white robes to wear—but also the emptying of their tombs by resurrection awaiting the future (Rev 6:9-11; cf. 14:13; 20:1-15). Visions of the Virgin Mary, to which Lüdemann himself appeals, have not generated belief in her resurrection so much as the reverse: belief in her assumption to heaven (though sometimes understood as *entailing* resurrection) has generated visions of her. Examples could be multiplied. Normally, visions of deceased people have not been thought to imply physical resurrections resulting in empty tombs; rather, they have been thought to consist of ghostly apparitions. So it is difficult to accept Lüdemann's thesis that reports concerning the emptiness of Jesus' tomb were made up because subjective visions of the postmortem Jesus were thought to imply his physical resurrection.[3]

---

3. The story found in Herodotus, *Hist.* 4.14-15, and cited by Lüdemann (*The Resurrection of Jesus: History, Experience, Theology*, trans. John Bowden [Minneapolis: Fortress, 1994], 119-20) mentions the disappearance of the body of a man thought to have just died, the disagreement of another man claiming to have just seen him and talked with him, the reappearance of the first man seven years later, another disappearance, and another reappearance elsewhere 240 years later than his first reappearance. But the story does not mention any resurrection; rather, it uses the Greek noun *phasma*, "apparition, phantom."

As to the appearances of Jesus as risen, there is some validity in Craig's argument that they were granted not just to believers but also to unbelievers, skeptics, and even enemies. At least there is if one grants that doubting Thomas and his fellow doubters among the apostles count as unbelievers and skeptics (Matt 28:17; Luke 24:11; John 20:24–25). James the brother of Jesus may also count; but though he is said not to have believed in Jesus during Jesus' public ministry (see John 7:3–5 with Matt 12:46–50; Mark 3:31–35; Luke 8:19–21), we are not told the state of his belief or unbelief at the time Jesus is said to have appeared to him. Surely Craig goes too far, however, to include Jesus' enemies, as though Saul of Tarsus (Paul) were not the only one, among those to whom Jesus appeared as risen. Again, the pruning of an overstatement would strengthen Craig's argument.

Over against Lüdemann's thesis that Peter's subjective vision of Jesus as risen sparked a series of copycat visions, Craig notes that the biblical narrative puts Jesus' appearance to women before the one to Peter (see esp. Matt 28:1–10 with Luke 24:1–35). But the appearance to women occurs in the story of their discovering Jesus' tomb to be empty; and in Lüdemann's view that story was made up, so historically speaking the chronological priority of Peter's vision remains.[4] It should have been enough for Craig that the patriarchalism of first-century Jewish culture makes extremely unlikely the concoction of stories in which women are the first to discover Jesus' tomb to be empty and the first to see the risen Jesus himself, and that the further away from its Jewish origin Christianity moved, the less likely a concoction of stories requiring the physicality of Jesus' resurrection. Gentiles did not project such a possibility (see Acts 17:32). If they entertained the possibility of an afterlife at all, it consisted at best of an immortality of the soul. These points are strong and sufficient.

On the other hand, Craig's point is weak that "hallucinations" (his pejorative term for the subjective visions that Lüdemann likes to talk about) cannot contain anything not already present in the mind.[5] How

---

4. Lüdemann does accept the historicity of Mary Magdalene's subjective vision *apart from* the story of an empty tomb (*Resurrection of Jesus*, 157–61, and esp. Gerd Lüdemann, *What Really Happened to Jesus: A Historical Approach to the Resurrection*, trans. John Bowden [Louisville: Westminster John Knox, 1995], 66).

5. With some justification Lüdemann complains about Craig's turning "visions" into "hallucinations." On the other hand, Lüdemann calls E. Earle Ellis, whom Craig cites for support, a "fundamentalist." That term, as the old saw puts it, connotes "too much fun, too much damn, and too little mental." But however much Lüdemann scorns Ellis's belief in the resurrection of Jesus, he knows right well that the record of advanced scholarship which Ellis established rivals his own.

does Craig know they cannot? He provides no evidence. To the contrary, if the conscious mind can think new thoughts, why not the subconscious mind too? And do we never dream anything hallucinatory? (Remember that Lüdemann compares visions to dreams.) Craig's "cannot" should be reduced at least to an improbability.

Craig goes on to argue that hallucinations would have projected Jesus into paradise to await resurrection at the end of the world. Well, Lüdemann thinks that visions of Jesus *did* project him into paradise. But according to Lüdemann, those who saw these visions went on to conclude not that Jesus was awaiting resurrection in paradise but that he was there because God had already resurrected him. Because of a widespread Jewish belief that the righteous dead were awaiting resurrection, however, probability lies here on Craig's side. For where else in ancient Judaism do we find the inference of a past resurrection from reception into heaven, as Lüdemann thinks happened in Jesus' case? No such inference was drawn concerning Adam, Abel, Seth, Moses, or the remaining righteous of the Old Testament, all of whom are said to have gained heavenly exaltation after their deaths (not to mention Enoch and Elijah, who never died in the first place).[6] To those Jews who believed in a resurrection of the righteous, it had the purpose of restoring physical life on terra firma, not in heaven, and in the age to come, not during the present evil age.[7] So an inference from present heavenly exaltation to a resurrection that has already taken place on earth, but without the accompanying enjoyment of life on a renewed earth, seems unlikely as well as unprecedented.

Against Lüdemann's hypothesizing a guilt complex in Paul to explain Paul's vision of Jesus (a subjective one in Lüdemann's view, of course),[8] Craig asserts that the evidence we have, insufficient for psychoanalysis though it is, shows the pre-Christian Paul not to have been weighed down with a sense of guilt: he himself says in Phil 3:6, "As to the righteousness in the law, I was blameless." But the details that Paul has just listed as the ingredients of his legal righteousness all have to do with externals: circumcision, nationality, tribal origin, cultural identity, sectarian membership, and the activity of persecution.[9] His blamelessness

---

6. 4 Ezra 14:9; T. Ab. 11, 13; Ascen. Isa. 9:8-9, 28; cf. Josephus, *Ant.* 4.8.48 §326.

7. See, for example, 2 Macc 7:1-23; 1 En. 24:1—27:5; 51:1-4; 2 Bar. 29:1—30:5; Sib. Or. 4:171-92; T. Ab. B7:16; Pseudo-Philo, Bib. Ant. 3:10.

8. See *Resurrection of Jesus*, 81-84.

9. "Regarding circumcision, an eight-dayer; born from the race of Israel [and] tribe of Benjamin; a Hebraist born from Hebraists; as to the law, a Pharisee; as to zeal, persecuting the church" (Phil 3:5-6).

had to do, then, with what others could observe. What was happening in Paul's own conscience is another question, and the possibility that Rom 7:7–25 describes a pre-Christian Paul who was suffering moral defeat within himself needs some consideration. Quite apart from the present debate, of course, the meaning of this latter passage is contested. Who is the "I" undergoing a moral defeat? At what time did, or does, that defeat occur? But just because the meaning *is* contested, Craig should not deny so confidently that Paul suffered a guilt complex before Jesus' appearance to him. On the other hand, Rom 7:7–25 specifies lust or covetousness, not the persecution of Christians that Lüdemann thinks had pricked Paul's conscience; and in Phil 3:6 Paul presents his zeal in persecuting the church as a basis for past Judaistic confidence, not as the seedbed for uneasy feelings of guilt that flowered into Christian conversion. So it is a tall order for Lüdemann to show that a guilt complex in Paul engendered a subjective vision of Jesus as physically risen from the dead. That Jesus had undergone the curse of crucifixion exacerbates the difficulty.[10]

If Craig's arguments veer toward overstatement, Lüdemann's careen from one fallacy to another. Overstatements may need no more than pruning, but fallacies need felling. Let us work through the fallacies in Lüdemann's arguments, then. Unfortunately, he presents the arguments so loosely that an intelligible discussion of them sometimes requires filling in gaps. We can only try not to misrepresent what he had in mind.

Matthew 23 says nasty things about the Jews, argues Lüdemann; and other parts of the New Testament, too, exhibit anti-Semitism. He says, in fact, that "a literal understanding of the New Testament story of the resurrection leads to anti-Semitism." Jesus therefore did not rise from the dead, we are presumably supposed to deduce.

First, however, Matt 23 says nasty things about "scribes and Pharisees" in particular, not about Jews in general; and the author of Matthew was almost certainly a Jew himself, writing for fellow Jews. Second, even if Matt 23 and the rest of the New Testament were as anti-Semitic as all hell (and anti-Semitism *is* hellish!), the story of Jesus' physical resurrection could still be historically true. A resultant anti-Semitism would not negate evidence of the event itself. Since when did a morally abhorrent outcome necessitate a denial of the originating event?

---

10. See Gal 3:13 for crucifixion as a curse. This curse also makes difficult Lüdemann's theory that Peter's subjective vision of Jesus was triggered by feelings of guilt for having denied Jesus (*Resurrection of Jesus*, 99–100, 176).

Third, why should we not think that a literal understanding of Jesus' resurrection leads to a loving, Christian evangelization of the Jews rather than to anti-Semitism? It certainly did in the case of the first Christians, who were themselves Jews. Even Paul, who described himself as an apostle to the gentiles, wrote that the gospel of the resurrected Christ was "to the Jew first" and that he could wish himself damned forever if it would do any good for the salvation of his fellow Jews (Rom 1:16; 9:1–3; cf. 11:1–36). If judgment was to come on unbelieving Jews, it was to come on them for their unbelief, not for their Jewishness, and from the hand of God, not from the hands of Christians. Nor does the New Testament limit such judgment to unbelieving Jews. Unbelieving gentiles are said to face the same prospect (Rom 2:1–12).

Then Lüdemann seems to argue that since the virgin birth of Jesus is unbelievable, so also is his resurrection, and that since his ascension and second coming are unbelievable, so also is his resurrection. And since Jesus did not come back in the first century, neither did he rise from the dead. Of course, Lüdemann gives us only his opinion that the virgin birth, ascension, and second coming are unbelievable; and he does not consider the possibility that evidence favoring the resurrection lends credibility to those other items. But even if we were to grant the unbelievability of those other items, the evidence favoring Jesus' resurrection would still stand. He might have been raised from the dead without having been born of a virgin, without having ascended to heaven, without having come back in the first century.

According to another argument, everyone wants immortality; and the disciples of Jesus wanted to remain his disciples but needed his resurrection if they were to do so. Lüdemann supposes that out of these twin desires arose the belief in Jesus' resurrection. But immortality does not require a resurrection of the body, only an ongoing existence of the soul. Nor does Lüdemann tell us how he knows the disciples wanted to remain disciples so badly that subjective visions of a resurrected Jesus were generated among them. We might think oppositely that the crucifixion would have dampened or drowned their ardor for discipleship (they are reported to have fled upon Jesus' arrest) had it not been for the resurrection. Even if not, we need only remind ourselves that throughout human history many religious leaders have died without having a belief in their subsequent resurrection evolve among those who continued to follow them.

To weaken Craig's argument that the burial of Jesus by Joseph of Arimathea serves as a necessary, supportive backdrop to the emptiness of Jesus' tomb, Lüdemann calls attention to a tradition that hostile Jews buried Jesus (Acts 13:29). But if the Gospels' increasingly favorable descriptions of Joseph arose out of unhistorical redaction, as Lüdemann thinks, nothing excludes the historical Joseph from the company of Jews hostile to Jesus, so that Joseph may have acted on their behalf. Then his burying Jesus would have had the purpose not of honoring him but rather of keeping the Mosaic law that a victim of hanging should not be left on a tree overnight but should be buried the same day (Deut 21:22–23; cf. John 19:31). Elsewhere Lüdemann himself offers this possibility.[11]

Here Lüdemann seems to have unwittingly left his flank exposed; for if Jesus' enemies buried him, they must have known the location of his tomb. Only if his disciples had buried him and kept the location secret from his enemies could the latter have been unable to point out a tomb containing Jesus' corpse. Well, not quite "only." Like Jesus' enemies, Lüdemann could propose a theft by Jesus' disciples. What Lüdemann does instead is to suggest that the disciples did not start preaching Jesus' resurrection till so much later than his death (fifty days later according to Acts 1:3 with 2:1, 24–28) that "you wouldn't see much left [of the body]." But you would see something, at least the skeleton; and you would see that the tomb was occupied, not empty. So Craig's question retains its force: Why did the enemies of Jesus not squelch the message of resurrection by exposing his remains?

In the Acts of the Apostles, Luke writes that between the passion and the ascension Jesus presented himself alive on earth during a period which lasted forty days (Acts 1:3). In listing the appearances of the risen Jesus, however, Paul does not mention that period (1 Cor 15:5–8). Therefore, Lüdemann infers, Paul did not know about it; and the early tradition that he did has to do with visionary appearances originating in heaven. Therefore again, the appearances listed by Paul did not take place during an earthly stay of forty days; Luke or someone before Luke made up that stay so as to accommodate the later-developed notion of a physical resurrection resulting in an empty tomb. Lüdemann does not say how he knows that Paul's nonmention of the forty-days' stay on earth spells

---

11. *Resurrection of Jesus*, 44, 173. There Lüdemann also argues that if Jesus' tomb had been empty, Christians would have venerated it. On the contrary, they did not venerate it precisely because it *was* empty. Tombs as such were not venerated. It was tombs containing remains of the deceased that were venerated.

Trimming the Debate between Craig and Lüdemann

ignorance of it. He would surely agree that Paul knew many things which go unmentioned in his letters. And how does Lüdemann know that the appearances listed by Paul originated in heaven rather than on earth? Or that they were nonphysical if they were heavenly and visionary? Or that Jesus was at first thought to have been nonphysically exalted to heaven immediately after his death rather than taken up physically forty days later?

Lüdemann does not offer an answer to these questions: Paul lists an appearance of the risen Jesus to him, uses the same language for that appearance as the language he uses for earlier appearances to others, and therefore implies that those earlier appearances originated in heaven just as the appearance to him did. Ironically though, it is in Acts, not in Paul's own letters, that we learn about the heavenly origin of the risen Jesus' appearance to Paul; and Lüdemann regards those accounts (there are three of them: Acts 9:1–9; 22:6–11; 26:12–18) as heavily laden with legendary elements.[12] By his own lights, then, he should be arguing for a late date in the heavenly localizing of Jesus, that is, for Luke's *having* to localize Jesus in heaven because he (Luke) had inserted the ascension between Jesus' earlier appearances and the appearance to Paul.

But let us suppose Paul himself had said that the risen Jesus appeared to him from heaven. Would his use of the same language for earlier appearances require that they too were thought to have originated from heaven? No, for that language has to do with the activity of appearing, not with the location of the object seen, nor, for that matter, with the object's physicality or nonphysicality. Even a vision so heavenly that the seer as well as the seen is said to have been located in heaven does not imply nonphysicality; for John the seer, having been transported to heaven (Rev 4:1),[13] sees Jesus as the Lamb slain but standing in God's presence (Rev 5:6). Jesus' standing rather than lying dead on an altar signifies his resurrection, and his slainness indicates that his resurrected body bears the scars of crucifixion, just as in the Gospel of John, which repeatedly uses the verb *standing* for appearances on earth of the risen but physically

---

12. Gerd Ludemann, *Early Christianity according to the Traditions in Acts: A Commentary* (Minneapolis: Fortress, 1989), 106–16. To preserve his hypothesis, however, Lüdemann is forced to treat as historical the heavenliness in Luke's accounts of Paul's vision. Historically, in other words, Paul was convinced he had seen Jesus exalted in heaven; and Luke's accounts reflect Paul's conviction though they contain much else that Lüdemann considers legendary (*Resurrection of Jesus*, 63–64).

13. That John's being "in [the] Spirit" (or "in spirit") does not mean "out of the body," see Rev 1:10; and Paul mentions the possibility of bodily transport to heaven for the seeing of "visions and revelations of the Lord" (2 Cor 12:1–2; cf. Gal 1:15–17).

scarred Jesus (John 20:14, 19, 26–29; 21:4). Whether seen on earth or in heaven, Jesus remains as physical after resurrection as he was before resurrection. Against both Lüdemann and Craig, then, the heavenliness of a vision does not imply nonphysicality.

Further concerning the language used by Paul and the tradition he cites, Lüdemann notes the aorist tense and passive voice of the Greek verb *ōphthē*, translated "appeared" or "was seen by." The New Testament does contain several instances of the verb in that form where someone or something appears in or from heaven (Acts 9:17; 26:16; Rev 11:19; 12:1, 3). But there are more instances where the objects seen have an earthly locale: Moses and Elijah on the Mount of Transfiguration (Mark 9:4; Matt 17:3; Luke 9:31); an angel of the Lord on the right side of the altar of incense in the temple at Jerusalem (Luke 1:11); an angel on the Mount of Olives just outside Jerusalem (Luke 22:43, where "from heaven" goes with "angel," not with "appeared"); fiery tongues resting on each of the disciples gathered in Jerusalem (Acts 2:3); Moses before two of his fellow Israelites in Egypt (Acts 7:26); an angel in the flames of a burning bush at Mount Sinai (Acts 7:30, 35); and the risen Jesus in the presence of his disciples during the forty days before his ascension (Acts 13:31). As to the possibility of physicality in the object seen, we should note the appearance of Moses in Egypt, where he got into a physical altercation with one of his fellow Israelites (Acts 7:27), and Jesus' appearances—portrayed in physical terms, as admitted by Lüdemann—between his resurrection and ascension.[14] In other words, *appeared* implies neither nonphysical substance nor heavenly location nor heavenly origin. The substance, the location, and the origin depend on other factors; Paul's citation contains no hint of exaltation to God's right hand. Therefore Lüdemann lacks a good basis for his opinion that the earliest tradition concerning the risen Jesus has him appearing from heaven in a nonphysical form.[15]

---

14. Compare Acts 13:31 with Luke 24:13–53 and Acts 1:1–11. See also passages in the Septuagint where physical objects, human and nonhuman, appear in definite locations on earth (Gen 1:9; 8:5; 46:29; Exod 10:28, 29; Lev 13:14, 57; 4 Kgdms 14:11; Song 2:12; 1 Macc 4:6, 19; 9:27; 2 Macc 3:25 LXX) and where the Lord or his angel appears in definite locations on earth (Gen 18:1; Exod 3:2; Judg 6:12 LXX, not to list passages where he appears on Mount Sinai).

15. The notion that a Jesus exalted to heaven must appear from there in a nonphysical form is further contradicted by the Gospel of John, which has Jesus ascending to heaven on Easter Sunday, during daytime, and follows up with several admittedly physical appearances on earth. That John has Jesus ascending on Easter Sunday is evident from the following data: (1) John 7:37–39 says that the Spirit was not yet given

Trimming the Debate between Craig and Lüdemann   201

On the contrary, other language in this earliest tradition favors at least the physicality of the risen Jesus, if not the earthly locale of his initial appearances as well, so that the stories of the empty tomb cannot be easily relegated to a secondary level of legend-making.[16] Craig argues correctly that the element of burial in the tradition requires that the element of resurrection means the raising of a dead body to new life. But his argument could profit from some elaboration. *Resurrection* means "standing up" (*anastasis*) in consequence of being "raised" (*egeirō* in the passive). Normally, dead bodies are buried in a supine position; so in conjunction with the mention of Jesus' burial the further mention of his having been raised must refer to the raising of a formerly supine corpse to the standing posture of a live body, just as also in Mark 16:6 ("He has been raised. He is not here. Look, the place where they laid him!") and Luke 24:36 ("He [the 'raised' Jesus—Luke 24:6] stood in their midst"; see also Luke 24:7, 23; John 20:14, 19, 26; 21:4; Acts 7:56; and again, Rev 5:6). There was no need for Paul or the tradition he cites to mention the emptiness of Jesus' tomb. They were not narrating a story; they were listing events. It was enough to mention dying, being buried, being raised, and being seen.

Physical resurrection resulting in an empty tomb is exactly what we should expect Paul to have understood and meant; for the had been a Pharisee, and the first-century Jewish historian Josephus, who claims to have been a Pharisee himself, says the Pharisees believed in physical

---

because Jesus was not yet glorified. (2) His glorification included his heavenly exaltation following earthly ministry (see, for example, John 17:5). (3) Yet Jesus bestowed the Spirit already on the evening of the first Easter Sunday (John 20:22). (4) Furthermore, on the first Easter Sunday morning Jesus told Mary Magdalene to stop holding on to him because he had not yet ascended to the Father; he ordered her to tell his disciples that he was ascending to his and their Father and God (John 20:17). (5) A week later, however, Jesus invited Thomas to touch him (John 20:26–27). (6) So Jesus must have ascended in the meantime—indeed, between the command in the morning that Mary stop holding on to him and the bestowal of the Spirit that evening.

16. Tied to a secondary level of legend-making is Lüdemann's assertion that "none of the four New Testament Gospels was written by the author listed at the top of the text." It is true that the titles starting "The Gospel according to" represent early church tradition, not original elements of the text. But the church tradition dates back very early, and Lüdemann's denial of Mark's and Luke's authorship would draw wide scholarly resistance. Furthermore, the New Testament identifies Luke as a companion of Paul, and Mark as a companion of both Paul and Peter. Moreover, the earliest post-New Testament tradition, now being dated at about AD 110 and before, says that in writing his Gospel, Mark drew on Peter's reminiscences. Consequently, Lüdemann may have less room for legend-making than he thinks. See Robert H. Gundry, *Mark: A Commentary on His Apology for the Cross* (Grand Rapids: Eerdmans, 1993), 1026–45.

resurrection, though he expresses the thought in a more Greek-philosophical mode: "The soul of good people passes into another body."[17] Moreover, Luke distinguishes the Pharisees' belief in resurrection from their belief in angels and spirits (Acts 23:6–8). The physicality of resurrection appears also in later rabbinic literature, where it is even debated whether dead bodies will rise wearing the same clothes in which they were buried.[18] To think that Paul had given up the Pharisaical view of resurrection as physical would take strong evidence to the contrary.[19]

But Lüdemann thinks he has such evidence. On the one hand, he argues, the structure of the tradition cited by Paul favors the idea that his mention of Christ's burial functions to guarantee the death of Christ over against gnostic denials of it. We do know that at a later date—say, toward the end of the first century or beginning of the second—some gnostics were denying the death of Christ.[20] But Paul wrote 1 Corinthians about half a century earlier,[21] and it is disputed whether Gnosticism had arisen in Corinth so early.[22] For the sake of argument, however, let us grant that it had. Lüdemann still has to contend with the facts that Paul is citing tradition, that Paul gave this tradition over to the Corinthians during his prior evangelization of them, that he had received the tradition earlier,[23] and that the tradition originated earlier still. Lüdemann himself traces the various elements making up the tradition, including the element of Christ's burial, back to Jerusalem in "the first two years immediately after the crucifixion of Jesus," that is, "between 30 and 33 CE."[24] Does

---

17. Josephus, *J.W.* 2.8.14 §163, where "another body" probably means a renewed body rather than brand new one.

18. See the citations in H. Strack and P. Billerbeck, *Kommentar zum Neuen Testament*, 4th ed. (Munich: C. H. Beck, 1965), 2:551; 3:475.

19. That he had not given it up, see Acts 23:6, though Lüdemann might deny the historical value of this detail (*Early Christianity*, 242–47).

20. Not always of Jesus, though, for some gnostics distinguished between a human Jesus who died and a divine Christ who did not.

21. Lüdemann prefers the date AD 49 (Gerd Lüdemann, *Paul, Apostle to the Gentiles: Studies in Chronology* [Philadelphia: Fortress, 1984], 263).

22. The Gospels of Luke and John were written later, but their reporting the physicality of Jesus' resurrected body, even if that reporting was directed against gnostics, does not imply unhistoricity. For anti-gnostic use of material does not demand anti-gnostic invention of it.

23. "For I gave over to you among the first things what also I had received, that Christ died" (1 Cor 15:3).

24. Lüdemann, *Resurrection of Jesus*, 38, also 25–26.

Lüdemann expect us to believe that a gnostic denial of Christ's death originated in Jerusalem, right where the crucifixion had taken place, right after Christ had died, so that burial was mentioned to counteract the denial? For lack of evidence there is not an ounce of scholarly consensus that a gnostic denial of Christ's death had arisen by that time in that place. The very suggestion that it had would likely be greeted with guffaws among scholars, whatever their position on the resurrection. And to save his argument that the mention of burial in this earliest possible tradition coming out of Jerusalem aims to prove the reality of Christ's death, Lüdemann cannot take refuge in a supposedly gnostic problem at Corinth two decades or so later, when Paul was writing 1 Corinthians.

Besides, burial is usually mentioned as a consequence of death, not as its guarantee. (After all, Romeo, it is possible to be buried alive!) So even though the mention of Christ's burial is literarily tied to his death, as Lüdemann avers, that linkage provides no convincing reason to infer a polemic against people who denied the reality of Christ's death. Nor do we have a convincing reason to join Lüdemann in his denial that the mention of Christ's burial implies an empty tomb as the result of resurrection (cf. Ezek 37:13, "when I open your graves and bring you up from them," and Dan 12:2, "Many of those who sleep in the dust of the earth will awake").

Further, a more careful reading of 1 Cor 15 shows that Paul cites the early tradition as common ground between him and his Corinthian audience. Not only did they receive that tradition by faith when he first preached it to them; they also presently "stand" in this tradition and "are being saved" by it so long as they persevere in it (1 Cor 15:1–2; cf. 2 Tim 2:17–18). By citing it, then, particularly by citing the parts about burial and appearances, Paul is not trying to convince incredulous Corinthians that Christ really did die and really was raised. They agree with Paul on these matters (an additional reason why he does not need to mention the empty tomb).

Having cited the tradition as common ground, Paul argues *from* Christ's resurrection, not *for* it. To what purpose does he argue? To the purpose of proving a future resurrection of Christian believers. *That*, not the past resurrection of Christ, is what some of the Corinthians are denying.[25] Paul even dares to risk the past resurrection of Christ, which they

25. "How is it that some among you are saying, 'There is no resurrection of the dead'? . . . If the dead are not raised at all, why are people even being baptized for them? . . . But someone will say, 'How are the dead raised? And with what kind of body

affirm with Paul, for the future resurrection of Christian believers, which some are denying: "But if there is no resurrection of the dead, not even Christ has been raised ... whom he [God] did not raise if indeed, then, the dead are not raised. For if the dead are not raised, not even Christ has been raised.... But now Christ has been raised from among the dead as the firstfruits of them who have fallen asleep [a euphemism for 'died']. For ... in the Christ, all will be made alive" (1 Cor 15:13, 15–16, 20, 22). Paul would hardly dare to risk the resurrection of Christ if some of the Corinthians were denying it because—real death being a precondition of resurrection—they had denied the reality of his death.

But after trying to show that Paul argues against a docetic view of Christ's death, Lüdemann reverses field by saying that Paul portrays the resurrection of Christ as spiritual, not physical. A spiritual, as opposed to physical, resurrection looks very docetic. So Lüdemann has Paul denying a docetic death but affirming a docetic resurrection, affirming a physical death but denying a physical resurrection! If Lüdemann were correct, Paul would have used the language of immortality apart from resurrection, not the language of resurrection, more specifically, resurrection of the body; for the language of immortality apart from bodily resurrection was current in Jewish literature of the period.[26]

Ah, but Paul describes the resurrected body as "spiritual," Lüdemann responds. Yes, agrees Craig, but spiritual in what sense? Craig's first answer: in the sense that the resurrected body is the mortal body that was laid in a tomb but is now improved, immortalized. Craig's second answer: a spiritual body does not mean a nonphysical body any more than the spiritual as opposed to fleshly Christians that Paul talks about earlier in 1 Corinthians are ghosts. Instead, spiritual Christians are those taught, filled, and led by the Holy Spirit, whose temple is their present physical bodies (see 1 Cor 2:10–16; 3:1; 6:19; 14:37; Gal 6:1).

Craig's second answer needs amplification. Spiritual gifts are gifts given by the Holy Spirit (Rom 1:11; 1 Cor 12:1; 14:1). The manna, the

---

are they coming?' Ignoramus!" (1 Cor 15:12, 29, 35–36). A fear that the Corinthians who were denying a future resurrection might take the further step of denying Christ's past resurrection may have led Paul to reinforce their belief in the latter by adding to the tradition his statement that the majority of the five hundred who saw Christ risen were witnesses still living, and also adding Christ's appearance to Paul himself. But since Paul indicates that the Corinthians believe in Christ's resurrection, it is better to regard these additions as simply reinforcing Paul's argument for a future resurrection.

26. See, for example, Wis 1–5 (esp. 3:1–4); 4 Macc (esp. 18:23); Josephus, *J.W.* 2.8.11 §§154–57 and *Ant.* 18.1.5 §18 (concerning the Essenes).

water-supplying rock, and the Mosaic law—all in the Old Testament—are spiritual in that the Holy Spirit gave them to the Israelites (Rom 7:14; 1 Cor 10:3-4). And the gospel is spiritual as given by the Holy Spirit (Rom 15:27; 1 Cor 9:11; see also Eph 1:3; 5:19; Col 1:9; 3:16 for blessings, songs, and understanding as "Spiritual" because they are given or inspired by the Holy Spirit). In other words, we should capitalize the adjective *Spiritual* and dismiss the idea of nonphysicality. In Paul's view, then, the resurrected body is Spiritual not in the sense of nonphysicality (he even switches back and forth between "body" and "flesh" in 1 Cor 15:35-41) but in the sense of its having been raised by God's Holy Spirit, which is none other than Christ's Spirit, rather than produced by natural generation, as in the case of our present bodies. Let Paul speak for himself in reference to the Spiritual body at resurrection: "The last Adam [Christ] became a life-producing Spirit" (1 Cor 15:45). We may add another of Paul's statements to good effect: "But if the Spirit of the one who raised Jesus from the dead dwells in you, the one who raised Christ from the dead will make alive also your mortal bodies through his Spirit that dwells in you" (Rom 8:11).[27]

Lüdemann's last argument for nonphysical resurrection in Paul comes out of the statement "Flesh and blood cannot inherit the kingdom of God" (1 Cor 15:50). But the immediately following statement reads, "Nor does perishability inherit imperishability." These two statements parallel each other, so that the phrase "flesh and blood" corresponds to "perishability." Together the terms refer to the present mortal body in respect to the perishability of its flesh and blood, not in respect to the physicality of its flesh and blood. For Paul proceeds to say that it is "*this* perishable body" that will put on imperishability and "*this* mortal body" that will put on immortality (1 Cor 15:51-55, esp. 53).[28] And since for

27. The force of this passage diminishes if one reads with certain manuscripts "because of his Spirit."

28. Elsewhere Lüdemann describes 2 Cor 4:6 as "a possible reflection of the Damascus event" and goes on to treat the possibility as an actuality by concluding that Paul's vision of Jesus near Damascus "had the character of light [as opposed to 'the seeing of a revived corpse']" (*Resurrection of Jesus*, 53, 163). But 2 Cor 4:6 reads that God "has shone in *our* hearts to give the light of the knowledge of God's glory in the face of Jesus Christ." The plural of the first-person pronoun includes at least Timothy, probably also Silvanus and Titus, if not the Christians in Corinth as well (2 Cor 1:1, 19; 2:13), and contrasts with Paul's using the singular of the first-person pronoun in 1:13—2:13. Surely Lüdemann does not include Timothy, Silvanus, and Titus—much less the Corinthians—along with Paul in the vision near Damascus. Paul's reference to the face of Christ would comport better with a resurrected body than with a featureless

Paul the resurrection of Christians will follow the pattern of Christ's resurrection, as Lüdemann agrees,[29] Paul must have thought that when Christ was raised, it was the perishable, mortal body of his earthly lifetime that put on imperishability and immortality, not that he was exalted to heaven in some nonphysical form.

But, says Lüdemann, physical resurrection would require a decaying corpse, "already cold and without blood in its brain," to be revivified. Yes, though he should have added immortalization to revivification. Here we have a definition, however, not an argument (as he seems to think). Compatible with the definition are reports that the risen Jesus ate food, but they prompt a question whether or not he had to use the restroom afterward. Apparently Lüdemann considers the question a *reductio ad absurdum*. Among other possibilities he might also have considered the one that eternal bliss includes the joys of elimination. Or are we too Platonically antiseptic for that?

"But Mark doesn't tell any story about the physical body [of Jesus] coming out of the tomb," says Lüdemann. Again, yes, and the same can be said of Matthew, Luke, John, and all other authors of the New Testament. But such a story is exactly what we would expect of a legend, and the apocryphal Gos. Pet. 9:35–10:42 makes up for its absence from the New Testament by describing Jesus' exit from the tomb. Instead of admitting that Mark's failure to include such a story favors the historicity of what he did report, Lüdemann infers that as in Paul (our earliest source) so also in Mark (our earliest Gospel) the resurrection of Jesus is still nonphysical: his body is "just not there" in the tomb. But to say so is to neglect other elements in Mark's report, namely, the announcements "He has been raised" and "He is going ahead of you into Galilee; there you will see him, just as he told you" (Mark 16:6–7). Does Lüdemann really think that Mark intends his audience to visualize the risen Jesus as a ghost traveling northward from Jerusalem to Galilee and appearing to his disciples in Galilee as a ghost?[30]

In sum, when Lüdemann's arguments are trimmed, little is left. The evolution of tradition he traces—from historical but subjective visions of a Jesus nonphysically exalted in heaven to objective but legendary sightings of a physically resurrected Jesus on earth—does not hold up light anyway.

---

29. Lüdemann, *What Really Happened to Jesus*, 103.

30. For further discussion see Robert H. Gundry, "The Essential Physicality of Jesus' Resurrection according to the New Testament," in *Jesus of Nazareth: Lord and Christ*, ed. J. B. Green and M. Turner (Grand Rapids: Eerdmans, 1994), 204–19.

under examination. When Craig's arguments are trimmed, a sturdy stock remains. Its strong branches support the decorative weight of additional arguments. As for Jesus himself, "He is risen indeed!"[31]

---

31. See further Robert H. Gundry, "The Essential Physicality of Jesus' Resurrection according to the New Testament," in *Jesus of Nazareth: Lord and Christ. Essays on the Historical Jesus and New Testament Christology*, Festschrift I. Howard Marshall; ed. J. B. Green and M. Turner (Grand Rapids: Eerdmans, 1994), 204-19.

Ingmar Bergman and *The Seventh Seal*

INGMAR BERGMAN WAS A Swedish cinematographer whose work belongs to what is called *serious cinema*. Ordinarily he wrote his own screenplays and directed the filming of them himself. The title of his classic film, *The Seventh Seal*, comes from the book of Revelation in the Bible and thus sets an apocalyptic tone to give a feeling that the film deals with ultimate issues, such as the ultimate reality for human beings, the actual or possible significance of human action, the meaningfulness or nonmeaningfulness of religion (particularly Christianity), and the dilemma of modern people.

When viewing the film we immediately notice that for Bergman the ultimate reality about human existence is death. The film begins and ends with death. At both beginning and end a carrion-feeding vulture circles ominously in the sky. One of the opening scenes features a horrid death-head. The closing scene features the dance of death. A chess game with the angel of death continues throughout the film. Death shows itself in many other ways as well. In other words, life is one long game to defeat death, but death always wins. This preoccupation with death, with the threat of nonexistence, with the fact that death haunts life, points up one of the existential aspects of Bergman's philosophy.

To come closer to the meaning of the film we need to recognize what kinds of people the main characters represent. The squire represents a sensual person. The naughty little ditty he sings toward the beginning of the film isn't a signal that we're about to see a sexy movie. Just the opposite, in fact. It's to tell us that the squire is a sensual man, so that when he later says to the girl whom he saves from death and refuses to rape, "I've wearied of that kind of love," we know that *he* knows what he's talking about. Bergman has turned preacher at this point. He's saying that the contemporary notion that sexual explorations bring meaning and fulfillment in life is a myth which needs to be demythologized. In other words, sex is highly overrated. The squire has tried it and failed. That same lesson is to be learned from the actor who was seduced and later cut down by death as he sought safety on the limb of a tree. Only, the actor was an ignorant fool being led to the slaughter like a dumb animal, whereas the squire is a worldly-wise man whose failure to find satisfaction in sensuality has bred cynicism. Though a man of action who does what he knows must be done, he does it with a cynical attitude.

We might well agree with Bergman that sensuality turns out to be meaningless. But this seems to be *all* that Bergman has to say. It needs to be added that sensuality isn't only meaningless. It's also wrong. Wrong because it violates the holy laws of God, which are rooted in his very nature. Bergman cannot say so, of course, because for him there is no such God.

Antonius Block, the knight in Bergman's film, is a refined, sophisticated modern man. He's disillusioned with organized religion (represented by the witch hunt) and with traditional causes (represented by the Crusades, from which he has returned to Sweden). He has lost his faith. But he's intelligent and sincere. He desires authenticity. He can't stand sham and pretense. He values honesty above all. He wants to believe, but he can't. There are too many intellectual problems. Yet he's facing death. For him he's facing certain nonexistence. He desperately tries to find *some* meaning, *some* significance in life before he dies. Time is running out. He must do something truly worthwhile *now*. The Crusades have proved a total loss so far as he is concerned. How can he possibly salvage some significance for his life?

On the other hand, we see the clown and his family. They're reminiscent of the holy family—Joseph, Mary, and the baby Jesus. But beyond that reminiscence, the clown represents the truly pious person. He has simple, openhearted faith. He sees visions that others scoff at, but he knows they're real. At least to *him* they are. Bergman has nothing but scorn for the professional religionists, but he portrays the clown sympathetically, even enviously. To Bergman, however, this true piety of the clown is nonrational, visionary, mystical. Bergman here reveals his view—a very common view nowadays—that the only valid type of religion consists in the new mysticism. For to him religion can't be truly rational.

The clown also represents a persecuted Christian. Note the inn scene, where he's badgered, mocked, and barely escapes with his life. He's also a happy Christian. Note the idyllic family scenes bathed in sunlight. He escapes death. He lives forever, or at least has hope, symbolized by the infant son who will "carry on" (compare the rising sun in the last scene). Bergman himself has said that each of his films ends with the possibility of hope. The rising sun and new day of the last scene doubtless represent this possibility of hope. But two things must be said about it: (1) The hope is entirely nonrational and mystical, a circumstance that leaves modern people in the dilemma that to believe they must sacrifice their intellects—something impossible to do and remain fully honest. And (2) the setting of the new day is back on the beach where the film started. We're supposed to infer that the chess game with death is going to be played all over again, the cycle's repeating itself with cruel monotony.

As a thoroughly modern man, Bergman himself is Block. But he wishes he could be the clown. He wishes he could believe but thinks his intelligence and knowledge as a modern, post-Crusades man denies him the luxury of faith if he's to remain true to himself. Here, though, we might disagree somewhat with Bergman. Antonius Block is a little *too* honest in his intellectual doubts to be a realistic figure. Most of us have to struggle to be honest, at least completely so. But not Block, and therefore he isn't a wholly believable figure.

To be sure, people do have intellectual difficulties. But such difficulties aren't peculiar to moderns. People have always had intellectual problems with the Christian faith. The apostle Thomas did. So did the Athenians who heard Paul preach. There was widespread disbelief in the Greco-Roman pantheon at the very time Christianity arose and spread. Bergman fails to point out that intellectual problems are all mixed up with moral problems, that faith demands commitment, obedience, rectitude, and a cutting down of human pride and pretensions of merit. As a result, it is probably impossible to disentangle genuine intellectual problems from the perversity of those who claim they can't believe. Part (not all) of their problem is that they *will* not believe. So Bergman proves too simplistic in portraying Block. His portrayal underestimates human depravity, doubtless because Bergman is portraying himself; and all of us are blind to our own dishonesties, though very keen-sighted in pointing out the dishonesties of others.

Does Block succeed in performing one significant act before death takes him? Yes. When he knocks some pieces off the chess board, death thinks that Block is trying to gain a fresh start in the game. But Block has tricked death by engrossing the attention of death on the chessboard, so that the clown and his family are able to escape. This trick constitutes the single significant act of Block, the one act that gives meaning to his life in the face of death. And so, since for Bergman there is no God to love anymore, love for neighbor becomes the *first* commandment instead of the *second*. As the clown and his family flee through the forest during the midnight storm, the wife asks her husband what is happening. The clown answers that the storm is passing over them. His answer alludes to the Passover story in the book of Exodus, where the angel of death (symbolized by the storm in the film) passed over the houses of the Israelites, God's people, but took the firstborn of the Egyptians.

But even that incident doesn't provide very great encouragement. In the castle scene toward the end, the girl who followed the squire to become his wife says, "It is finished." The statement is, of course, borrowed from one of the Seven Last Words of Christ from the cross (see John 19:30). In Bergman, however, it means, "This is the end; there is no more." It's a cry of despair, or of brave resignation, or perhaps of relieved acceptance of death as an escape from the horrors of life. In any case, the meaning is far different from the biblical connotation of the statement. On the lips of the dying Jesus, "It is finished!" means not only, "Death has come; I'm about to die," but also, "It is accomplished! The work of redemption is done!" It's a cry of victory in death, even through and by means of death. For out of Christ's death comes eternal life. Here lies a big difference between the gospel and humanism.

The task of Christians is to show that believing in Jesus can be intelligent and truly pious and openhearted at the same time. But care must be taken not to lose the simplicity of faith in attempts to make it intellectually respectable. Absent that simplicity, Bergman and those like him will not be attracted to it.

Frederick the Bruce

IN THE FIRST QUARTER of the fourteenth century Robert the Bruce reigned over Scotland. In the second half of the twentieth century another Scot named Bruce—Frederick Fyvie Bruce ("Fred" to his friends, "Professor Bruce" to his students, or simply "F.F.B.")—reigned, it could be said, over worldwide evangelical biblical scholarship. The comparison stops there, however, because the irenicism of Frederick the Bruce contrasted sharply with the militancy that characterized Robert the Bruce, a warrior. Suitably to this contrast, Robert failed on a couple of occasions to capture Elgin, the hometown of Frederick (hereafter, F.F.B.). Tim Grass's biography, *F. F. Bruce: A Life*, deals with the life of F.F.B.[1]

An alert by way of full disclosure: I was a doctoral student of F.F.B., his first one (so far as I know) during his first year at England's Victoria University of Manchester. On the other hand, I hardly came to know him: a fifteen-to-twenty-minute academic conversation once a month for a year, and never any socializing in each other's homes or elsewhere. He hadn't yet established a seminar. I took not even one class that he taught, and I heard him give only one special lecture. At our first meeting in his office we agreed on a dissertation topic. He suggested half a dozen books for me to start with; and on receiving a draft of my dissertation, he told me to use "vicegerent" rather than the "viceregent" that I had written. Apart from the negligible monthly conversations already mentioned, plus one later-related exception, that was it. So the biography taught me a lot that I didn't know about my former doctoral supervisor. It even prompted me to read in addition his autobiography, *In Retrospect: Remembrance of Things Past* (Grand Rapids: Eerdmans, 1980).

1. Grand Rapids: Eerdmans, 2012.

Tim Grass, author of the biography, has tried not to duplicate the autobiography. Inevitably there is some overlap, but the biography grows out of a great deal of additional research. Representing the research is a thirteen-page select bibliography that includes manuscripts, private papers and correspondence, files, unpublished theses/dissertations, books, articles, and websites, besides a thirty-six-page, chronologically ordered bibliography of F.F.B.'s writings (not including more than two thousand of his book reviews!), a chronological outline of significant events in F.F.B.'s life (1910–1990), and sixteen photos in addition to the handsome headshot on the book cover and spine.

F.F.B. grew up in the Open Brethrenism of northeastern Scotland, his father being a farm worker-turned-itinerant evangelist whom F.F.B. often accompanied on preaching engagements and for whom on these occasions he read out Scripture passages. The local revival that started in 1858 gave birth to this Brethrenism, and to the end of his days F.F.B. personally and financially supported—despite his scholarly pursuits, one is tempted to say—the Christian evangelism and worldwide missionary work for which the Brethren are deservedly famous. Nor did dedication to scholarship curb his piety, as evidenced for example in the practice of family devotions (Bible reading and prayer) after breakfast each morning, plus frequent preaching (not just lecturing).

At the same time, northeast Scottish Brethrenism and F.F.B. himself were mildy Calvinistic (lacking belief in double predestination, limited atonement, and, in F.F.B.'s case, perseverance of the saints). Like his father and unlike most (Plymouth) Brethren, F.F.B. was nondispensational, once telling me that he did not know of anyone in the UK who still believed in a pretribulational rapture of the church (surely an overstatement designed to debunk the popularity of that belief in the US). According to Grass, F.F.B. even inclined later in life to postmillennialism. He definitely shifted from believing in the saints' resurrection at Jesus' return to believing in its taking place at their deaths if they did not survive till that return.

Other positions of his, often not well-known in broad evangelical circles, also made him theologically suspect among many Brethren: opposition to their allegorical interpretations of the Old Testament tabernacle and narrative; advocacy of women's liberation in the church (but with a caution not to upset Christian harmony thereby); appreciation of Barthianism (which appreciation may have contributed to his encouraging me to spend a half year at Basel University, where Karl Barth held court but did not win me over); ecumenical sympathies (as opposed to ecclesiastical separatism); belief in three Isaiahs and in a second-century date for Daniel (though inclusive of sixth-century materials); denial of historical inerrancy in the Bible (though arguing for its essential historicity); post- and therefore non-Pauline authorship of 1–2 Timothy and Titus; reticence to harmonize apparent discrepancies in Scripture; sympathetic assessments of Marcion, Pelagius, and F. C. Baur (usually considered heretics by orthodox Christians); acceptance of Rudolf Bultmann as a true Christian (despite Bultmann's condemnation of a theological interest in the historical Jesus contrary to F.F.B.'s own position that apart from the Jesus of history there is no gospel); openness to "fellowship with the Pope and Ian Paisley, though preferably not at the same time!"; willingness to acknowledge a strong case for including the Old Testament apocrypha in Protestant editions of the Bible; and disapproval of moves in the 1970s to tighten the doctrinal basis of the Tyndale Fellowship for Biblical Research, of which he was an early leader (a disapproval that recalls his saying to me, "Creeds are better sung than signed," as though singing fosters a more devotional and less pilpulistic understanding of them).

Alongside these sometimes mildly liberal tendencies, however, Grass points out balancing elements of both theological and behavioral conservatism. F.F.B. championed the Westminster Confession's statement on the divine authority of Scripture, with emphasis on its and John Calvin's view of the Scripture as self-authenticating through the inward witness of the Holy Spirit: hence, infallibility as regards the matters of salvation and godliness that the Bible was meant to address. F.F.B. also defended arguments from fulfilled prophecy and miracle and affirmed the moral corruption of human beings, salvation by grace through faith without any contribution of human achievement, Christ's authority to execute judgment, the Christian gospel as the sole way of salvation (What would F.F.B. make of current interreligious dialogue?), and evangelism and godly living—rather than scholarship for its own sake—as the purposes for biblical research. In his view, foreign missions should concentrate on church-planting, not on the establishing of schools, hospitals, and similar Christian institutions. (The church-planting concentration is presently being diluted somewhat by evangelicals' marrying social activism with evangelism.) F.F.B. feared that hostile governments might take over Christian social institutions, and he likewise had no use for the institutionalizing of ecumenism. But his social conscience led him to deplore the materialism of First World countries and cultures at the expense of poor countries. As to domestic culture, F.F.B.'s children were not allowed out to play on Sundays (where was Paul, his beloved "Apostle of Liberty"?), and the Bruces waited till their children had grown up before exercising Christian liberty by drinking alcohol at home (whereas imbibing has now become so prevalent among evangelicals that the practice of total abstinence amounts to an exercise of Christian liberty).

Peppering F.F.B.'s biography are some personal tidbits of interest. As a youngster at Elgin Academy he wrote an article claiming that the Scots had descended from ancient Egyptians and Assyrians and that the Stone of Scone had been Jacob's pillow, mentioned in Gen 28. Asthma apparently kept F.F.B. from participating in sports, and certainly from serving later in the military. Nonmechanical, he never learned to drive an automobile, which he considered a waste of time when train riding provided him opportunity to work. Technologically backward, he never learned to use a computer for word processing. During the last year of his life he bought an electric typewriter but did not use it and instead continued using a small manual typewriter. Nor during his last years did he keep up with new developments in biblical criticism: structural, sociological, feminist, postcolonial, deconstructive et al.

While still a teenager and not yet baptized, F.F.B. argued in print against infant baptism. His courtship of Anne Bertha (Betty) Davidson, who became his wife, lasted seven years, a good theological number, though on our very first meeting he told me emphatically, "Mr. Gundry, I am a historian and philologist, not a theologian." In connection with that courtship and marriage, one should not miss the hilarious example of F.F.B.'s humor on page 21 of the biography. Twirling a walking stick while strolling along and holding it out when crossing a road exhibited a certain flamboyance.

During World War II F.F.B. served as a nighttime air warden and fire-watcher and started writing his commentary on the Greek text of Acts in an air-raid shelter. Multitasking had him engaging in conversation and seminar discussions while writing letters, marking essays, and correcting proofs. In the *Harvester*, a Brethren publication, he answered no fewer than two thousand questions sent in by readers during the years 1952–1975. His lectures consisted in monotone reading, often from proofs of one of his books. Though a supervisor of doctoral students, he held reservations about the research doctorate; and he himself never earned a doctorate. Pressure to propose "some new thing" tended to produce unlikely hypotheses, he thought; and he himself proposed no new idea, at least not a noteworthy big one. Touting the BA as superior to Oxford's DPhil, the Oxford philosopher John Lucas expressed to me the same sentiment. Had F.F.B. influenced him, or was it "in the air (or 'clouds')" that the earned doctorate was invented for aspiring Americans?

F.F.B. was good at talking and playing with children, as on the one occasion when I introduced my own very young daughters to him in his office. But he fell short in small talk with adults; and in serious talk his comments were notably brief as well as clear and coherent, as I found out when expecting a full hour's conversation about my doctoral research only to get about a quarter hour of "yes," "no," or a sentence or two in answer to my questions, plus ten or so minutes of informal but labored conversation over tea and biscuits. According to Grass, later doctoral students fared better (as did my four-year-old daughter when asking F.F.B. whether he had any children), doubtless because they had conversational skills superior to mine. Grass also describes F.F.B.'s book reviews as "kindly," to which description I might add that the effusiveness of the blurbs he wrote for others' books became something of a joke. (But who is complaining? Not his beneficiaries!)

More than one acquaintance of F.F.B. has remarked his powers of memory. Though not referenced by Grass, F.F.B.'s doctoral student Moisés Silva tells of asking him whether a Hebrew word might carry a meaning favored by its Old Testament context but unattested in Hebrew lexicons, and having F.F.B. respond in the affirmative by reciting on the spot a line in one of Bialik's modern Hebrew poems that features the word in exactly the meaning Silva had suggested. (When it comes to prodigious memory, though, F.F.B. had his peers at Manchester, among them the Jewish scholar P. R. Weis, co-editor with H. H. Rowley of the *Journal of Semitic Studies*.)

All of which gives rise to the question, *What was it about F.F.B. that vaulted him to unequalled prominence among evangelical biblical scholars?* Grass answers this question admirably well. First to mention is F.F.B.'s sheer intellectual brilliance. Academic prizes were showered on him at Aberdeen University. Called the most brilliant student there of his generation, he earned such high grades that more than forty years later I heard them lauded during a meeting of the Society for New Testament Studies at that university. He took his Cambridge degree, with first-class honors (as at Aberdeen), in two years rather than the usual three. Aberdeen University awarded him an honorary DD, and the University of Sheffield an honorary DLitt. Given the prestige of his predecessors in the Rylands Chair of Biblical Criticism and Exegesis at the University of

Manchester—A. S. Peake, C. H. Dodd, and T. W. Manson—his appointment to that chair constituted an honor in and of itself. According to a story making the rounds at the university, H. H. Rowley was reported to have said upon reading F.F.B.'s commentary on the Greek text of Acts, "I don't care if he's a Jehovah's Witness, let's give him the chair" (or words to that effect).

Elections to the presidencies of the Society for Old Testament Study and of the Society for New Testament Studies (SNTS), and as a Fellow of the British Academy, which then awarded him the Burkitt Medal in biblical studies, paid further tribute to his intellectual brilliance. F.F.B. recognized the danger in these honors, however. After hearing accolades from some of his former students in a private meeting following the presidential address he gave to the SNTS, he responded—not unappreciatively, but self-deprecatingly—that "it does good to no man's soul to hear such things said about him." (Grass regrets that F.F.B.'s response was not recorded, but together with others I was there to hear it.) By the way, during F.F.B.'s presidential address a well-known anti-evangelical, later to become president of the SNTS himself, was sitting beside me and after the address said to me, "I expected to hear some evangelical twaddle but have to admit that this man knows a lot."

So adding to the prominence of F.F.B. among evangelical biblical scholars was the vast breadth of his learning. He started as a scholar in the Latin and Greek classics, beginning with Latin at the age of eleven and with Greek at the age of thirteen. His studies in the classics continued throughout his years in Aberdeen and Cambridge, and his first employments at the universities of Edinburgh and Leeds remained in that field; so he was self-taught in biblical studies, the field into which he shifted at the universities of Sheffield and Manchester. His undergraduate studies included English, logic, and moral philosophy; and he taught himself enough church history to write a three-volume survey of it. One can taste the flavor of all this learning in a dissertation title of his: "The Latinity of Gaius Marius Victorinus Afer, with appendices on his Biblical text and on the vocabulary of Candidus the Arian."

At the University of Vienna F.F.B. studied Sanskrit, Indo-European philology, the Hittite language, and more Greek. He learned Hebrew and Middle Irish; and his book reviews evince a knowledge of Dutch, French, German, Italian, and Spanish. According to Grass, F.F.B. studied Coptic at Manchester in 1962–1963. Maybe so, but his special lecture on the Gospel of Thomas a year or two earlier left me with the impression that he had already learned Coptic in preparation for the lecture. Because of his vast learning, in any case, "he has been called 'evangelicalism's Erasmus'" (so Grass). Yes! But I have to note that during my time in Manchester it was F.F.B.'s colleague Arnold Ehrhardt whom we called "Erasmus," his having told me once, "I feel competent to teach both law [as he had done at the University of Freiburg im Breisgau], church history, and theology," and then added the fillip, "in a *German* university." No disservice to F.F.B., though; and testifying further to the breadth of *his* learning were his presidencies of the Manchester Egyptian and Oriental Society, the Yorkshire Society for Celtic Studies, and the Victoria Institute, plus his editorship of the journals of the latter two societies, of the *Palestine Exploration Quarterly*, and of the *Evangelical Quarterly*.

Contributing yet further to the preeminence of F.F.B. in evangelical biblical scholarship was the panache that attached to his attainment of posts in secular universities, most gloriously the Rylands Chair at Manchester, whereas other evangelical biblical scholars of note—especially Americans—taught only in evangelical theological seminaries, which did not offer PhD programs for students who might carry forward the scholarly legacy of their teachers. At Manchester, F.F.B. supervised about fifty doctoral students from all around the world; and his fame was such that he also lectured all around the world, not to mention the worldwide circulation of his many books and articles, both scholarly and popular. They lacked very much theological development and practical application, but their clarity of style and down-to-earth explanations of what our ancient texts meant have drawn much admiration and reflect his classical training.

In the evangelical world at large F.F.B.'s influence diminished with the rise to prominence of Martin Lloyd-Jones and especially of John R. W. Stott, neither of them a scholar of F.F.B.'s caliber but richly gifted in other respects. Grass judges correctly that F.F.B. paved the way for evangelicals' acceptance of critical methods in biblical research and for the acceptance of evangelicals in the wide world of biblical scholarship. He was not alone in doing so, however. One thinks of the Americans Ned B. Stonehouse and George E. Ladd, among others.

My own association with F.F.B. has led me to review mainly his life as delineated in Grass's book rather than to evaluate Grass's treatment as such. (It is very good.) I hope to be forgiven for having interjected reminiscences of mine, but their occasions were so few as to be memorable. A last reminiscence: During the oral defense of my dissertation the external examiner, who was theologically liberal, asked me a question rather obviously designed to test my theology. Before I could answer, F.F.B. told him, "We're here to examine Mr. Gundry's scholarship, not his theology." End of interrogation. Thank you, Professor Bruce.

www.ingramcontent.com/pod-product-compliance
Lightning Source LLC
Chambersburg PA
CBHW022014220426
43663CB00007B/1072